The Denninghoffs

1989

JOHN TAYLOR

Mormon Philosopher, Prophet of God

JOHN TAYLOR

Mormon Philosopher, Prophet of God

Francis M. Gibbons

Deseret Book
Salt Lake City, Utah

Printed in the United States of America

ISBN 0-87747-714-0
Library of Congress Catalog Card Number 84-73532

First printing March 1985

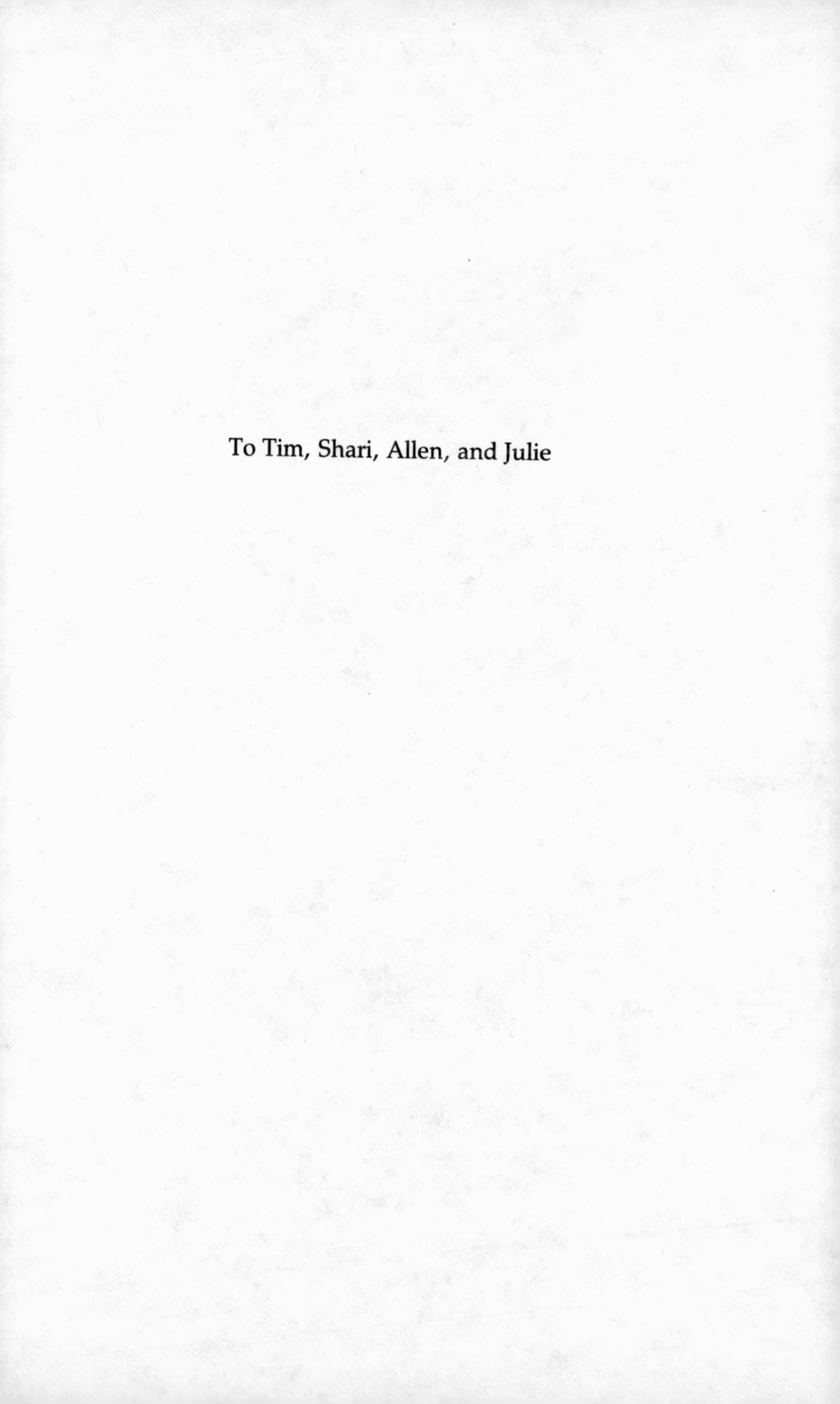

To Tim, Shari, Allen, and Julie

Contents

Key to Abbreviations

BHR B. H. Roberts, *The Life of John Taylor* (Salt Lake City: George Q. Cannon and Sons, 1892)

HC Joseph Smith, *History of the Church of Jesus Christ of Latter-day Saints*, 7 vols., 2nd ed. rev. Edited by B. H. Roberts (Salt Lake City: The Church of Jesus Christ of Latter-day Saints, 1932–51)

JD *Journal of Discourses*, 26 vols. (London: Latter-day Saints' Book Depot, 1854–86)

MS *Millennial Star*

PPP Parley P. Pratt, *Autobiography of Parley Parker Pratt*, 5th ed., edited by Parley P. Pratt, Jr. (Salt Lake City: Deseret Book Company, 1961)

Chapter One

Conversion

Parley P. Pratt, a modern apostle, arrived in Hamilton, Ontario, Canada, in April 1836, uncertain about what he should do. Being a man of keen spiritual perceptions, and a pragmatist as well, it is curious that he would have traveled the long distance from Kirtland, Ohio, to this place without formulating a definite itinerary and course of action. But he was a man of faith also, and it was his faith in a prophecy uttered by fellow apostle Heber C. Kimball that had impelled him to leave a sick wife, a partially completed home, and a mountain of debt in Kirtland to undertake a mission to "Upper Canada." Elder Kimball's prophecy had come at a crucial time when Parley was debating whether to fulfill his domestic responsibilities or to heed the apostolic oath and covenant he had taken on February 21, 1835. Once his visionary friend had spoken, however, there was no doubt, at least no doubt about the choice between home and his ministry. "Thou shalt go to Upper Canada," Heber C. Kimball had told him, "even to the city of Toronto, the capital, and there thou shalt find a people prepared for the fullness of the gospel, and they shall receive thee, and thou shalt organize the church among them, and it shall spread thence into the regions round about, and many shall be brought to the knowledge of the truth and shall be filled with joy."

(PPP, pp. 130-31.) But Elder Pratt was doubtful on arriving at Hamilton as he pondered how to reach Toronto. He was penniless, which suggested that he walk. But the spring thaw had made it certain that such a journey would be slow, tedious, and muddy. The only alternative was to take a lake steamer, an option that lacked viability at the moment as he did not have the two-dollar fare.

In his perplexity, the Mormon missionary followed the example of Joseph Smith, the founder of The Church of Jesus Christ of Latter-day Saints: He went to a secluded place in a nearby forest and there implored the Lord for help to enable him to book passage for Toronto. Rising from his knees, he walked back into Hamilton and engaged several people in conversation on the street. "I had not tarried many minutes," Elder Pratt wrote of the incident, "before I was accosted by a stranger, who inquired my name and where I was going. He also asked me if I did not want some money. I said yes. He then gave me ten dollars." (PPP, pp. 134-35.)

Arriving in Toronto that evening, Elder Pratt went directly to the home of John Taylor, whose name and address had been given to him by Moses Nickerson, a business acquaintance of Mr. Taylor's, who had accompanied Elder Pratt part of the way from Kirtland.

The householder who received Elder Pratt was a fine specimen of manhood. Standing just under six feet tall and weighing 180 pounds, John Taylor greeted the stranger with the delightful accent that marked him as a native of northern England. And his verbal greeting, cordial but restrained, was accompanied by a careful appraisal of the American, made with his searching gray eyes. Had the visitor been asked, he doubtless would have pronounced his host a handsome man with his even features; his virile physique, made strong by manual labor from his youth; and his wavy brown hair, already flecked with gray at the temples despite his youthful age of twenty-eight.

The initial cordiality with which John Taylor received Elder Pratt cooled when he learned that the visitor was a

Mormon. Having served as a preacher in the Methodist church, the immigrant had heard many derogatory reports about this new American sect and had closed his mind against it. Therefore, he did not show an interest in hearing the visitor's message nor in helping him to find lodgings or a place in which to hold meetings. Disappointed at this rebuff, the missionary checked in at a public house and the next day began canvassing Toronto's ministers and civil officials, seeking accommodations for public meetings. These efforts proved fruitless.

With all doors closed against him and with the rapid depletion of the funds donated by the stranger in Hamilton, the apostle was discouraged. This led him to seek out another place of seclusion for secret prayer, which he found in a grove of pine trees on the outskirts of Toronto. There he knelt again, acknowledging his failure to find an open door on his own initiative and imploring divine aid in the fulfillment of his mission. Returning to the city, he called again at the home of John Taylor and his wife. While he was there Mrs. Walton, a friend of the Taylor's, came to visit. In a conversation with Leonora Taylor, Mrs. Walton was told about Elder Pratt, about his claim of apostleship, and about his inability to find a place to preach. Learning this, the friend offered lodgings and the use of her parlor for his meetings.

Thus Parley P. Pratt began to proselyte among a group of Bible students in Toronto, most of whom were nominal members of the Methodist church. John Taylor was one of the leaders of this group, most of whom had begun to question the tenets and practices of Methodism because they did not conform to biblical teachings. Thus they met together periodically to study the Bible, to discuss its doctrines, and to pray for guidance.

Overcoming his initial reluctance to listen to Elder Pratt, John Taylor began to attend the meetings held at Mrs. Walton's and at other homes that were ultimately opened to the visitor. It soon became apparent that this American was a skilled and knowledgeable teacher, well schooled in the

Bible. Finally realizing that he had been misled about the Latter-day Saints, John not only attended these meetings but he began an independent study of the doctrines the newcomer taught. This study was facilitated when he wrote down eight sermons Elder Pratt delivered and carefully compared them with the Bible. He also reviewed evidences of the authenticity of the Book of Mormon and Doctrine and Covenants. Commenting later on these studies, the investigator said, "I made a regular business of it for three weeks and followed Brother Parley from place to place." Finally convinced of the truthfulness of what they had been taught, both John and Leonora Taylor were baptized into The Church of Jesus Christ of Latter-day Saints on May 9, 1836. And in the twilight of his life, the husband said of the incident, "I have never doubted any principle of Mormonism since."

With the baptism of the Taylors, Mrs. Walton, and others in the study group, a branch of the Church was established in Toronto as Heber C. Kimball had predicted. Other events also demonstrated the truth of the remaining portion of Elder Kimball's prophecy about the Church spreading from Toronto "into the regions round about." Elder Pratt wrote about this phase of his Canadian ministry: "The work soon spread into the country and enlarged its operations in all that region. . . . My first visit to the country was about nine miles from Toronto, among a settlement of farmers, by one of whom I had sent an appointment beforehand. John Taylor accompanied me—this was before he was baptized—we rode on horseback. We called at a Mr. Joseph Fielding's, an acquaintance and friend of Mr. Taylor's. This man had two sisters, young ladies, who seeing us coming ran from their house to one of the neighboring houses, lest they should give welcome, or give countenance to *"Mormonism."* Mr. Fielding stayed, and as we entered the house he said he was sorry we had come, he had opposed our holding meeting in the neighborhood; and, so great was the prejudice, that the Methodist meeting house was closed against us, and the minister refused, on Sunday, to give out the appointment sent by the farmer." (PPP, p. 151.)

The initial repugnance of the Fieldings toward Mormonism progressively moderated into tolerance; then into curiosity, investigation, and intellectual acceptance; and finally into spiritual conversion. The Fieldings were to play important roles in the unfolding drama of Mormonism, especially Joseph, who a year after his conversion would be found back in his native England under extraordinary circumstances, and his sister Mary, who would later become the wife of Patriarch Hyrum Smith and the mother of Joseph F. Smith, the sixth president of The Church of Jesus Christ of Latter-day Saints.

Within two years after his baptism, John Taylor was called as a member of the Quorum of the Twelve Apostles. In this he saw the fulfillment of a spiritual impression he had first received as a teenage boy in England and that had been affirmed intermittently thereafter. The impression first came one day in the country outside Penrith, England, as he walked with a companion to a preaching assignment as a Methodist "exhorter." Suddenly, moved by a spiritual impulse, he stopped in the middle of the road and, turning to his companion, said, "I have a strong impression on my mind, that I have to go to America to preach the gospel!" After migrating to Canada and marrying Leonora Cannon, he occasionally related this experience to his wife, who would ask whether his work as a Methodist preacher fulfilled that impression. Invariably he would answer, "This is not the work; it is something of more importance." (BHR, pp. 28, 30.)

It is a mark of John Taylor's sensitivity that he knew beforehand he was to be called by God to a great work.

Chapter Two

English Roots

After his conversion, John Taylor learned of still another portion of Heber C. Kimball's remarkable prophecy to Parley P. Pratt that foreshadowed the extension of Mormon proselyting to the land of his birth. When Elder Kimball had pictured how the Church would be established in Toronto and then spread to the surrounding areas, he had added: "And from things growing out of this mission, shall the fulness of the gospel spread into England, and cause a great work to be done in that land." (PPP, p. 131.)

John Taylor took the first official step in the process that led to the establishment of The Church of Jesus Christ of Latter-day Saints in the British Isles and to the conversion of tens of thousands of investigators. While John Taylor served as the leader of the Latter-day Saints in upper Canada, his friend and recent convert, Joseph Fielding, asked that he write a letter to Joseph's brother, James, who was a protestant minister in Preston, England, a small community between Liverpool and Milnthorpe, John Taylor's birthplace. This letter, which told of the restoration of the gospel through the Prophet Joseph Smith, appears to have been the first instance in which word of this event had reached England from the pen of an official of the Church.

The year following John Taylor's conversion, Joseph

Fielding and others accompanied Heber C. Kimball on the first LDS missionary expedition to England. Arriving at Liverpool, the elders promptly went north to Preston, where their first sermons on British soil were delivered in the Reverend James Fielding's church. And the first Mormon converts, who were drawn from the minister's flock, were baptized in the River Ribble, which flows by Preston.

That first trickle of conversions, which in the years ahead would burgeon into a mighty flood, came from the area where John Taylor was born and to which he would shortly return to help carry on the work that, as Elder Kimball had prophesied, would grow out of Parley P. Pratt's ministry in and around Toronto.

The reports of the work at Preston that reached John Taylor doubtless aroused many nostalgic feelings and remembrances of his infancy and youth. Milnthorpe lies to the north of Preston, not far from the head of Morecombe Bay, and near Windemere, sometimes called the Queen of English Lakes. In this pleasant place John Taylor was born on November 1, 1808, to James Taylor and Agnes Taylor Taylor. Although the father was trained to work the land, he accepted a government position when John was six and moved his family from Milnthorpe. The itinerant nature of his work with the excise required that he move about, although his headquarters were in Liverpool.

In 1819, when John was eleven, his father moved the family to a small farm in Hale, Westmoreland. The farm had been devised to him by an uncle, William T. Moon. There, for three years, the son got "mixed up with ploughing, sowing, reaping, haymaking and other farm work" while attending school at nearby Beetham. At age fourteen he was apprenticed to a cooper in Liverpool. After a year, his employer's business failed, and John then moved to Penrith, Cumberland, where he began to learn the turner's trade, an occupation that provided sustenance for him and his family during most of his young adulthood.

In Penrith the intellectual and spiritual qualities of James and Agnes Taylor's son began to flower. His heredity and environment were conducive to this. From his well-educated father, who was proficient in Greek, Latin, and higher mathematics, he had early acquired a liking for study, analysis, and reflection. And from both parents he had inherited a strong mentality and by them was thoroughly trained in the catechism and prayers of the Church of England, into which he had been baptized as an infant. The father and mother also exemplified in their conduct the religious principles they sought to inculcate in the son.

The physical surroundings at Penrith are such as to arouse the dormant spiritual sensitivities of even the most worldly. And for one as inherently spiritual as was John Taylor, they were especially compelling. The name given to the valley in which Penrith is situated, the Vale of Eden, suggests beauty and fertility and the impression it conveys to those who visit it. The valley is located between the Pennine and Cumbrian mountains, the highest in all England, through which flow the Eden River on its northwesterly course toward the Solway Firth. Nearby, nestled between the mountain peaks and fed by the snows that blanket them much of the year, lie fifteen picturesque lakes from which the area derives its name, the Lake District. The heavy rainfall, the resulting dampness and luxuriant vegetation, and the drifting, changing cloud formations that now and then lie brooding on the mountaintops lend an air of romance and mystery to the scene. Adding to this provocative mood are ancient druidical ruins, the famous Lowther Castle, Eden Hall, and Shap Abbey, all of which lie within a radius of six miles. Some have surmised that these spectacular scenes of nature and these ancient remnants of man's creativity contributed significantly to the development of the English literary school known as the Lake Poets. William Wordsworth, Robert Southey, and Samuel Taylor Coleridge were members of this school, and all were contemporaries of John Taylor. One may infer that the poetic imagery found in many of Elder Taylor's sermons and writings were inspired in part by the sensory impressions he absorbed during the five years he lived in Penrith.

During this period John Taylor's mind turned away from the rigid forms and orthodoxy of the Church of England to the more vibrant attitudes and practices of Methodism. Such a change could have been predicted for one who, as a small boy, had seen in vision an angel holding a trumpet to his mouth and sounding a note of comfort or warning to the world. Nor was it likely that the cold and uncongenial Church of England could for long hold a sensitive boy who often when alone and sometimes in company "heard sweet, soft, melodious music, as if performed by angelic or supernatural beings." (BHR, p. 28.)

Confident that the younger, more aggressive church would better satisfy his spiritual needs and provide a better outlet and forum for his religious zeal and commitment, John Taylor joined the Methodist church at age sixteen and was soon designated as one of its exhorters. This role entailed visiting Methodist groups and congregations in the neighborhood where he expounded biblical doctrines, testified of God's reality and goodness, and admonished his hearers to live a strictly moral life.

Judging by the extensive knowledge of good literature he showed in his maturity and by the literary impulses that pervaded the Lake District, John Taylor combined his biblical studies with an extensive review of the classics during his Penrith interlude. During his young impressionable years, he learned the theoretical and practical lessons good literature had to teach. And it was by this means that he learned good sentence structure and absorbed the poetic instinct for clear and succinct exposition.

After five years of tutelage as a turner at Penrith, John moved to Hale, where his father helped set him up in business. He operated his business successfully for four years until his departure for Upper Canada in 1832. The ship on which he sailed encountered a storm so violent that the seasoned captain and his officers feared she would founder. The twenty-four-year-old turner, who was making his first voyage, entertained no such fear. "So confident was I of my destiny," he wrote of the incident, "that I went on deck at midnight and amidst the raging elements felt as calm as though I was sitting in a parlor at home. I believed I should reach America and perform my work."

Such was the certitude with which John Taylor approached the shores of America in the year 1832. Docking at New York City, he spent several months there and in Brooklyn and Albany appraising the economic conditions and casting about for employment. Finding nothing that suited him, he went on to Toronto, where his parents had settled two years before. In this bustling port city of about nine thousand, comprised mostly of British immigrants, the newcomer opened a wood-turning shop and settled down to establish an economic base and to pursue his destiny in a new land.

Chapter Three

Marriage and Migration

By the time of his arrival in Toronto, John Taylor was a man with fixed priorities. While it was necessary first to arrange for living accommodations and gainful employment, these were merely the means to an end and, therefore, were subordinate to his principal goal of preaching the gospel. So he promptly affiliated with a Methodist society upon his arrival and was soon engaged in "exhorting" as he had done in England.

The membership of John's new congregation included an attractive, vivacious immigrant from the Isle of Man (via England), Leonora Cannon. Leonora's father, George, a sea captain who operated out of Peel on the Isle of Man, was a descendant of Scotsmen who had fled to that sanctuary in the Irish Sea because of religious and political difficulties in their native country. Moving to England as a girl after the death of her father, Leonora migrated to Canada as the companion and aide of the wife of the private secretary to Lord Aylmer, the governor general of Canada.

In the beginning, Leonora seems not to have been impressed by the handsome young turner recently arrived from England. Indeed, after becoming acquainted through church social activities, she rejected his proposal of marriage without any apparent hesitancy. Later, however, she had a vivid dream in which she saw herself in such a relationship with the newcomer as to convince her she was to be his wife. The couple was married on January 28, 1833, and set up housekeeping in somewhat cramped but comfortable quarters adjacent to the husband's wood-turning shop. Here Parley P. Pratt found and converted the Taylors under the circumstances already explained.

At the time of their baptism, John and Leonora had two children: George John, two years old, and Mary Ann, age four months. Despite the pressures of maintaining his young family in a strange environment, Elder Taylor found the time to devote himself to his new ministry. This was made possible in large part by the competence and maturity of Leonora, who was twelve years older than her husband and therefore much more experienced than he in managing affairs. And any domestic difficulties and inconveniences the Taylors experienced because of the husband's preoccupation with his business and church work were bridged over by the sense of enthusiasm their conversion had produced.

It is apparent that Parley P. Pratt immediately recognized the potential of this immigrant couple, as he ordained the husband an elder shortly after his baptism. Almost immediately, John began to preach the doctrines of his adopted religion, thereby beginning the fulfillment of the prophecy he had uttered years before on the country road near Penrith.

The effective proselyting of Parley P. Pratt and the augmenting strength provided by converts like the Taylors resulted in a rapid growth of the Church in Upper Canada. So promising were the prospects that Orson Pratt and Orson Hyde of the Twelve were sent to assist with the work. After a productive summer of baptizing and organizing, the three apostles departed for Kirtland in the fall of 1836, leaving the promising young John Taylor in charge.

The following spring, the new Mormon leader in Upper Canada traveled to Church headquarters in Kirtland. With him were Isaac Russell and several other Toronto brethren.

John's main purpose in making this trip was to meet and to receive counsel from the head of the Church, Joseph Smith. He was richly rewarded in this aim as he not only met and received counsel from the young prophet, who was just three years older than John, but he was entertained in the Smith home. Such an intimate association with the man who had conversed with Deity filled the new convert with a sense of awe that was not to abate throughout his life.

If Joseph Smith did not perceive the qualities of loyalty and mental toughness in his new follower when they first shook hands, he was soon to learn about them. At the time a spirit of dissension and hatred had settled upon the small community that only a year before, when the Kirtland Temple was dedicated, had experienced a spiritual refulgence unknown since Pentecost. This sudden change from light to darkness in Kirtland coincided with the economic panic that swept over the country in 1837, causing hundreds of bank failures, including failure of the bank in Kirtland, which had been organized by Joseph Smith and his associates. Unaware that what Kirtland faced was part of a national phenomenon, and anxious for a local scapegoat, many pointed the finger at the community's most prominent citizen, Joseph Smith, who also was the chief officer of the defunct bank. So when Elder Taylor and his friends arrived from Toronto, they found the Prophet in a state of siege, being attacked on all sides. Apart from the trauma of seeing the head of his newly found church pilloried in this way, the Canadian convert was appalled to find that his mentor, Parley P. Pratt, had succumbed to the popular uproar and had begun to criticize and condemn Joseph Smith. When Elder Pratt endeavored to infect his student with the same venom, he was sobered by this perceptive answer: "If the work was true six months ago, it is true today." And when the impact of that statement had registered with his friend, John added the necessary corollary: "If Joseph Smith was then a prophet, he is now a prophet." (BHR, p. 40.)

There were those other than Elder Pratt who learned that John Taylor was a convert of extraordinary boldness and intelligence. At a meeting in the Kirtland Temple during which Warren Parrish, a former secretary to Joseph Smith, had denounced the Prophet, John Taylor arose and reminded his listeners of something they seemed to have forgotten: "It was Joseph Smith, under the Almighty, who developed the first principles, and to him we must look for further instruction." Then, comparing his querulous brethren to those who had railed at Moses, he added: "The children of Israel, formerly, after seeing the power of God manifested in their midst, fell into rebellion and idolatry, and there is certainly very great danger of us doing the same thing." (Ibid., p. 41.)

Although the town was in chaos, John Taylor seems to have left Kirtland with a sense of peace and achievement. While the turmoil that was evident on all sides could have upset one of weak conviction or shallow understanding, it was easily reconcilable by the visitor who, through his Bible studies, was familiar with the cantankerous nature of the Israelites and with the destructive and confusing effect of evil forces. And his contacts with the Prophet Joseph Smith had confirmed his perceptions of the man and his work, thereby fulfilling the purpose of his visit.

The spiritual effect of Elder Taylor's stay in Kirtland probably exerted an influence on the unusual manifestation he experienced on his way home. Arriving at Queenstown near Niagara Falls on Sunday, his party found an isolated place below the falls where they knelt in prayer. As John Taylor implored the Lord for help in finding a place in which to preach in Queenstown, he spoke in tongues. Although he was well acquainted with other spiritual phenomena, with visions, dreams, and promptings, never before had the traveler experienced the exhilarating excitement of speaking in tongues.

It is difficult to assess the impact of this experience. One as spiritually minded as John Taylor could well have regarded it as a benediction to his Kirtland pilgrimage and a mark of heavenly approval of his work. Whatever else it may have achieved, its effects can be traced into the zeal he brought to the work after arriving home.

Not long after Elder Taylor returned to Toronto a man from Kirtland named Sampson Avard appeared, bearing a document from his high priests quorum that designated him as the presiding officer of the Church in the Toronto area. Although the three apostles had put Elder Taylor in charge and had not released him, the new convert, whose knowledge of Church procedure was still rudimentary, yielded the reins of leadership to the stranger from Kirtland. This led to the first reprimand John received from a leader of his adopted church. The reprimand came from the Prophet Joseph Smith who, accompanied by Sidney Rigdon and Thomas B. Marsh, went to Toronto in August of 1837. On his arrival, Joseph sought out Elder Taylor to arrange for a series of meetings and thus learned about John's abdication to Sampson Avard. This evoked some pointed though kindly instructions about the principles of authority, delegation, and accountability, instructions that were never forgotten and which the student often used in the decades ahead.

The attitude with which Elder Taylor received this mild censure is suggested by his comments about President Smith's visit: "This was as great a treat to me as I ever enjoyed," wrote he. "I had daily opportunity of conversing with them, of listening to their instructions, and in participating in the rich stores of intelligence that flowed continually from the Prophet Joseph." (BHR, p. 43.)

While following the meeting schedule arranged by John Taylor, the Prophet's party encountered Sampson Avard, whom the Mormon leader rebuked severely. This devious man, who was in league with the dissidents in Kirtland, caused more turmoil the following year in Missouri when he fabricated the story that Joseph Smith had organized a band of murderers called the Danites.

During his tour of the new branches in Upper Canada, Joseph Smith, who was a good judge of character, had the opportunity to scrutinize John Taylor carefully. What he found was a man who was teachable but not servile. He was intelligent, articulate, and tough-minded. And, perhaps more important to Joseph than any of these qualities, was the fact that John Taylor had experienced a spiritual conversion. His faith and commitment did not consist of a mere intellectual assent but were based upon a sure knowledge acquired by a means other than the physical senses.

On returning to Kirtland, Joseph Smith found that the conditions there had deteriorated beyond repair. Several members of the Twelve were in open rebellion. Although the Prophet had frankly acknowledged his inexperience and ineptitude in business matters, which was in part the cause of the difficulty, his critics were unwilling to overlook his weaknesses and concluded that since he was in error in this matter, he was also in error in matters pertaining to the Church. His most outspoken critics among the Twelve at this time were William E. McLellin, Parley P. Pratt, Luke S. Johnson, William B. Smith, John F. Boynton, and Lyman E. Johnson. Of these, Elder Boynton was disfellowshipped on September 3, 1837, and was excommunicated three months later. The disfellowshipment of Elder Boynton marked the first official crack in the Quorum of the Twelve after its formation in February 1835. As Joseph Smith considered the need to replace Elder Boynton, his mind fixed upon the able young wood turner in Toronto whose loyalty was unquestioned and whose native abilities held the prospect of extraordinary growth in the years ahead. So in the autumn of 1837, Joseph Smith wrote to John Taylor in Toronto, calling him as a member of the Quorum of the Twelve Apostles. To have fulfilled in this way the spiritual impression he had received near Niagara Falls as he spoke in tongues added strong impetus to Elder Taylor's zeal. Years later in reflecting on his call to the Twelve and the feelings it evoked, he wrote: "I looked upon it as a life-long labor, and I considered that I was not only enlisted for time, but for eternity also, and did not shrink now, although I felt my incompetency." (BHR, p. 48.)

Before his call to the Twelve, John Taylor had purchased property in Kirtland with the intention of moving there to start a business in partnership with Henry Humphrey. However, due to the worsening of conditions in Kirtland, Joseph Smith requested that Elder Taylor move with his family to Far West, Missouri. Because his business in Toronto had suffered financially through the priority he gave to his church duties, John lacked the means to outfit teams for such a long trip. Nevertheless, he advised Leonora to prepare to leave on a certain day. To the importunate questioning of his wife about how he proposed to travel that long distance without money, the husband gave only the vague answer "I don't know; but the Lord will open out the way." (BHR, p. 49.) Not long afterward, a friend, John Mills, who originally had planned to move to Kirtland, decided instead to go to Far West and invited Elder Taylor and his family to travel with him. Learning that his leader lacked means either for outfitting or expenses, Brother Mills insisted that the Taylors accompany him at his own expense and that he did not expect reimbursement. Later, other members in Toronto contributed food and money. By this means, the Taylor family was able to leave on the day the father had designated, fully supplied with every necessity.

Aside from the striking example of self-confidence this incident provides, it furnishes insight into a fixed characteristic in John Taylor's makeup. He would never ask a human being for help. When needs arose, as they often did throughout his life, he would implore the Lord for assistance and direction, but never other people. This quality was rooted both in his native independence and dignity and in his assurance that God would reward him with the blessings that he sought in faith. Once he and two brethren were planning to sail for Liverpool from New York but did not have enough money to pay for even one passage. Nevertheless, he instructed one of his companions to make reservations for three. The answer given to the question of his incredulous friend was much like his response to Leonora when she wondered how the Taylors would get to Far West without money. He told him in essence that God is the ruler of all things and that from His enormous treasures of wealth, He would provide the pittance necessary to get them to Liverpool. Within a short time, John's faith was rewarded when several members of the Church came forward independently to proffer help.

So it was a man of enormous zeal and faith who departed from Toronto with his family and friends shortly after the first of the year in 1838. A sleigh had been fitted out to accommodate the families of Elder Taylor and Brother Mills while they drove wagons loaded with their food, furnishings, and clothing. The low temperatures that refrigerate the Great Lakes during the winter months had frozen the ground, thereby simplifying and speeding their travel, which took them first to Kirtland, where Elder Taylor had business to transact.

Chapter Four

To Missouri and Beyond

The conditions at Kirtland were both better and worse than John had left them a few months before. A single event lay at the root of these opposites—the departure of Joseph Smith, his family, and his close associates in mid-January. Joseph Smith's departure had reduced the level of hatred and enmity among the dissidents in Kirtland, which in turn had a quieting effect on the community. At the same time, Joseph's departure, as far as John Taylor was concerned, had robbed the place of its main attraction.

Although the frenzied and hateful atmosphere at Kirtland had moderated, there was a residue of ill will reserved for anyone who continued to honor and follow the Prophet Joseph Smith. Being not only a follower but also an outspoken and militant one, John was treated with open hostility. The few meetings he attended in the temple during his short stay were barren of spirituality and friendliness. It was with a sense of relief, therefore, that Elder Taylor and his party left Kirtland and headed for Missouri.

The impending thaw caused the travelers to convert the sleigh into a wagon. With this and the freight wagons brought from Toronto, the party set out. Their meager cash resources made it necessary that Elder Taylor and his friend, John Mills, work their way across Ohio, Indiana, and Illinois while trekking toward Missouri. When in need of money they would lay over temporarily to enable the men to ply their artisan skills. The stay in Indianapolis was extended to two months because Leonora gave birth to her third child, Joseph James, while they were there, and it was necessary to give her time to recuperate. In addition to working part-time in a cabinet shop, John built a sturdy wagon as Brother Mills had decided to remain there a while longer.

All along the way, Elder Taylor took the opportunity to preach the gospel. The reception he received ranged from friendly to hostile, depending on his audience and the attitude of the townspeople. In communities where the Saints and their doctrines were unknown, or where a spirit of tolerance prevailed, Elder Taylor was able to preach unrestrained. But occasionally animosities generated by apostates or rival churches interfered. One such place was a small community near Columbus, Ohio, where a group of troublemakers, on learning that Elder Taylor had scheduled a preaching service, decided to tar and feather him. When a few Church members heard about the plot, they went to John and urged him to cancel the meeting as they lacked the strength to protect him. Expressing thanks for their concern, the traveler decided not to follow their counsel but to fulfill his appointment. At the meeting, the English convert proceeded to lecture his audience about the blessings of freedom guaranteed by the American constitution, about the valor of their forefathers in fighting for liberty, and about the yearnings of downtrodden people around the world to live under the American flag. Having laid that groundwork, the artful speaker suddenly shifted his focus. "But, by the by," he said quietly, "I have been informed that you purpose to tar and feather me, for my religious opinions. Is this the boon you have inherited from your fathers? Is this . . . your liberty?" After letting the implications of this accusatory question seep in, the speaker offered himself as a sacrifice to their "goddess of liberty" and, bearing his breast to the crowd, said, "Gentlemen come on with your tar and feathers, your victim is ready; and ye shades of the venerable patriots, gaze upon the deeds of your degenerate sons! Come on, gentlemen! Come on, I say, I am ready!" (BHR, pp. 54-55.)

Whether enthralled to inaction by the Shakespearean eloquence of the speaker or shamed to silence by his ironic sarcasm, the would-be tormentors made no move. Instead, they remained quiet and attentive while the speaker expounded the doctrines of Mormonism for three hours.

The courage, the poise under pressure, the eloquence, and the combativeness of John Taylor revealed by this incident were to surface again and again under varying circumstances. It was these qualities that would later earn him the title of the Champion of Right, by which he often was referred to among the Latter-day Saints.

If Elder Taylor entertained any idealistic views about the land of Zion, they were shattered when his party arrived at DeWitt, Carroll County, Missouri, in the late summer of 1838. This small town, strategically located on the Grand River near its confluence with the Missouri River, had been settled by a number of Latter-day Saint families. Throughout the summer, these families had been threatened by mobs intent on driving them from the state. Soon after Elder Taylor and his party arrived in DeWitt, the place was besieged by still another mob numbering about 150 and led by two protestant ministers. Aroused by the injustice of seeing the lives and property of harmless Saints threatened by a lawless mob, John, despite a painful injury to an arm (suffered when he had fallen from his wagon), decided to help provide the protection that the law had withheld. "I therefore threw off the sling and bandages from my lame arm," he wrote, "suppressed my repugnance to fighting, borrowed a gun, bought a brace of pistols, and prepared myself at least for defensive measures." (BHR, p. 57.)

Fortunately a temporary truce was negotiated with the mobbers, enabling John Taylor and his party to travel on to Far West.

The fears and apprehensions aroused in Elder Taylor by the mobbers at DeWitt did not abate upon his arrival in Far West. Reports and rumors of burnings, killings, and rapine were everywhere. Notwithstanding, a semblance of order and purpose was present as the Saints continued with their daily occupations and carried on the work of the Church as if conditions were normal. The Prophet Joseph Smith welcomed Elder Taylor warmly, advising him that his call to the apostleship had been confirmed by a formal revelation, received on July 8, 1838, in which John E. Page, Wilford Woodruff, and Willard Richards had received similar calls. (See D&C 118.)

Shortly thereafter, at a quarterly conference of the Church held in Far West on October 6, 1838, Elder Taylor was approved by the conference to fill one of the vacancies in the Twelve. However, he was not ordained until December 19, 1838, when at a meeting of the high council he was ordained by Brigham Young and Heber C. Kimball.

The process of John Taylor's call and ordination to the apostleship assumes special meaning in light of the alleged binding effect of revelations he received prior to his death and which were promulgated thereafter by certain individuals. Even though Joseph Smith advised him in the fall of 1837 he would be called to the Twelve, and even though that notification was affirmed by a formal revelation in July of the following year, his call was not efficacious and binding until he was approved by a constituent assembly of the Church and until he had been ordained by those having the requisite authority.

Shortly after his arrival in Far West, Elder Taylor was launched on his literary career. This came about when he and several other brethren were appointed to a committee to prepare a report to the Missouri legislature outlining the persecutions of the Latter-day Saints in that state. While other members of the committee, which included Brigham Young and Heber C. Kimball of the Twelve, provided important information, the laborious process of composition was left largely to Elder Taylor and Edward Partridge, the

Presiding Bishop of the Church. Until this time, John's literary efforts had been limited almost exclusively to intermittent correspondence. But the Prophet Joseph Smith apparently inferred a writing potential from John's dignified and impeccable speaking style and saw to it that he would play a key role in preparing the report, which was presented to the Missouri legislature on December 19, 1838, by John Corrill, a Latter-day Saint, who was a member of that body. As already indicated, this was the same day on which Elder Taylor was ordained to the apostleship. And at the meeting where the ordination took place, John was appointed to serve on still another special committee, this one to prepare a report to the national government, detailing the grievances of the Latter-day Saints arising out of their mistreatment in Missouri.

While nothing of a concrete, positive nature resulted from either of these reports as far as the Church was concerned, they were of special importance to John Taylor. The knowledge he gained in conducting the research was to prove invaluable to him, as was the experience he gained in literary composition. Perhaps more important than anything else, his service on these committees demonstrated his loyalty and ability, marking him in the minds of his leaders as a man of stature who could be relied upon.

Through the connivance of officials of the Missouri militia and certain nominal members of the Church, the Prophet Joseph Smith, his brother, Hyrum, and other Church leaders were arrested in Far West the last of October. This began several months of incarceration for Joseph Smith, first in Independence and then in Richmond and Liberty Missouri.

With the Prophet in custody, the Quorum of the Twelve Apostles assumed the administrative leadership of the Church. Most of these brethren lived in or near Far West, a town of about three thousand, which at that time was the state's largest community north of the Missouri River. Here Joseph Smith had engaged in his first effort at city planning, having laid out the town on four sections, two miles square, with wide streets and four-acre blocks, each block containing four one-acre lots. In the center of town was a large public square on a gently rising knoll from which most of the community could be seen, as also the farms and wooded areas beyond. The public square included a temple site, where the Saints intended to duplicate what had been done at Kirtland.

Because of the governor's order to exterminate the Mormons, the massacre of nineteen Latter-day Saints at nearby Hauns Mill, the arrest of Joseph Smith, and the demands of the Missouri militia and the mobs that the Mormons leave the state, it was clear to John Taylor that his stay in Far West would be brief. So he and Leonora and their three children settled into cramped temporary quarters while John plied his craft and fulfilled his responsibilities as a member of the Twelve. John's preoccupation with his duties imposed upon Leonora most of the domestic burdens. These were made lighter by the companionship of some of her friends from the Toronto area who also had migrated to Missouri at the suggestion of Joseph Smith. Among these was Mary Fielding, whom John had been instrumental in converting and who later had married Hyrum Smith, the Prophet's brother.

It is inferred that Mary Fielding Smith took special comfort from Leonora's presence when, two weeks after her husband was arrested and taken to Independence, she gave birth to her first child, whom she named Joseph Fielding Smith. Had Leonora possessed the intuition to perceive it, she doubtless would have been surprised to see that within a few decades Mary's baby would be a counselor to her husband in the First Presidency of the Church. And had such foresight been granted to her, she would have been equally surprised to see that her nephew, George Q. Cannon, then only eleven years old and a nonmember resident of Liverpool, England, would then be her husband's other counselor in the First Presidency.

It was during this period that John Taylor first came under the tutelage and direction of Brigham Young, whom he would later succeed as the President of the Church. There was thus formed a personal relationship between these two extraordinary men who were at once so alike and yet so different. The similarities in the two were at the spiritual level; the differences could be traced chiefly to their earthly backgrounds.

Both Brigham and John were intelligent, strong-minded men who had joined the Church in their maturity and whose conversions had been accompanied by powerful spiritual manifestations. Both had spoken in tongues shortly after their baptism and by this means had been given spiritual insight into their life missions. Both were staunchly loyal to the Prophet Joseph Smith, never deviating from his instructions and example, even after the Prophet's death. And both had experienced intellectual as well as spiritual conversion and therefore were committed to the doctrines of the Church, including the doctrines of the gathering and of building the kingdom of God on the earth.

But this pair had come from widely different backgrounds, which affected their outlook and perceptions. Elder Young had spent his infancy, childhood, and young adulthood in rural communities in Vermont and New York, communities with the comparatively unknown and undistinguished names of Whitingham, Sherbourne, Aurelius, Auburn, Port Byron, and Mendon. Moreover, most of these communities were on the American frontier of that day, in the midst of an as yet untamed and uncultivated forest land. Therefore, the first essential step of a farmer before he could apply his agricultural skills was to clear the land of trees, stumps, boulders, and underbrush. This tedious work monopolized practically all of the time of a farmer and his family. Such a preoccupation with the business of wresting a living from the soil left little time for cultural and intellectual pursuits, even had the facilities for such been available.

When in his mid-teens Brigham Young discontinued working on his father's farm to learn the crafts of glazing and painting, the physical demands upon him became less arduous, allowing for more leisure. But the opportunities for intellectual or cultural expression were woefully lacking in communities whose main object was to tame and subjugate the wilderness. In such an environment, the natural tendency was for one's intelligence and energies to be directed toward practical, temporal goals—clearing and tilling the land; constructing buildings, bridges, roads, and canals; and raising and training or butchering livestock—in short, bringing order out of the chaos of a wild environment.

John Taylor, on the other hand, was born in an area that had been under cultivation for hundreds of years. Nearby were large commercial centers that over the centuries had acquired the jewels of civilization: libraries, museums, theaters, and universities. And while the tilling of a farm in England was no less laborious than in America, still the absence of the extensive preparatory work, the presence of long-established procedures, and the more slow-paced and contemplative quality of the English character introduced a sense of peace and repose that was often absent from the driving, sometimes frenetic, character of the American Yankee. These altered circumstances enabled English farmers, like John Taylor's father, to acquire a solid classical education. And, of course, during the few years the father served as a civil servant in Liverpool, the son was exposed to the cultural advantages of that ancient city and to the cosmopolitan veneer that attaches to any great seaport.

So the different environments in which Brigham Young and John Taylor were reared to maturity were calculated to prepare one to tame a wilderness and the other to combat the intellectual enemies of the Church with Mormon doctrine and philosophy and well-honed sentences. And each recognized and honored the other in his special role and abilities. Brigham, for instance, declared John to be the most powerful editor and writer in the Church, and at the general conference following Brigham Young's death,

Elder Taylor said of his departed leader, "Brigham Young needs no fictitious aid to perpetuate his memory; his labors have been exhibited during the last forty-five years . . . in the building of cities throughout the length and breadth of this Territory." (JD 19:123.)

This is not to suggest that these two did not show any aptitude or skill beyond the limits of their special competence. Quite the contrary. The extensive writings and sermons of President Young reveal a terse, pithy style that is both entertaining and convincing. And, for his part, Elder Taylor showed considerable organizational and administrative skill, especially during the trying years he spent on the underground. Whatever conflicts arose between these two powerful men traced chiefly to the perception by one that the other had not quite measured up to his own high standard in the field of his special abilities.

But it is clear that any differences between John Taylor and Brigham Young were swallowed up by their religious convictions and by their overriding commitment to the apostolic responsibilities they had assumed. It was in this spirit that they and the other members of the Twelve rallied together during the crisis in Missouri to preserve some semblance of order among the Latter-day Saints while the President of the Church was in jail and while enemies on all sides were exerting pressure upon them to leave the state.

Anxious to conduct the affairs of the Church according to the wishes of its president, Elder Taylor and other members of the Twelve made periodic visits to the jail in Liberty, Missouri, where Joseph and Hyrum were incarcerated. Never before this had John been inside a prison. The repulsive impression created by the squalor of this place would remain with him throughout his life. He found a squat stone structure that measured twenty-two and a half by twenty-two feet. Its builders had boasted it was escape proof, a boast resting on the building's double oak walls filled with four feet of rock. The intense gloom of the jail's interior was barely affected by the thin shafts of light admitted through two small iron-barred windows. And the fetid odors that permeated the entire structure were nauseating to one who entered the building from the fresh outdoors. One can easily imagine how repugnant it was for John Taylor, who was the soul of cleanliness and gentility, to enter the jail and there to see his ideal and exemplar confined under such squalid conditions.

The next time Elder Taylor saw the interior of a jail was at Carthage, Illinois, where he would join his leader in confinement, witness his martyrdom, and barely escape death himself after being severely wounded.

Given the conditions that existed in Missouri at this time, the question was not whether the Saints would leave the state, but when and whence. The answer came in January when, through pre-arrangement with local political leaders, the Twelve shepherded the Saints from Missouri across the Mississippi River to Quincy, Illinois. Loading his family and their belongings on the wagon he had made while en route to Far West, Elder Taylor joined the caravan of destitute but doggedly determined Latter-day Saints who made their way to what they knew was only a temporary stop in their continuing exodus.

Chapter Five

Back to England

A revelation received in July 1838 had directed the Twelve to depart from Far West on April 26, 1839, for a mission abroad. (See D&C 118.) Knowledge of this revelation had been widely circulated among both members and non-members. And with the evacuation of the Saints from Missouri, the mobbers there, being aware of the revelation, had boasted that it would never be fulfilled. The members of the Twelve were equally determined that it would not fail.

The intent of the apostles to fulfill this mandate was not formed in ignorance of the dangers involved. Elder Taylor, in detailing the events of this bold venture for the *Millennial Star*, characterized the Missourians of that day as men who "would as soon have shot us as they would a dog." (MS 2:12.) Disregarding the hazards, the Twelve began to make preparations in mid-April for the trip to Far West. They were heartened and spurred on later by reports of the escape of Joseph and Hyrum Smith from their captors in Liberty.

Joined by a number of other brethren, the Twelve set out from Quincy with their wagons and mounts. Fording the river, they traveled through the wooded, rolling countryside of northeast Missouri without any extraordinary effort at concealment. On April 25, they met elders Clark and

Turley about thirty miles from their destination. This pair had been appointed as a committee to supervise the evacuation of the Mormon stragglers. They joined the group from Quincy, thereby swelling its number to thirty. The last leg of the journey was timed to enable the travelers to arrive in Far West under the cloak of night.

Bright moonlight bathed the sleepy, almost deserted village, and all was peaceful and quiet except for the noises made by the snorting and trampling of the horses and the rumbling and squeaking of the wagons. The Twelve and the others went methodically about the work that had brought them there. They rolled a stone weighing about a ton to the temple's foundation. During the ceremonies that followed, it was laid as the southeast cornerstone by Alpheus Cutler, who had superintended the excavation for the foundation. The group sang two hymns, including W. W. Phelps's "Adam-ondi-Ahman." The five members of the Twelve who were present, Brigham Young, Heber C. Kimball, Orson Pratt, John E. Page, and John Taylor, joined in ordaining Wilford Woodruff and George A. Smith to the apostleship, with Brigham Young acting as mouth in the ordination of Elder Woodruff and Heber C. Kimball acting as mouth in the ordination of Elder Smith. Also, a majority of the quorum then being present, the Twelve excommunicated several persons who had apostatized during the frenzied struggles connected with the expulsion of the Saints from Missouri. And each of the seven apostles prayed aloud in turn, according to seniority, beginning with thirty-eight-year-old Brigham Young and ending with twenty-one-year-old George A. Smith.

By the time the ceremonies ended, dawn had come to Far West, enabling John Taylor to inspect in the light of day what was once a thriving community but now had the aspect of a ghost town. Many of the homes had been burned, some by the mobbers as a means of punishing and terrifying the Saints, and others presumably by the owners to prevent their enemies from enjoying a windfall. Most of the buildings that remained unburned had been ransacked and stood empty and desolate. On all sides was convincing evidence that the hand of industry and thrift had been withdrawn from Far West. Doors and gates swung ajar, fences were in disrepair, barns and corrals stood empty, and grass had begun to grow across some of the roadways.

With the completion of the work at the temple, there was nothing to detain Elder Taylor and the others in Far West since all the Saints who intended to leave had been evacuated. So, in company with his friends, John returned to Quincy to make preparations for his mission abroad. His first concern was to find suitable lodgings for Leonora and the children. The solution, although not entirely to the Taylors' liking, was a room in an old army barracks in Montrose, Iowa, across the river from Nauvoo, Illinois. But John's impending departure for England made it impossible to build a new home.

The crudity and inconvenience of these quarters were compensated for by the good neighbors the Taylors found in Montrose. Brigham Young, Orson Pratt, and Wilford Woodruff and their families, along with other Latter-day Saints, had taken up temporary residency in the same barracks. Although they lived in poverty, there was a healthy spirit of optimism and self-confidence among these refugees. And the communal type of living gave some comfort to John and the other members of the Twelve, knowing there would be friends nearby to help their families while they were away.

It was during this summer that Elder Taylor received still another writing assignment. Joseph Smith, who had been asked by the editor of the *St. Louis Gazette* to do it, in turn asked John to prepare an account of the Mormon persecutions in Missouri. John accepted willingly and spent most of the summer gathering the facts and marshaling them into a convincing indictment of the lawlessness and bigotry practiced on the Saints in Missouri. Whatever the reason, the editor refused to publish the article when it was submitted, although as we shall see, the author later published it at his own expense.

Elder Taylor departed from Montrose for England on August 8, 1839. At the time, Leonora and the children were ill with the malarial fever that had afflicted most of the Latter-day Saints during the summer. Their condition and the uncertainties about the future had caused John to wonder whether his departure should be delayed still longer. However, words of encouragement from Leonora, his remembrance of the stressful circumstances under which Parley P. Pratt had left his family in Kirtland to proselyte in Toronto, and his ingrained sense of apostolic duty impelled him to leave. After bidding a tearful good-bye to his wife and children, the apostle walked resolutely to a skiff that waited at the river's edge, waved a last farewell to the family, and crossed the Mississippi to Nauvoo, where he was to meet his companion, Wilford Woodruff, who had gone ahead.

He found Elder Woodruff at the Nauvoo river landing shivering with the ague and hardly in any condition to begin a lengthy trip abroad. But, after conferring with Joseph Smith and other Church leaders, it was decided to leave anyway, presumably on the assumption that there is never a perfect time to launch any enterprise.

Following a mandate given to Joseph Smith and Oliver Cowdery in the early days of their ministry, the apostles were instructed to fulfill their mission abroad without purse or scrip. And they were promised they would receive "in the very hour" what they needed "for food and for raiment, and for shoes and for money, and for scrip." (See D&C 24:18.) John and Wilford reaped the firstfruits of this promise on the outskirts of Nauvoo. There they met fellow apostles Heber C. Kimball and Parley P. Pratt, who were trimming logs for cabins they had under construction. Desiring to help their brethren along the way, Parley donated an empty purse he had, and Heber gave the pair a dollar to put into it. From that moment, John was not without means during his mission, slender though they were at times, means that came from the liberality of the people.

Like the widow's barrel of meal, there was always enough with some to spare.

Three days after leaving Nauvoo, the missionaries reached Macomb, Illinois, which was the temporary residence of Zebedee Coltrin, one of the original presidents of the First Quorum of Seventy. Zebedee was a man of faith who would later migrate west during the exodus and who would pass away in Spanish Fork, Utah, four days before John Taylor. With the aid of Elder Coltrin and Don Carlos Smith, the Prophet's youngest brother, who also lived in Macomb, a series of meetings was arranged where the two apostles spoke. The result was the baptism of the pair's first convert on this mission, George Miller, a well-to-do farmer in the area, who, five years later, would become the Second Bishop of the Church.

The new convert donated a horse to the missionaries, and the other Saints chipped in nine dollars as the elders left Macomb with Brother Coltrin, who had offered to drive them to Springfield in his wagon. At the state capital, where two years before young Abraham Lincoln had begun his career as a prairie lawyer, John Taylor formally began his career as a published author. Organizing the extensive notes he had compiled during the summer into an eight-page pamphlet, John decided to publish it under the imposing title "A Short Account of the Murders, Robberies, Burnings, Thefts, and Other Outrages Committed by the Mob and Militia of the State of Missouri, upon the Latter-day Saints, The Persecutions They Have Endured for their Religion and their Banishment from the State by the Authorities Thereof." To finance the publication of two thousand copies of this tract, Elder Taylor, with Wilford Woodruff's consent, sold the horse George Miller had given to them. Some of the tracts were given to Zebedee Coltrin to sell, with proceeds to be given to Sister Taylor and Sister Woodruff. The remainder was kept by the two apostles for later distribution or sale.

Aside from its literary qualities, the most distinguishing

feature of this work is the impressive accumulation and arrangement of facts to support the author's thesis. John Taylor did not deal in generalities or speculation, but in specific examples of the unlawful burdens that had been heaped upon the Latter-day Saints. There was no hint here of the philosophical tone that would characterize some of his later writings. Rather, it was similar in spirit and purpose to the writings of the noted religious and political pamphleteers of the past. Elder Taylor's obvious intent was not to tickle the intellectual fancy of his readers, but to convince them that a great wrong had been committed that ought to be corrected. It is to be inferred that the persuasive power of this short pamphlet weighed heavily in Joseph Smith's decision to appoint John Taylor as the editor of the Church publications at Nauvoo upon his return from England.

Having delivered his first written message to the world, thereby acquiring the title of "author," Elder Taylor and his companion continued their journey toward the east coast. Up to this point, John had enjoyed good health. Indeed, it would appear that of all the members of the Twelve who had left Nauvoo that season, he was the healthiest. But the malarial fever that had afflicted so many of the Saints at last proved to be impartial. It struck John as his party approached Germantown, Indiana. "When I got out of the carriage . . .," he wrote of the incident, "I dropped down senseless in the highway, and [it] was some time before I recovered." (MS 2:13.) The same thing happened the next day with more serious consequences, as it was only with great difficulty he "was restored to animation."

It being apparent his convalescence would take time, the patient urged Elder Woodruff to continue his journey eastward, with the understanding they would rendezvous in New York before going abroad. So the ailing apostle was left alone in Germantown in the care of an innkeeper, Jacob Waltz, and his wife, who nursed him back to health. After a two-week confinement, the fever broke, and a weakened and emaciated John Taylor began to grope his way back to activity. His first thoughts were of his neglected ministry, so with the encouragement and aid of the Waltz family and others who had befriended him, the apostle scheduled a series of meetings in a nearby chapel whose doors had been opened to him. So debilitating had been his illness that most of the missionary's sermons were delivered while he was seated.

As usual, Elder Taylor did not complain about his misfortune, nor did he ask for help from those around him. This intrigued those who knew of his illness and of his apparent lack of means, especially in contrast with other ministers of their acquaintance who were exceedingly aggressive in soliciting donations. At length one of the townsmen approached the apostle and, asking pardon for intruding into his private affairs, said several friends, knowing of the heavy expense he had incurred while ill, wanted to assist him financially. The answer was typical: "I preach without purse, . . ." he told the visitor, "leaving the Lord to manage those matters you speak of in His own way; and as you have been prompted by the Lord and your own generous impulses, I shall thankfully receive whatever assistance you are disposed to render me." (BHR, p. 70.) The donation from the visitor, added to some slender means he had received from other benefactors, enabled John to pay for all the expenses he had incurred while in Germantown and to leave that place with a small nest egg.

The next major stopping place was Dayton, Ohio, where, after preaching for several days, Elder Taylor suffered a relapse and was confined to bed for another two weeks, this time in the home of a Brother Brown.

As John was preparing to leave Dayton, George A. Smith arrived with a party that Elder Taylor joined for the trip to Kirtland. Here they met Elders Brigham Young and Heber C. Kimball, who had preceded them there; and after John had recovered sufficiently from still another siege of illness, the enlarged group traveled on to New York without incident.

Elder Taylor was welcomed into the apartment of Parley P. Pratt on arriving in New York City. Although a penny was all the cash he had when he arrived, when some of the brethren asked John about his finances, he answered that he had "plenty of money." This was reported to Parley P. Pratt, who went to his friend and, explaining that he needed several hundred dollars to publish a manuscript and had heard that John had means, asked for a loan. Parley was told he could have all the money his fellow apostle had, and, reaching into his pocket, John Taylor produced the penny. After a good chuckle, Brother Pratt asked his Toronto convert what he meant by giving out that he had plenty of money. "Yes, and so I have," John answered. "I am well clothed, you furnish me plenty to eat and drink and good lodging; with all these things and a penny over, as I owe nothing, is not that plenty?" (Ibid., p. 73.)

Parley urged at the next meeting of the Manhattan Branch that the members chip in to help pay Elder Taylor's steerage fare to Liverpool. John objected and instead encouraged anyone who had surplus money to donate it to help publish Parley's manuscript. After the meeting, Elder Woodruff expressed chagrin that his companion had declined this proffered aid, as he had booked passage on the assumption they would leave soon for England to fulfill the mission that had already been delayed for more than six months. John said if he believed they should leave immediately, to make reservations for both of them on the packet ship *Oxford*. When asked how they would pay the fare, Elder Taylor answered, "Oh, there will be no difficulty about that. Go and take a passage for me on your vessel, and I will furnish you the means." (Ibid., p. 74.) When their friend Theodore Turley said he would like to join them, Elder Taylor asked Wilford to book passage for him too.

This demonstration of faith was rewarded later when several members came forward, unsolicited, to donate money for the elders' passage. It was enough to get them to England with some loose change to spare. So when John Taylor reached his native land at Liverpool, he still had "plenty of money," according to his reckoning.

Chapter Six

With the Twelve in Great Britain

After spending two days in Liverpool, where John acted as guide in showing his companions the city he knew so well, the trio left for Preston on January 13, 1840. There Elder Taylor found that his Canadian friend Joseph Fielding presided over the thriving Preston branch, which traced its origin to the proselyting of Heber C. Kimball and his associates beginning in 1837. After a few days of visiting and "rejoicing before God" that they had been enabled thus far to brave the storms and opposition, the two members of the Twelve, who were the senior apostles in the British Isles (Brigham Young and four other members of the Twelve would not arrive until April) convened a priesthood council where a plan was formulated to carry on their work. It was decided that Elder Woodruff would go to Staffordshire, Elder Turley to Birmingham, and Elder Taylor, accompanied by Joseph Fielding, to Liverpool.

John and his companion were warmly received in Liverpool as guests at the home of George Cannon (Leonora's brother) and his wife, Ann Quayle. This pair and three of their children, including twelve-year-old George Q. Cannon, were among the first converts Elder Taylor and his companion baptized in Liverpool.

Aside from working with the relatives and friends of members, as in the case of the Cannon family, the missionaries at first followed the proselyting approach used by Heber C. Kimball and his associates in Preston: They sought opportunity to speak in chapels belonging to other Christian denominations. So, the Elders visited many leading ministers in the city, most of whom, John wrote, were so "wrapped up in sectarianism that there was very little room for the truth in their hearts." (MS 2:15.) An exception was found at a chapel on Hope Street where, following the pastor's sermon, John arose and asked permission to make a few remarks. His request was granted, and, moving to the vestry, the apostle addressed twenty of the leaders and exhorters of the church. The result was inconclusive. Some wept with joy, John reported, while others were "hardened" and "raged" against the elders.

Ultimately, the doors of the churches were closed to the missionaries, who then rented a hall where they began to hold regular preaching services. Many of the attenders were attracted to the message, and from these the companions began to reap a harvest of converts. By April 16, 1841, when Elder Taylor filed a report with Parley P. Pratt, editor of the *Millennial Star,* the branch in Liverpool numbered over two hundred. (Ibid.)

On April 6, 1840, Elders Brigham Young, Heber C. Kimball, Parley P. Pratt, Orson Pratt, and George A. Smith, of the Twelve, and Elder Reuben Hedlock disembarked at Liverpool from the packet ship *Patrick Henry.* Learning of their arrival, Elder Taylor met them the next day. After savoring the joy of being reunited with his brethren and after being briefed on affairs in America, John reported on his work in Liverpool and introduced the new arrivals to his converts, who most likely were overwhelmed by the presence of six apostles in their midst.

After a few days, the party traveled north to Preston. There Elder Wilford Woodruff joined the other brethren, and a majority of the quorum being present, there was held the first official meeting of the Twelve outside the American continent. Other aspects of this gathering further enhanced its historical significance. The minutes of the meeting, prepared by John Taylor, who served as its clerk, reveal that Brigham Young was sustained as the president of the Twelve; Willard Richards was ordained to the apostleship; and approval was given to publish the Book of Mormon, a hymn book, and a periodical named the *Latter-day Saints' Millennial Star*. At the same time, Elder Taylor was reassigned to labor in Liverpool and its environs and also was appointed to assist in compiling the hymn book and in publishing the Book of Mormon.

Returning to his field of labor, John resumed his ministry there and continued to proselyte enthusiastically as in the past. He also began to devote more time to training the new members in the doctrines of the Church and in its administrative procedures. This was a task that would increasingly occupy the time of Elder Taylor and his brethren of the Twelve as they sought to alter the attitudes and habits of masses of converts who had entered the Church with diverse backgrounds, temperaments, and capabilities, and to mold them into "the body of Christ." (1 Corinthians 12:27.)

It was during this period that for one of the few times in his career Elder Taylor did not follow a customary habit of his, and in the process learned a valuable lesson. The incident grew out of a decision by Brigham Young that the wife of Parley P. Pratt be allowed to join her husband in England while he served as the editor of the *Millennial Star*. Learning of this, John went to Elder Young, in violation of his habit of imploring God but not men for desired blessings or privileges, to request permission for Leonora to join him. Clothing his petition in its most attractive dress, he pointed out that apart from the aid and comfort she would be to Elder Taylor personally, Leonora would also be a definite boon to the work because of her intimate, first-hand knowledge of English ways and customs and her numerous relatives and acquaintances in Great Britain. To John's chagrin, his request was denied, not because of any preferential treatment to be given to Elder Pratt, but because it was intended that Parley's stay in the British Isles would be much longer than Elder Taylor's.

The embarrassment to a man of his independence and sensibilities of being turned down in this way doubtless had a profound effect, so much so that there appears to be no other recorded instance in which John Taylor overtly sought special treatment or favor. Seemingly, the cost of a favor was too high for him if it had to be purchased with a loss of independence or self-esteem.

The assignment to compile a hymn book was given to a committee of the Twelve chaired by Brigham Young. John Taylor and Parley P. Pratt were the other members. As the work progressed, the differences in approach between an aggressive executive and two editors and literary men became glaringly apparent. President Young was concerned primarily with financing and expediting the printing of the book so that it would be in the hands of the British Saints as soon as possible. John and Parley, on the other hand, were equally concerned about the quality of the hymns, about the make-up of the volume, and about proofreading of the galleys to guard against typographical errors. President Young was prepared to sacrifice literary perfection on the altar of speed, and being the chairman of the committee, his views prevailed, sometimes to the annoyance of his precise brethren. This was nothing more than the kind of collision that occasionally occurs between powerful men of different talents and temperaments but does not indicate a dislike for each other, as some have implied.

By July the work in Liverpool had progressed to the point that John felt it was timely to obtain more spacious accommodations for his meetings. So in the middle of the month he contracted for the Music Hall in Bold Street, which had a seating capacity of about fifteen hundred. He intended to deliver a series of lectures there. But because access to the hall could not be obtained for several weeks, he decided to take the opportunity to visit Ireland.

Among Elder Taylor's Liverpool converts was a convivial Irishman named McGuffie, fondly called Brother Mack, who had many acquaintances in Newry, County Down, Ireland. In company with Brother Mack and a young convert from Manchester named William Blake, John sailed from Liverpool on July 27, 1840. Landing at Warren Point, near the present border separating Ireland and Northern Ireland, the three missionaries went immediately to Newry. There, through the influence of Elder McGuffie, arrangements were made for a meeting in the Session House, where John Taylor preached the first sermon by a Latter-day Saint on Irish soil. Several hundred attended the meeting. Their response to the message was hardly ecstatic as judged by the small handful that turned out to hear the Mormon apostle the next night. This tepid reception caused Elder Taylor to dismiss the idea of holding additional meetings in Newry, and plans were made, accordingly, to leave for Belfast the next morning. That night, John had a vivid dream in which a man appeared, urging that he remain in Newry to preach. The next morning the dream was enacted in reality when the same man stopped the apostle as he and his companions were leaving town, imploring him to stay. As he had received no spiritual impulse to heed this request, Elder Taylor declined, notwithstanding the extraordinary way in which he had received foreknowledge of it. However, he advised the man that Elder McGuffie would soon return to Newry to continue the teaching he had begun.

A fourth man, Thomas Tate, an investigator, joined the party at Newry. John had met this man in Liverpool earlier and at that time had prophesied that he would eventually join the Church. Arriving at the Four Towns of Bellimacrat, a typical well-scrubbed Irish community, Elder Taylor preached in a barn owned by a Mr. Willie. Gauged by the unusual events of the next day, the impact of this sermon far exceeded that of the apostle's effort in Newry. As the quartet traveled toward Belfast, Elder Taylor engaged Mr. Tate in conversation, developing some of the themes discussed or hinted at the night before. As the discussion progressed, the investigator became convinced that the doctrines expounded by the Mormon apostle were true. Reaching the crest of a hill, the gospel student saw a lake ahead, and, alluding to Philip's baptism of the eunuch, said, "See, here is water; what doth hinder me to be baptized?" (Acts 8:36.) Satisfied that Thomas Tate was prepared for the ordinance, Elder Taylor then baptized him in the clear, cold waters of Loch Brickland near Lisburn, Northern Ireland. The event marked the first convert baptism in Ireland performed by an official of The Church of Jesus Christ of Latter-day Saints.

Arriving at Lisburn, the missionaries could find no suitable building in which to meet, so they preached outdoors. Elder Taylor delivered four meaty sermons in the marketplace to large crowds who paid respectful attention to the handsome man with the English accent who spoke of a restoration of the gospel and of singular spiritual experiences of a young prophet in America. While the listeners seemed to be intrigued by what they heard, none came forward seeking baptism.

It was John's original intention to hold meetings in Belfast, but scheduling complications made that impossible. Booking passage on a North Channel packet ship, he sailed through the Firth of Clyde and twenty miles up the Clyde River to the ancient city of Glasgow, where elders Hedlock, Clark, and Mulliner had been laboring. There he preached to the members of the small branch that had been organized and to the investigators with whom the three elders were working. He did the same in nearby Paisley.

The aura of apostolic authority that enveloped the visitor had a dual and, in a sense, a conflicting effect upon the Glasgow Saints. They felt an overflowing love toward him because of his role as a special witness of the Lord Jesus Christ, but, because of their respect for him, they were reluctant to be too familiar with him. Still, Elder Taylor's democratic yet dignified demeanor removed most feelings of reticence so that his visit was characterized by a remarkable show of affection by the Glasgow Saints. They crowded around him following each meeting pleading for special blessings, and when it came time to depart, they implored him to remain yet a while longer. But the apostle's schedule of meetings in the Music Hall made it imperative that he leave.

In Liverpool Elder Taylor found that his missionary force had been augmented by the arrival of Elder Curtis and Elder Winchester from the states. Their effective labors, added to the work of other Mormon missionaries in the city, had swelled the size of the Liverpool Branch, and these, plus numerous investigators, friends, and a few curiosity seekers brought sizable audiences to the Music Hall in Bold Street to hear Elder Taylor. In a series of lectures during several weeks, he traced the course of the apostasy, detailed the circumstances surrounding the restoration, outlined the events that were yet to occur in the unfolding drama of the gathering and second coming, and expounded from the scriptures, ancient and modern, all of the basic doctrines of the Church. In this kind of setting, John Taylor's talents were displayed to the best advantage. His knowledge, platform presence, delivery, and spirituality combined to bring understanding and conviction to those who listened with open minds and hearts.

Soon after completing his series of lectures in the Music Hall, the apostle embarked for the Isle of Man in company with Hiram Clark and William Mitchel. This trio landed at Douglas, the island's capital and largest city, whose harbor was choked with fishing craft and whose ancient streets and buildings bore the imprint of its Viking, Gaelic, and British heritage. After surveying the prospects during a canvass of the area, the brethren decided that Brothers Clark and Mitchel would go north to Ramsey while Elder Taylor would remain in Douglas. The apostle accompanied his associates out of town on the road to the north and, finding a secluded place, stopped for a council meeting.

Following a fervent, kneeling prayer, the companions found three stones, which they placed at the foot of a tree on which were carved the date and the names of the missionaries. Elder Taylor then ordained Brother Mitchel a deacon, conferred a special blessing on Elder Clark, and joined them in an impromptu testimony meeting where they sang, prophesied, and spoke in tongues. Being thus spiritually energized, John returned to Douglas to face what proved to be the most determined opposition he had experienced since first arriving in Great Britain on his mission.

Following the pattern of his earlier work in Liverpool, Elder Taylor sought out a suitable hall for preaching. The one selected, the Wellington Rooms, was located in a marketplace and, with its thousand-seat capacity, was reputed to be the largest hall in the city. To stimulate an interest in the lectures he planned to deliver, Elder Taylor contacted many of the residents who knew Leonora and her family. In addition, he made the acquaintance of some of the community leaders, including Mr. Cain, a bookbinder and seller, who also was a Primitive Methodist preacher. This man was later to render an important service to the Mormon apostle.

Predictably, the lectures by the stranger in the Wellington Rooms aroused a furor among the local clergy as they began to see some of their parishioners being baptized into The Church of Jesus Christ of Latter-day Saints. The most vocal of these was the Reverend Thomas Hamilton, who, failing to deter the lecturer by creating rowdy disturbances at his meetings, challenged him to a debate. Elder Taylor accepted in a lengthy letter that narrowed the issues to the subjects discussed in his lectures, defined the procedure to be followed, and suggested that Mr. Cain serve as the chairman of the meeting. The challenger accepted these conditions, and the debate was held amidst an atmosphere of high excitement and a good deal of acrimony generated by the volatile Reverend Hamilton. But the outcome was the opposite of what he had intended. He found his opponent too much to handle, doctrinally, oratorically, and intellectually. As a result of the debate, Elder Taylor discovered that his message was more widely disseminated than ever, and the tide of public opinion was running in his favor because of the crude tactics of his opponent. When he was complimented for having bested his rival, the newcomer brushed it off by explaining that the challenger was, after all, "a very ignorant man."

Other local divines, observing the humiliation of the Reverend Hamilton in a head-on confrontation with John Taylor, sought other forums in which to oppose him. One merely began to devote the sermons in his own church to attacks upon Elder Taylor and Mormonism. John Taylor answered him in another series of lectures delivered in the Wellington Rooms. Another, Mr. J. Curran, published a series of scurrilous articles in the local press. Elder Taylor responded by writing lengthy, answering letters to the editors of the *Manx Liberal* and the *Manx Sun*. Still another, the Reverend Robert Heys, printed and distributed three tracts denouncing the doctrines expounded by the eloquent Mormon elder. John Taylor responded to each one, answering point by point the arguments of accusations made by his critics. So the controversy between the lone visiting missionary and the corps of hostile critics who opposed him waxed and waned.

In reporting to the editor of the *Millennial Star*, Elder Taylor furnished this summary of his labors on the Isle of Man: "I had much opposition, but the truth has come off triumphant, and there is now in that place about 100 members, 2 elders, 4 priests and 2 teachers; and the work of God is rolling on." (MS 2:15.)

Returning to Liverpool, the apostle busied himself with his duties there, preaching as before, supervising the activities of the missionaries placed under his charge, and instructing the new converts in their duties. He also visited and preached in other English cities, including Birmingham, Sheffield, and Manchester. Being headquartered in the major British port used by the Latter-day Saints, he became heavily involved in directing the emigration to the United States of the British converts. Unlike today when new members are urged to remain in their native countries, converts then were encouraged to migrate to the United States as part of the "gathering." Prompted by counsel from their leaders and, in many instances, moved by inner spiritual impulses, the converts began to emigrate soon after the Twelve commenced proselyting in the British Isles. These new members funneled into Liverpool, where Elder Taylor and others arranged for their transportation to the United States. In 1840, the first year during which the Twelve proselyted in Britain, 290 saints emigrated from Liverpool; during the following year, that number swelled to 705. (Richard L. Evans, *A Century of "Mormonism" in Great Britain* [Salt Lake City: Deseret News Press, 1937], p. 245.)

In early April 1841, nine members of the Quorum of the Twelve Apostles convened in Manchester to review the achievements of the previous year and to lay plans for the future. At that time it was decided that Orson Hyde, who had arrived late in England, would continue on his mission to Jerusalem, that Parley P. Pratt would remain in Manchester to publish the *Millennial Star*, and that the other seven brethren would return to the United States. Accordingly, John Taylor and six of his brethren, Brigham Young, Heber C. Kimball, Orson Pratt, Wilford Woodruff, George A. Smith, and Willard Richards sailed from Liverpool on the packet ship *Rochester* on April 20, 1841, bound for the United States. As this small group of energetic men recapped a ministry of a little more than a year, which they had commenced penniless, they could count among their achievements the baptism of hundreds of converts; the publication of the Book of Mormon, a hymn book, and thousands of copies of the *Millennial Star* and assorted tracts; the emigration of scores of converts; and the establishment of branches in "every noted town and city in the kingdom of Great Britain." (MS 26:7.)

Chapter Seven

Surprises and Challenges at Nauvoo

After a month-long, turbulent crossing of the Atlantic, the apostles docked at New York City, renewed acquaintances with the Manhattan Saints, and made their way to the Ohio, where they boarded a riverboat, the *Cicero*. Not as speedy as its namesake was eloquent, the *Cicero* set some sort of a record for slowness, taking nineteen days to negotiate the leg of the journey between Pittsburgh and Nauvoo. The main difficulty lay in an extraordinarily low water level, following a minimal spring runoff. The captain and crew of the struggling craft were kept busy dodging sandbars or fighting their way off them. It took three days, for instance, to free the boat from one particularly large specimen.

Elder Taylor and his friends stepped ashore at Nauvoo on July 1 to the stirring strains of a brass band and the warm greetings of family and friends. Missing from the welcoming party was Leonora, whom John found bedridden and near death in her cramped Montrose apartment. Never having recovered from the illness that afflicted her when he had left almost two years before, Elder Taylor's stoical wife had concealed her true condition in the letters she had sent abroad, sugarcoating the circumstances at home so as not to create a distraction from the missionary's work. Convinced that only the intervention of heaven could restore his weak and emaciated wife to health, John summoned the brethren from the other apartments in the barracks to assist in administering to her. Twenty elders crowded into the tiny room where Leonora lay, and with her three young children looking on in wonderment, this sensitive, resilient woman was anointed and blessed by the humble men who knelt around the sickbed. Soon after the administration, Leonora relaxed into a dewy slumber, and the next morning she arose with seeming vigor. While her eventual restoration to robust health was gradual with intermittent relapses, the turning point in her condition could be traced to the incident in Montrose when the twenty elders joined in fervent prayer for her recovery.

Forseeing a period free from assignments that would take him away from Nauvoo, the returned apostle moved promptly to prepare more suitable living accommodations for his family. Purchasing a lot on the corner of Parley and Granger streets, he built a new frame house into which the Taylors moved on October 1, 1841. In the meantime, he was ushered into the inner circle of high Church and community leadership with appointments to the city council, the board of regents of the University of Nauvoo, and judge advocate of the Nauvoo Legion with the rank of colonel. Moreover, his ties to the Prophet Joseph Smith were cemented more closely during this period, largely through John's literary competence. Joseph put his articulate disciple to work preparing an additional petition to Congress seeking redress for the damages suffered by the Saints in Missouri, and another summary of the wrongs inflicted on the Mormons by the Missourians. And, more important to Elder Taylor's editing and writing career, the Prophet began to ease him into key positions on the Church publications, the *Times and Seasons* and the *Wasp*. The *Times and Seasons* had been edited by Joseph's brother Don Carlos Smith until his death on August 7, 1841. Soon after, the

Prophet became the editor of that publication, and Elder Taylor his assistant. However, because of Joseph's preoccupation with other weighty responsibilities, Elder Taylor was from the beginning of his connection with the *Times and Seasons* its chief editor in fact if not in name. And a year later, the formal title was conferred upon him.

The *Wasp* had been edited previously by William Smith, another of the Prophet's brothers. The name of this weekly implies its tone and purpose under William Smith's direction. He was a proud, vocal, and combative man who used the pages of the *Wasp* to excoriate the enemies of the Church and, almost incidentally, to report the local happenings. A favorite target for his abuse was Thomas Sharp, the acerbic editor of the *Warsaw Signal*, who traded blow for blow with his rival.

William's interest in running for the legislature afforded an opportunity for the Prophet to make a needed change in the management and policy of the *Wasp*. It was then that Elder Taylor was placed in charge. The change in the tenor and quality of this publication was almost instantaneous. After editing only a few issues, Elder Taylor was instrumental in having it renamed the *Nauvoo Neighbor*. Moreover, John's erudite, precise literary style added a touch of class the paper had lacked previously and improved its readability and readership.

One significant change the readers of these two Church newspapers detected after Elder Taylor's voice became predominant was the subtle introduction of a wry sense of humor. Many saw in his stories and parables only a theme for laughter or jest, something to lighten the burden of the day. But often, the stories were designed to poke gentle fun at the ministers and divines who persistently attacked the Church. So with tongue in cheek he once posed the question whether anyone knew of an established minister who had been spiritually prompted to serve a less affluent congregation. Again, he told the parable of a man who had an artificial leg that so much resembled a real one in appearance that he began to believe in its reality, even to the extent of blaming a cold he contracted on the fact that the wooden leg got wet.

But for the most part, Elder Taylor was conservative in his reporting and editorializing, resorting to satire or caricature only when necessary to defend the doctrines and aims of the Church or its leaders. Otherwise he commented or reported on events, personalities, and issues, whether religious or political, in his usual objective, dignified, and highly literate style.

Elder Taylor and his fellow apostle, Wilford Woodruff, who was associated with him as business manager of the *Nauvoo Neighbor* and the *Times and Seasons*, earned their living from the revenues generated by these publications. When this was found to be insufficient, they had to improvise imaginatively to develop other sources of income. This led them into job printing, bookbinding, and, ultimately, into selling books, boots, and seeds. They also took an excursion into franchising in partnership with Wilson Law, obtaining the exclusive right to sell Neal's Lamps in Hancock County.

Although at this time Nauvoo was in the midst of a vast building boom with domestic and business structures mushrooming all over the city, the economy generally was not robust. Money was in short supply, which encouraged bartering. So, John and Wilford sometimes found it necessary to accept payment for some subscriptions in commodities or services. But the absence of monetary liquidity, the lack of complexity in the governing laws, and the practice of most Nauvoo residents to raise family gardens and to keep a cow and chickens added a touch of rural security and placidity to the life of this rapidly growing urban center. And life there for the Taylors assumed a more prestigious aspect when John completed negotiations to acquire the printing office and an adjacent two-story brick house, both of which still stand.

However, the apparent rise in family influence and affluence was accompanied by an unexpected upheaval in the family structure. The source of this upheaval was Elder Taylor's entry into the system of plural marriage. This was the most difficult ordeal John was to encounter during his long journey along the pathway of Mormonism. The privations and indignities he suffered during the dark days of his exile could not compare with the emotional trauma he suffered in accepting and living this principle. "I had always entertained strict ideas of virtue," he said in explaining his conversion to the doctrine, "and I felt as a married man that this was to me, outside of this principle, an appalling thing to do. The idea of going and asking a young lady to be married to me when I already had a wife! It was a thing calculated to stir up feelings from the innermost depths of the human soul." (BHR, p. 100.)

The novelty of this principle, which seemed to run counter to the concepts of morality he had observed from childhood, caused Elder Taylor and the other members of the Twelve to procrastinate in accepting it. At length the Prophet confronted John in a way that left no middle ground on which to stand. He left this account of the dilemma Joseph created for him: "We [the Twelve] seemed to put off, as far as we could, what might be termed the evil day.

"Some time after these things were made known unto us, I was riding out of Nauvoo on horseback, and met Joseph Smith coming in, he, too, being on horseback. . . . I bowed to Joseph, and having done the same to me, he said: 'Stop;' and he looked at me very intently. 'Look, here,' said he, 'these things that have been spoken of must be fulfilled, and if they are not entered into right away the keys will be turned.'" (Ibid., pp. 100-101.)

Whatever meaning Joseph Smith attached to these words, John interpreted them to mean that his failure to accept them would be a rejection of the Prophet and, therefore, of God. At that moment, the depth of Elder Taylor's conviction about the prophetic role of his friend and about the divine source of the principles he had revealed stood on trial. His answer, although lacking in enthusiasm, was prompt and unequivocal. Said he, "Brother Joseph, I will try and carry these things out." (Ibid., p. 101.)

John's obedient but unenthusiastic response doubtless was prompted in large part by the likely effect it would have upon Leonora. This queenly woman, who was then forty-seven years old, was weighed down with grief, having laid to rest her fifteen-month-old baby and namesake, Leonora Agnes, in early September 1843. The impact on his aging, grieving, much-loved companion by taking a younger wife would have been of predominant concern to a man of John Taylor's sensibilities. Because she had heard rumors about plural marriage from both apostate and friendly sources, Leonora was not surprised when her husband broached the subject. But she was agitated, not only for the reasons that had agitated John and his brethren in the Twelve, but because of her fading youth and the emotional trauma of having another admitted to the intimate relationship with her husband that until then she had enjoyed alone.

But in Leonora Cannon, John Taylor had found a woman who was his intellectual, emotional, and spiritual peer. So, after the expected period of struggling against this new imperative her adopted religion had laid upon her, she yielded and accepted the idea that her husband was to become a polygamist. Indeed, as was true in most such cases, she counseled with him about who the plural wife should be. Out of this came the mutual decision that John would approach Leonora's thirty-two-year-old cousin, Elizabeth Kaighin, who also was born on the Isle of Man and was baptized by Parley P. Pratt in Toronto on the same day the Taylors were baptized. The common blood and ancestry of this pair, their shared British heritage, and their commitment to the doctrines of Mormonism helped smooth the path for Elizabeth's marriage to John Taylor on December 12, 1843.

While the common assent of all concerned lifted this trio over the first obstacle that confronted anyone who walked the pathway of polygamy, there were other formidable barriers ahead. Not the least of these was the economic challenge of adding the expense of another household to an already overloaded budget. The reordering of duties and privileges became a problem, especially for Leonora, who had to assume more responsibility for the care and training of her children. Although all three were mature adults, there was always the hazard of hurt feelings and unintended slights. And socializing became awkward, if not impossible, because at this time, the doctrine had been introduced to only a select few in whom the Prophet had implicit confidence. And these and other difficulties were multiplied and magnified as John married other polygamous wives—Jane Ballantyne on February 25, 1844; Mary Ann Oakley, January 14, 1846; Sophia Whitaker, April 23, 1847; and Harriet Whitaker, December 4, 1847. And on September 26, 1856, after the exodus, and after the teaching and practice of polygamy had been publicly announced, Elder Taylor was married to his seventh wife, Margaret Young.

What impelled John and these intelligent, virtuous women, who bore him thirty-five children, to enter into a practice that was foreign to their background and upbringing, and that heaped upon them the abuse and scorn of a hostile and unforgiving society? The answer is to be found in the unquestioning confidence all eight of them had in the revelation given to the Prophet Joseph Smith. Of this John wrote in explaining his acceptance of the doctrine, "The revelation says that 'All those who have this law revealed unto them must obey the same.' Now, that is not my word. I did not make it. It was the Prophet of God who revealed that to us in Nauvoo, and I bear witness of this solemn fact before God, that He did reveal this sacred principle to me and others of the Twelve, and in this revelation it is stated that it is the will and law of God that 'all those who have this law revealed unto them must obey the same.'" (Ibid., p. 100.)

At the time of Elder Taylor's marriage to Elizabeth Kaighin, the conditions in Nauvoo were confused and stressful. At the root of the problem lay a rupture within the high councils of the Church over the issue of polygamy. John C. Bennett and William Law, former confidants of the Prophet, had become disaffected over this issue, among others, and had begun to attack Joseph. They formed the nucleus of a group of dissidents, apostates, and enemies whose opposition had exceeded the bounds of debate and invective and had crossed into the realm of intimidation and threats of physical violence. This resulted in a beefing up of the Nauvoo police force in December 1843, the month in which John Taylor married Elizabeth.

The agitation caused by this upheaval was heard and felt far beyond the boundaries of Illinois and was fueled, in large part, by the publication of a series of libelous letters John C. Bennett wrote for the *Sangamo Journal* in Springfield, Illinois, in 1842. These were later revised and published in a book entitled *The History of the Saints: or, an Exposé of Joe Smith and Mormonism.*

The fury of the resulting debate stirred up a national issue that was kept alive by enemies, apostates, and politicians who used the novelty of it to whip up support among voters who were anti-Mormon or who were genuinely troubled about the social and moral implications of polygamy.

In an effort to learn the attitude of national presidential candidates toward the plight of the Latter-day Saints, Joseph Smith wrote to each of them asking their views about the efforts of the Saints to obtain redress for the wrongs they had suffered in Missouri. These inquiries were either ignored or were answered in a noncommittal way. It was against this background that the Twelve held a special meeting in the office of Joseph Smith on January 29, 1844. Out of that meeting came the decision to support the Prophet's candidacy for the presidency of the United States. Because of his skill in writing, his experience in Nauvoo government, and his knowledge of media procedures gained in his publishing and editorial work, John Taylor was appointed as the Prophet's campaign manager.

In a lengthy editorial that appeared in the *Neighbor* in February, Elder Taylor explained why the Latter-day Saints could not support the candidates (Henry Clay and Martin Van Buren) put forward by the two major political parties and the reasons why his candidate had entered a race he could not conceivably win.

Mr. Clay was dismissed summarily as a viable candidate because of his federalist views, which were opposed to the ends the Saints sought to attain in their controversy with Missouri. And as to Mr. Van Buren, the editor observed, "We have been informed from a respectable source that there is an understanding between Mr. Benton of Missouri and Mr. Van Buren, and a conditional compact entered into that if Mr. Benton will use his influence to wipe away the stain from Missouri, by a further persecution of the Mormons, wreaking vengeance on their heads, either by extermination or by some other summary process" that Mr. Van Buren would reward him appropriately. The editor went on to say, "We could scarcely credit the statement and we hope yet, for the sake of humanity that the suggestion is false; but we have too good reason to believe that we are correctly informed."

Any question about the forcefulness and clarity of John Taylor's writing as a political commentator is removed by these sentences which explain why his candidate had decided to run: "One great reason we have for pursuing our present course is that at every election we have been made a political target for the filthy demagogues in the country to shoot their loathsome arrows at. And every story has been put into circulation to blast our fame, from the old fabrication of 'walk on the water' down to the 'murder of Governor Boggs.' The journals have teemed with this filthy trash and even men who ought to have more respect for themselves . . . have made use of terms so degrading, so mean, so humiliating, that a Billingsgate fisherwoman would have considered herself disgraced with. We refuse any longer to be thus bedaubed for either party; we tell all such to let such filth flow in its own legitimate channel for we are sick of the loathsome smell. . . . Under the existing circumstances, we have no other alternative and if we can accomplish our object, well; if not we shall have the satisfaction of knowing we have acted conscientiously, and have used our best judgment; and if we have to throw away our votes, we had better do so upon a worthy rather than upon an unworthy individual who might make use of the weapon we put in his hand to destroy us."

A week after the decision was made to support Joseph Smith's candidacy, the Prophet's campaign manager invited the candidate, his brother Hyrum, Sidney Rigdon, the Twelve, and their wives to a social at the Taylors' lovely new home adjacent to the Times and Seasons office. There, according to the Prophet's journal, the group "took supper and had a very pleasant time." (HC 6:197.)

The next day, February 7, 1844, Joseph, with the assistance of Elder Taylor and other members of his staff, completed his major campaign tract, "Views of the Powers and Policy of the Government of the United States." This thoughtful document affirmed the duty of government to promote freedom and to protect life and property. It also advocated the abolition of slavery, the creation of a national bank, and the avoidance of entangling foreign alliances. Tracing the evolution of the government of the United States, it lauded many of the earlier presidents for their judgment and sagacity, and then, in a sentence that bears the mark of John Taylor's pen, it derided one of the Church's favorite objects of scorn: "At the age, then, of sixty years, our blooming Republic began to decline under the withering touch of Martin Van Buren!" (HC 6:203.)

Within two months, the campaign was in high gear. At the annual conference of the Church in early April, 344 brethren volunteered to electioneer for Joseph throughout the country. All of the Twelve, except Elders John Taylor and Willard Richards, joined the campaigners in the field. These two apostles were excused from this duty to enable them to serve as staff for the candidate at campaign headquarters. And as to John, his continuing responsibilities in editing the *Times and Seasons* and the *Neighbor* also required his presence in Nauvoo. It was this circumstance that resulted in Elders Taylor and Richards being the only members of the Twelve who were in the area at the time of the martyrdom. And their presence in the Carthage jail when the mob did its bloody work illustrates their loyalty to Joseph Smith and the tie that binds the Twelve to the First Presidency.

In less than two weeks after the April conference, the decision of a Church court diverted Elder Taylor's attention from the campaign and set in motion a chain of events that brought him to the edge of death. On April 18, 1844, William Law, William's wife, Wilson Law, and Robert D. Foster were excommunicated for "unchristianlike conduct." (HC 6:341.) These four formed the nucleus of a vocal group of apostates in Nauvoo who had banded together in opposition to Joseph Smith. When their ties to the Church had been officially severed, they moved to acquire a voice by which their opposition could be amplified. The means sought to accomplish this was the establishment of their own newspaper. On May 7, their press arrived at Doctor Foster's. Three days later, there appeared a prospectus of the new publication, which, it was announced, would bear the provocative name *The Expositor*. And on June 7, the only issue of this gossipy sheet hit the streets of Nauvoo with a thunderous impact. In it Joseph Smith was portrayed as a fallen prophet, driven by ambition and more interested in power than in Christian purity. It also pictured the Church's missionary effort abroad as a devious ploy to trap unsuspecting females into polygamy; and, it labeled Joseph as venal, dictatorial, and blasphemous.

The unwelcome appearance of this journal posed a cruel dilemma for both Joseph Smith and John Taylor. Joseph could not deny the germ of truth that lay beneath the *Expositor*'s monstrous lies and distortions, namely that he and others in the Church had begun to teach and to practice polygamy. Nor was it feasible to admit the charge at the time, as to do so would have given credence to the libelous charges with which the paper abounded. Therefore, employing a rhetorical tactic with which he was familiar, editor John Taylor completely ignored this charge, focusing instead on the paper's glaring falsehoods and its strident tone.

But, in the view of the leaders of the Church then in Nauvoo, it was insufficient merely to answer the *Expositor*. It seemed imperative to them that they silence it. And this presented John Taylor with one of the most stressful dilemmas he ever faced. It posed the stark issue of whether he, the proprietor and editor of the city's two most prominent newspapers, would be a party to the suppression of a new competitor, however offensive it might be. Apart from that disturbing aspect of the matter stood the question of freedom of speech and the press, which John Taylor ardently supported. This alone would have argued in favor of not interfering with the new publication.

But there were weighty, competing considerations that were elaborated by Joseph Smith at an all-day meeting of the Nauvoo city council on Saturday, June 8. He contended that allowing the paper to continue publishing its libelous trash would create a mob spirit in the city, which would be far more chaotic than would be the results of closing the paper down.

This position was the one finally adopted by the council, which on the following Monday declared the *Expositor* to be a nuisance and ordered that it be abated. Indicating the depth of his acceptance of this view, John Taylor made the motion on which the decision was based. The order was carried out promptly when the *Expositor*'s press was destroyed, the type was scattered, and the papers in the office were burned.

It must not be inferred that Elder Taylor and the other members of the city council were blind to the repercussions that might result from this bold act. "They felt that they were in a critical position," John wrote later, "and that any move made for the abating of that press would be looked upon, or at least represented, as a direct attack upon the liberty of speech, and that, so far from displeasing our enemies, it would be looked upon by them as one of the best circumstances that could transpire to assist them in their nefarious and bloody designs." (BHR, p. 118.)

It is obvious, therefore, that Elder Taylor and the council confidently expected that abating the *Expositor* would generate a violent storm of protest and that this would, to an extent, be playing into the hands of their enemies. But they surely failed to see that it would ultimately result in the martyrdom of Joseph and Hyrum and the almost fatal wounding of Elder Taylor, or they would not have entered upon that course.

The expected storm arose with sudden fury. The newspapers in nearby Quincy, LaHarpe, and Warsaw trumpeted the event with their loudest and most discordant blasts. Thomas C. Sharp, the acid-tongued editor of the *Warsaw Signal*, perhaps still smarting from the insults William Smith had heaped upon him in the *Wasp*, outdid himself with this chilling threat: "We hold ourselves at all times in readiness to cooperate with our fellow citizens . . . to exterminate, utterly exterminate, the wicked and abominable Mormon leaders."

It was amidst the furor stirred up by such attacks, and the gossip and recriminations that inevitably followed, that Joseph, Hyrum, John Taylor, and fifteen other defendants were charged with inciting to riot by the court in nearby Carthage. In the meantime, Elder Taylor sought to counter the negative effects of the anti-Mormon press by publishing in the *Neighbor* and the *Times and Seasons* the city council's version of what had happened and the reasons for its actions. This effort was aborted at first when the papers were destroyed in the post office. Later, John was able to get some of them through to the readers by mailing them beyond a radius of thirty miles from Nauvoo.

Along with these happenings, there were some frantic legal maneuverings in behalf of Elder Taylor and his codefendants when petitions for habeus corpus were filed before and were granted by the Nauvoo court and Justice of the Peace Daniel H. Wells. This only served to intensify the attacks upon the Church and its leaders by the anti-Mormon press and to create angry demands that the defendants be delivered to Carthage promptly to answer to the court where they had been charged.

While all this was going on, Joseph Smith declared martial law in Nauvoo because of the menacing tone of the enemies outside the city and reports that armed mobs were being raised to attack the Saints. Learning of the events that threatened to erupt into a shooting war, Illinois Governor Thomas Ford traveled to Carthage to attempt to mediate the dispute. Arriving there on June 21 and establishing his headquarters at the Hamilton House, he dispatched a letter to Joseph Smith requesting that the Prophet send to Carthage one or more well-informed and discreet persons "who will be capable of laying before me your version of the matter." (HC 6:521.) Selected to perform this service were John Taylor and J. M. Bernhisel, who traveled to Carthage that night bearing affidavits and other documents detailing the events from the perspective of the Latter-day Saints.

The two Mormon representatives found Carthage to be little less than an armed camp, overflowing with militia, mobbers, and apostate Mormons, all hostile to them and their cause. They registered at the Hamilton House, where the governor was staying. Also registered there were the Higbees, the Laws, and other apostates who had precipitated the present crisis. Forewarned about the atmosphere of tension and hostility that pervaded this place, the two visitors brought handguns with them for protection, which they placed beneath their pillows on learning that a violent enemy named Jackson occupied an adjoining room.

Although Elder Taylor had honed his speaking skills amidst the rough-and-tumble of heckling debate in Great Britain and frontier America, he was hardly prepared for the wild scene when he and Elder Bernhisel made their presentation to Governor Ford the next morning. Instead of hearing it in private where he could have considered their views in a measured, objective way, the governor insisted on opening the hearing to the public. Given the composition and temper of Carthage's populace at that time, Mr. Ford's decision ensured that the visitors' views would be presented in the presence of a hostile and clamorous audience. Even then, the conditions would have been bearable had the governor conducted the hearing in an orderly way. But he did not. Instead, showing a politician's penchant for popular acceptance, he permitted the spectators to interject their comments and criticisms at will. "Such an interview!" (BHR, p. 124.) John said of the ordeal. Throughout it, angry voices could be heard from the audience, challenging, denying, or contradicting statements with which they disagreed.

Under such circumstances, it is not surprising that Illinois' chief executive turned a deaf ear to John Taylor's plea that Joseph Smith not be required to appear in Carthage. Nor would he approve the Saints bringing arms with them for self-protection. Instead, he pledged his faith as governor and the faith of the State of Illinois that Joseph and his friends would be protected, and that he would guarantee their safety. Later events were to prove either that the governor lied to the Mormon elders, or he promised more than he could deliver.

Elders Taylor and Bernhisel, accompanied by Captain Yates, left Carthage in the early evening on Saturday, June 22, bearing a lengthy memo from Governor Ford. Arriving in Nauvoo at 10:00 P.M., they went immediately to the Mansion House, where Joseph Smith read the decision. The kernel of the governor's wordy message was embodied in these sentences: "I require any and all of you who are or shall be accused to submit yourselves to be arrested by the same constable, by virtue of the same warrant and be tried before the same magistrate whose authority has heretofore been resisted. Nothing short of this can vindicate the dignity of violated law and allay the just excitement of the people." (HC 6:536.)

While the decision, which affected John Taylor as well

as the Prophet and the other defendants, was not unexpected, the governor's characterization of the mob spirit that prevailed as "the just excitement of the people" added still another layer of apprehension to the burden of care already carried by the brethren.

This development caused Joseph Smith to contemplate fleeing west. Indeed, he crossed the river to Montrose later that night for this purpose but returned the following evening when stung by a false accusation of cowardice. The next day, Monday, June 24, 1844, Joseph, Hyrum, John Taylor, and the other defendants left Nauvoo on horseback in the cool morning hours, headed for Carthage and their date with destiny and (for Joseph and Hyrum) death.

Chapter Eight

Martyrdom and Its Aftermath

The arrival of the horsemen in Carthage was delayed until almost midnight, occasioned by the need for Joseph Smith to return to Nauvoo with an Illinois militiaman after the group had reached Albert Fellows's farm, just a few miles from their destination. Three surprises awaited Elder Taylor upon his arrival. The first was the confused and circus-like atmosphere that pervaded this usually sleepy town so late at night during the week. It was as if everyone had stayed up just to look at the Mormons as they surrendered to the Carthage officials. Second, in the forty-eight hours since John had left on Saturday, the number of troops had swelled alarmingly, and most of them were camped on or were loitering around the town square. Ostensibly, these troops had been mustered by the governor to protect the prisoners or to guard against the possibility of armed resistance by the Nauvoo Legion. Ironically, part of these troops later became the instrument of death in the martyrdom of Joseph the Prophet and his brother Hyrum, and in Elder Taylor's almost fatal wounding. The third surprise came the following afternoon when, at their arraignment, all the defendants in the inciting-to-riot suit were released on bail except Joseph and

Hyrum, who earlier had been spuriously charged with treason. It was this unexpected turn of events that resulted in the confinement of Joseph and Hyrum while their sixteen co-defendants were set free. However, John Taylor, Willard Richards, and others, voluntarily shared the confinement of the Smith brothers to keep them company and to render clerical and counseling assistance as necessary.

On Wednesday night, June 26, four others in addition to the two prisoners shared the upper room debtors' cell of the Carthage jail: Elders Taylor and Richards and Dan Jones and Stephen Markham. Early in the morning on Thursday, the Prophet sent Dan Jones to inquire about a gunshot that was heard during the night. He was never able to return to the jail. After lunch, when Elder Richards took ill, Stephen Markham was sent out to get medicine. Like Dan Jones, he was never able to return. This reduced to four the number of occupants of the cell: Joseph and Hyrum Smith, John Taylor, and Willard Richards. It was this quartet who would play the leading roles in the drama of blood and death that would be enacted in their cramped cell just a few hours later.

Thus began an afternoon that would be etched vividly and forever on John Taylor's memory. As summer had been ushered in officially six days before, it was warm but not hot. Therefore, it was shirt-sleeve weather, and the brethren were dressed casually and comfortably. Wanting to use their enforced idleness profitably, they had brought the scriptures and the works of Josephus to jail with them. Intermittently, excerpts from these writings were read aloud and discussed. Also discussed were the legal maneuverings that had brought the Smith brothers to this end, the threats of assassination that had floated around Carthage during the previous several days, and the ominous presence of the Carthage Greys who had been appointed to guard the prisoners. There is nothing to indicate, however, that there was any discussion about Joseph's presidential campaign, which had been all but forgotten in the excitement that followed the destruction of the *Expositor* press.

In the late afternoon, Elder Taylor, who had a fine baritone voice, sang all fourteen verses of "A Poor Wayfaring Man of Grief." Sung without accompaniment, this mournful hymn aroused melancholy feelings in the brethren, which seemed to be not unpleasant to their senses, however, as the Prophet asked John to sing it a second time, which he did.

About five in the evening, the chief jailer, who had treated the prisoners and their guests with civility, became concerned for their safety when he learned that Elder Markham had been forced to leave town. For this reason, it was decided to transfer them from the debtors' cell to the criminal cell, where it would be easier to protect them. However, after discussion, it was also decided to delay the transfer until after the brethren had eaten their dinner in the more congenial surroundings of the debtors' cell.

As one of the guards departed after leaving food, a loud commotion was heard outside, punctuated by several shots. Looking down from a window, Elder Richards saw a large group of armed men with blackened faces, some of whom surrounded the building, while others pushed the guards aside and rushed upstairs. Because of the speed with which they occurred with hardly any warning, the events that followed within the next few minutes would forever remain a blur to John Taylor and Willard Richards. But a few of the fleeting images in this kaleidoscope of terror stood out in memory; these the two apostles later reported.

As the four brethren heard the noise of many feet mounting the stairs, accompanied by shouts of coarse profanity, they reacted instinctively, reaching for whatever weapons of defense lay at hand. John grabbed a gnarled cane Stephen Markham had left behind, which its owner called his "rascal beater." Joseph reached for a gun Cyrus Wheelock had smuggled into the prison for self-defense, and Elder Richards picked up John's cane. These three then took positions by the door. Hyrum was standing in the middle of the room, and before he could move out of the line of fire, he was cut down by a fusillade of four balls fired by members of the mob who had partially forced open the door. As he fell, Hyrum cried, "I am a dead man." Reacting instantly, Joseph called out, "Oh, my poor, dear brother Hyrum" and, thrusting his gun out the opening in the door, fired several times. In the meantime, John and Willard were flailing away with their canes, trying to ward off the guns that were thrust into the room.

It soon became apparent that this effort at self-defense was futile, as the pressure on the door increased when other mobbers forced their way up the stairs and onto the landing, adding their weight and firepower to the attack. It was then, in terror and confusion, that Joseph and John made an abortive attempt to escape through the two windows, either without knowing or, in the pandemonium that reigned in the cell, forgetting that the jail was ringed with other disguised gunmen who were as intent on killing as were those who had forced their way inside. John sprang to the front window. Hardly had he reached it than he was struck mid-thigh of the left leg by a ball fired from within. The impact of this shot, added to the forward momentum of his attempt to jump, would have propelled him to the ground, had it not been for a fortuitous shot from outside that struck his vest pocket watch, throwing him back into the room and onto the floor. He immediately began to scramble, dragging himself along the floor toward the protection of the bed that stood in the corner. During that agonizing effort, while the room reverberated with the deafening sounds of the gunfire, Elder Taylor was shot three more times, one bullet striking below the left knee, a ball he carried to his grave; the second tore away the flesh from his left hip; the third struck his left arm above the wrist, coursing downward until it came to rest just under the skin in the palm of his left hand.

Meanwhile, Joseph sprang to the side window, and as

he teetered on the sill, a shot from inside threw him to the ground below, where his body came to rest by a well. As the Prophet fell, someone shouted that he had leaped from the window, which was the signal for all the assassins who were inside to run from the building. It was this hasty exit of the gunmen, lucky in its timing, that again saved John Taylor from almost certain death; it also saved Willard Richards, who had been pinned behind the door when it was forced open, from all harm except a scratch from a bullet that grazed his left earlobe.

Like jackals frightened from their prey by an armed hunter, the assassins scurried from the scene once it had been confirmed that Joseph Smith was dead, thereby indicating that his murder was the mob's chief object and that the killing of Hyrum and the wounding of Elder Taylor were mere incidentals to their main purpose.

The flight of the gunmen from the jail ended the danger of further injury to the two apostles who remained inside. They did not know this at the time, however. Willard, seeing Hyrum lying dead in the middle of the floor, and apparently assuming that John, who was concealed beneath the bed, had suffered the same fate, glanced hurriedly out of the side window to see Joseph lying motionless on the ground below. Then he walked toward the door. As he did so, John called out, asking that he be taken along. Elder Richards complied promptly, dragging his bleeding companion into the criminal cell, where he threw a filthy mattress over his body to conceal it. Elder Taylor could have been spared this nauseous experience had either of the brethren recalled that the trail of blood, leading from the debtors' cell to his new place of hiding, would have revealed John's whereabouts to even the most casual observer.

Having concealed his companion, Elder Richards left the jail to check on the condition of the Prophet; finding him dead, he returned to report. "I felt a dull, lonely, sickening sensation at the news," John wrote later. "When I reflected that . . . the Prophet of the living God, had fallen . . . it seemed as though there was a void or vacuum in the great field of human existence to me. . . . Oh, how lonely was that feeling! How cold, barren and desolate!" Then followed these introspections on Joseph's character, and the great void his death would create: "In the midst of difficulties he was always the first in motion; in critical positions his counsel was always sought. As our Prophet he approached our God, and obtained for us His will; but now our Prophet, our counselor, our general, our leader was gone, and amid the fiery ordeal that we then had to pass through, we were left alone without his aid, and as for our future guide for things spiritual or temporal, and for all things pertaining to this world or the next, he had spoken for the last time on the earth!" (BHR, pp. 140, 141.)

Satisfied now that there was no further danger from the mob, Willard dragged John out of the criminal cell to a landing from which the wounded apostle could see the corpse of Hyrum lying in the middle of the debtors' cell. "There he lay as I had left him," John wrote later in a reflective mood. "He had not moved a limb; he lay placid and calm, a monument of greatness even in death. . . . Poor Hyrum! he was a great and good man, and my soul was cemented to his. If ever there was an exemplary, honest and virtuous man, an embodiment of all that is noble in the human form, Hyrum Smith was its representative." (Ibid., p. 142.)

Although Elder Richards was a doctor, his medical skills were not such as to enable him to render surgical aid to his wounded friend. So there now stepped forward from a crowd of curiosity seekers a doctor, Thomas L. Barnes, who offered help John doubtless wished later he had withheld. In examining the patient's wounds, the volunteer discovered the ball under the skin of John's left hand. Even without the benefit of an antiseptic or surgical instruments, Doctor Barnes decided that on-the-spot surgery was vital. Using a dull pen knife, he managed to open a jagged incision and, using a pair of carpenters compasses, pried out the half-ounce ball. Elder Taylor's stoical endurance of this butchery elicited from the doctor the questionable praise that the patient had nerves "like the devil."

After witnessing this crude surgery, the onlookers were agreed that the victim should be moved to the Hamilton House, where he would be more comfortable and where better facilities for his care were available. They were halted in this design, however, by these abrupt words: "I don't know you," said John. "Who am I among? I am surrounded by assassins and murderers; witness your deeds! Don't talk to me of kindness and comfort; look at your murdered victims! Look at me! I want none of your counsel nor comfort. There may be some safety here; I can be assured of none anywhere." (Ibid., p. 143.)

In the meantime, the coroner, Robert F. Smith, had been summoned; he was the justice of the peace and had issued the warrant for the arrest of Joseph and Hyrum on the spurious charge of treason. As Mr. Smith examined Hyrum's body in the adjoining room, Elder Taylor overheard the name of Francis Higbee mentioned. Speaking loudly, he called out, "Captain Smith [a title the coroner claimed as an officer of the Carthage Greys] you are a justice of the peace—I want to swear my life against that man." (Ibid.) It is reported that on hearing about this, Francis Higbee hurriedly left Carthage out of fear, a fear that soon gripped most of the apostates and non-Mormons in town. This apprehension was rooted in uncertainty about the reaction of the Latter-day Saints in Nauvoo when they learned of the martyrdom of their leaders.

By 6:30 P.M. Carthage had begun to assume the aspect of a ghost town as the fear of Mormon retribution had prompted many to flee. Even the Hamiltons were preparing to abandon their hotel, at least temporarily, to avoid the anticipated scourging. However, upon learning about John Taylor's serious condition, and yielding to the persuasion of Elder Richards, they remained and welcomed the wounded apostle, who was then moved to the hotel from the jail.

Prior to the move, the two members of the Twelve had

counseled together about the steps to be taken in the interests of the Church. They shared the concern that some of the Saints might attack Carthage in retaliation. To minimize this possibility, it was decided to send a conciliatory message to the Saints in Nauvoo. Written from the Carthage jail and dated at "8 o'clock 5 min. p.m. June 27, 1844," it read: "Joseph and Hyrum are dead. Taylor wounded not very badly. Our guard was forced, as we believe, by a band of Missourians from 100 to 200. The job was done in an instant, and the party fled toward Nauvoo instantly. This is as I believe it. The citizens here are afraid of the Mormons attacking them; I promise them no." It was signed by Elder Richards and then, following a postscript, was countersigned by Elder Taylor, who had insisted that the extent of his injuries be downplayed.

The note was entrusted to George D. Grant for delivery; he was intercepted en route by Governor Ford, who was returning from Nauvoo and insisted that the messenger go back to Carthage with him. The governor's purpose was to delay announcement of the massacre in Nauvoo so as to enable him to assemble the court records and to leave with them and his staff before the anticipated Mormon assault, an assault that never materialized.

It was not until the next day, June 28, that Elder Taylor's wounds were dressed. And on the day following, Leonora and John's parents arrived in Carthage to lend comfort and support. By this time, the excitement and emotional trauma produced by the shooting had begun to subside. In their place grew an increasing awareness of the physical discomfort that to a large extent had been deadened by a preoccupation with external events. During the day the pain intensified, especially in the left thigh, which had become swollen and discolored. When a competent doctor called to pay his respects and to inquire about the wounded man's health, Elder Taylor requested that he remove the bullet from his left thigh. There being no anesthetic, Elder Taylor stoically endured the probing surgery until the physician found and removed the slug, which had been flattened against the bone to the approximate size of a twenty-five-cent piece. From that time, the patient began to mend.

After several days of convalescence, it was decided to move the apostle to Nauvoo. Because a jolting ride over an unpaved road would have been too painful, his friends first began to carry him on a litter. And when the uneven cadences of the litter-bearers created jarring discomfort, he was placed in a sleigh that slid smoothly over the prairie grass alongside the road.

The approach of Elder Taylor's caravan had been announced in Nauvoo by horsemen who had gone ahead. Numerous Saints, impelled by a love for their wounded leader and by the unaccountable mystique that surrounds one who has played a role in a tragic or historic event, walked or rode along the highway toward Carthage. The first of these welcomers met the sleigh-borne apostle five miles from Nauvoo. As the enlarged procession moved forward, it was augmented at intervals as other members and friends from Nauvoo were met along the way. Escorted to his home, John was welcomed by the other members of his family and thoughtful neighbors who lavished upon him every service and attention that generosity could conceive. He later wrote about the contrast between this treatment and the indignities he had suffered in Carthage, "Never shall I forget the difference of feeling that I experienced between the place that I had left and the one I had now arrived at. I had left a lot of reckless, blood-thirsty murderers, and had come to the city of the Saints, the people of the living God; friends of truth and righteousness, all of whom stood there with warm, true hearts to offer their friendship and services, and to welcome my return." (Ibid., p. 149.)

Soon after, Elder Taylor discovered a new theme for appreciative reflection. When Willard Richards delivered a bag containing some of the valuables that had been removed from John's clothing after he had been wounded, John learned for the first time how his life had been saved by the watch in his vest pocket: "I shall never forget the feelings of gratitude that I then experienced towards my

Heavenly Father," he recorded. "The whole scene was vividly portrayed before me, and my heart melted before the Lord. I felt that the Lord had preserved me by a special act of mercy; that my time had not yet come, and that I had still a work to perform upon the earth." (Ibid., p. 150.)

Chapter Nine

Reorganization and Renewal

Since Elders Taylor and Richards were the only members of the Twelve in Nauvoo at the time, the initiative of leadership rested with them. Two main concerns confronted the Church at the onset: quelling any intention to retaliate for the murders, and assuring the Saints that the Church was intact and moving forward despite the martyrdom. A step was taken promptly to resolve the first concern when Elder Taylor published conciliatory resolutions of the city council in the *Times and Seasons.* In addition to endorsing the efforts of Governor Ford to preserve order, these resolutions warned that the city officials would not allow any "revenge on the assassinators" of Joseph and Hyrum. Instead of an appeal to arms, they appealed to the majesty of the law and expressed a willingness to "leave the matter with God" should the law fail. The city council also pledged "that no aggressions by the citizens of said city shall be made on the citizens of the surrounding country." (HC 123:151.)

Steps to resolve the second concern included a statement from Elders Taylor and Richards (joined in by W. W. Phelps) addressed to the Church as a whole (see HC 152, 153) and a letter from the two apostles to Reuben Hedlock, presiding Elder in England, and to "the Saints in the British Empire." (MS 5:76.) The essence and tone of the general letter is embodied in this statement: "Be peaceable, quiet citizens, doing the works of righteousness, and as soon as the Twelve and other authorities can assemble, or a majority of them, the onward course to the great gathering of Israel . . . will be pointed out." (HC 7:152.) The special letter to Great Britain gave some of the details about the murders the Saints there would not have heard about and offered these words of counsel about the stability and continuity of the Church: "God has not left his church without witnesses: as in former days, so shall it be in the latter days. When one falls, another will rise to occupy a similar station. Our Heavenly Father has always had a leader to his people, and always will have; and the gates of hell can never prevail against the chosen of heaven." (MS 5:78.)

The first member of the Twelve to join Elders Taylor and Richards after the martyrdom was John's mentor, Parley P. Pratt, whose preaching had brought John into the Church. These three brethren began to counsel together, pending the return of the other members of the Twelve. After rendering what assistance they could to the grieving families of the martyrs, and after comforting and reassuring the Saints who mourned the loss of their leaders, this trio focused on the serious question of succession in Church leadership. Sidney Rigdon, a longtime associate of Joseph Smith, and one of his counselors, had arrived in Nauvoo shortly after Elder Pratt. President Rigdon promptly began to hold secret meetings with William Marks, the president of the Nauvoo Stake, and others to discuss the appointment of new Church leadership. Learning of these efforts, the three apostles invited Sidney to meet with them at John Taylor's home to discuss the matter. Elder Pratt left this record of that meeting: "On being informed of this untimely and underhanded attempt, I called upon Elder Rigdon to meet with us—that is, the three of the Twelve then in the city, at the home of brother Taylor, who was still confined with his wounds, and there we expostulated with him, and showed our reasons for being opposed to such a course." (PPP, pp. 334-35.) While the brethren were unable to dissuade Elder Rigdon from holding a meeting to discuss the appointment of a "guardian" for the Church, he did agree to defer holding it until after the other members of the Twelve had returned.

In the meantime, the apostles learned of an effort by William Marks and Emma Smith, Joseph's widow, to appoint a trustee in trust for the Church. Parley P. Pratt was designated to attend a meeting held for that purpose in Emma's residence, the Mansion House. Speaking in behalf of the three, Elder Pratt vigorously opposed that move, the result being that the meeting was adjourned without any action being taken.

By Saturday, August 7, eight members of the Twelve were in Nauvoo, all except Elders Orson Hyde, John E. Page, William Smith, and Lyman Wight. Under the direction of Brigham Young, these eight met at the home of John Taylor on that day to prepare for a priesthood leadership meeting to be held that evening in the Seventy's Hall and for a general meeting to be held the following morning at the temple site. At that time it was decided that Brigham Young would act as a spokesman for the quorum of the twelve at these meetings.

Because his wounds had not healed completely, Elder Taylor was unable to attend these two meetings. However, a majority of the Twelve was present at both of them, and the representations made by the quorum spokesman had John's approval.

At the Sunday morning meeting, Sidney Rigdon spoke for an hour and a half, presenting his claim to be the guardian of the Church. In his speech that followed, President Young merely relied on the order of the priesthood as it was defined in the revelations given through the Prophet Joseph Smith: "The Twelve are appointed by the finger of God, . . ." he told the large audience gathered on the temple grounds, "an independent body who have the keys of the priesthood—the keys of the kingdom of God to deliver to all the world: this is true, so help me God. They stand next to Joseph, and are as the First Presidency of the Church." (HC 7:233.)

When the question of who would lead the Church was put to a vote, the Saints present overwhelmingly accepted the leadership of the Twelve. While there were many aftershocks following this event, which resulted in the creation of several splinter groups, August 8, 1844, marked the beginning of the dominance of the Twelve in Church administrative affairs, a dominance that would continue until the reorganization of the First Presidency in December 1847.

The Twelve lost no time in taking the reins of leadership. Numerous council meetings were held to chart their course, most of which were held at John Taylor's home to accommodate his physical disabilities. Out of these meetings came a united plan to move forward on both temporal and spiritual fronts. The completion of the temple was high on the list of priorities. At the same time, the Saints were encouraged to complete or to improve their Nauvoo holdings and to spruce up their homes. Also, the Twelve reached out beyond the confines of the city to encourage those with means to invest in Nauvoo enterprises. Elder Taylor enthusiastically endorsed these initiatives, in connection with which he spearheaded the formation of a "Trades Union" whose goal was to establish industries that would produce everything necessary to make the community self-sustaining as well as provide a surplus for exportation.

All this was subordinate to the chief object of expounding the gospel at home and abroad in order to prepare a people worthy to receive the Savior at his second coming. So, shortly after the Twelve assumed the direction of the Church, they adopted a resolution "to bear off the kingdom of God in all the world, in truth, honesty, virtue and holiness, and to continue to set their faces as a flint against every species of wickedness, vice and dishonesty in all its forms." (MS 26:167.)

This aggressive activity did not go unnoticed by the

enemies of the Church, who had been lulled into momentary inactivity and silence by the enormity of the martyrdom. They quickly aroused, however, on discovering they had erred in assuming that the power of Mormonism derived from the charisma of the Smith brothers. Emboldened by the inability or unwillingness of government to obtain convictions for the murders of Joseph and Hyrum, and worried about the vigor and efficiency with which the Twelve had undertaken the leadership of the Church, the enemies reverted to a tactic that had proven successful in the past. That was to heap on the Saints the blame for any crime or misconduct that occurred in the area. So, unfounded charges of thievery and counterfeiting began to be leveled at the Mormons, charges based solely on suspicion and the malignant intent of the accusers. To counter charges that the City of Nauvoo was harboring those who had committed these alleged crimes, the city council ordered an investigation that failed to uncover any evidence to support the charges. Predictably, this did not satisfy the accusers. In an effort to do so, Governor Ford, who avowedly was no friend of the Mormons, conducted an independent investigation, which produced this report included in the Governor's 1845 message to the Illinois legislature: "I have investigated the charge of promiscuous stealing and find it to be greatly exaggerated. I could not ascertain that there was a greater proportion of thieves in that community than in any other of the same number of inhabitants and perhaps if the city of Nauvoo were compared with St. Louis, or any other western city, the proportion would not be so great."

Undeterred by these reports, the enemies of the Church pressed forward with their campaign of vilification, a campaign that soon embraced overt acts of arson and assault. In Morley and other outlying Mormon settlements, houses and grain stacks were burned, forcing families to live in makeshift shelters or with family or friends.

About this time, a mass meeting of non-members was held in nearby Quincy, out of which came a resolution that the only answer to the numerous problems between the Saints and their enemies in Illinois was for the Mormons to leave. The Twelve had reached the same conclusion independently, the plans were laid accordingly for the Saints to depart in the spring of 1846.

The preceding autumn was a time of feverish activity in Nauvoo as the members of the Church prepared for a mass exodus toward a destination that was vaguely identified among them as "the Rockies" or merely "the west." Elder Taylor's editorial in the December 1, 1845, issue of the *Times and Seasons* provides insight into the nature of these preparations, the spirit of those involved in them, and their attitudes toward those who had made the exodus necessary: "Peace and union reign at Nauvoo," wrote John, "and as to business, every Saint that means to keep the commandments of the Lord, and prepare for the revelations of Jesus Christ, is earnestly employed in fitting out for the intended removal next spring: or, as a willing and obedient people, many are engaged upon the temple. . . . The mob, as usual, are busy in manufacturing lies about the Saints, and what they lack is gratuitously supplied by apostates who naturally drop down among the dregs of society. . . . We believe also, that the mob keep up the old system of plundering and crying mad-dog in order to prejudice the community against the saints." The piece concluded with these words of admonition: "We can say in the voice of truth, Brethren; be just—be wise—be watchful—be prayerful and put away all evil."

However, the prospects of delaying an orderly departure of the Saints until the spring were put in question by the harassing action of their enemies, who inundated them with a flood of vexatious suits and writs. The turmoil this created, added to the intermittent burning of the homes or haystacks of the Saints and occasional assaults, murders, or intimidating threats prompted Governor Ford to send a company of militia under Major Warren to keep the peace. Whether through ineptness or a malignant intent, the major's presence served only to perpetuate rather than to thwart the harassments to which the Mormons had been subjected. The frivolous suits continued as before. Illegal writs were issued for the arrest of the Twelve. And the assaults, trespasses, and intimidations were not diminished. Under these provocations, Elder Taylor openly declared that he would no longer submit to such indignities and lawlessness. Because Brigham Young had made similar statements, Major Warren sought an interview with the leading brethren, where he lectured them on their duty to uphold the law and to sustain those appointed to enforce it. This hypocrisy aroused the lion in John Taylor, the wounded survivor of the Carthage blood bath, who then delivered a stinging rebuke the major most likely never forgot. "You talk, sir, about the majesty of the law," Elder Taylor began quietly. "Why, sir, the law to us is a mere farce." The speaker then related how he and the others went to Carthage under a solemn promise of protection made by Governor Ford and of the tragic results. "I was shot nearly to pieces," he said, "and two of the best men in the world were shot dead at my side. This is a specimen of your protection!"

Correctly assessing that a discussion of Carthage would wholly undercut his premise of the law's majesty, the major attempted to focus the discussion on the present only, but was brought up short by the skillful apostle: "I will touch upon the things of the present in a moment," he said. "You may think this outrage was an outbreak—a sudden ebullition of feeling that the governor could not control; but, who was it that did this deed? The governor's troops, sir, were among the foremost of that bloody gang. And where, sir—tell me, where is our redress? You talk about the majesty of the law! What has become of those murderers? Have they been hung or shot, or in any way punished? No, sir, you know they have not. . . . They are now applying the torch to the houses of those they have so deeply injured."

Elder Taylor continued in this vein at length, showing the inconsistency of requiring rigid adherence to the law by the Saints while allowing their enemies both literally and figuratively to get away with murder. He ended with this blunt warning: "And you will talk to us of law and order and threaten us with punishment for disobeying your commands and protecting our rights. What are we? Are we beasts? I tell you for one, sir, I shall protect myself, law or no law, judge or no judge, governor or no governor. I will not stand such infernal rascality, and if I have to fight it out, I will sell my life as dearly as I can."

Apparently convinced that this forthright man with the English accent meant what he said, the major decided to return and seek counsel. He returned in a few days with a letter from Attorney General Brayman that asked whether Elders Taylor and Young were serious in refusing to subject themselves to the law. Denying they had taken this position, and affirming that their grievances resulted from the faulty administration of the law, John added this final warning: "I have endured as much as I feel willing to endure under this government. I feel myself oppressed and wronged. . . . I do not mean to be taken by any unjust requisition and thrust into prison; if I am, I must go there dead; for they shall not take me there alive. I have no personal feelings against you, Major Warren, but I will not put up with these accumulated wrongs."

Later in reflecting on the boldness and belligerency of these words, Elder Taylor said he was "surprised" at himself but that he did not doubt he was "directed by the spirit of the Lord." Subsequent events revealed that at the time of this confrontation, Major Warren had in his possession writs to serve on the Twelve. However, the vehemence of Elder Taylor's response caused him to fear there would be bloodshed were he to do so, which caused him to refrain from serving them.

Despite these stressful events and the added pressures to complete the temple and to prepare for the exodus, John was able to maintain a consistent balance in his personal life and his business enterprises. He continued to publish the *Times and Seasons* up to the very end. Indeed, the last issue of this publication, whose masthead carried the motto Truth Will Prevail, was issued February 15, 1846, just the day before Elder John Taylor and his family crossed the Mississippi River to join the Camp of Israel. That issue, in addition to a lengthy excerpt from the history of Joseph Smith (which had been serialized in the *Times and Seasons* for many months) contained a letter from Wilford Woodruff dated December 18, 1845, at Liverpool, England. A foreword to this letter, written by Elder Taylor, serves as a fitting preamble to the exodus of the Latter-day Saints from Illinois: "Every Saint that reads it," John wrote of his friend's letter, "will see at once the handy work of God in the great moves of The Church of Jesus Christ of Latter-day Saints. . . . Although we have to flee from the presence of freemen, or civilized society, mark the act: watch till the end of the matter, and then judge whether God has a hand in it or not." And in the previous issue of the *Times and Seasons* published February 1, 1846, an article about chartering a ship, the *Brooklyn*, to transport some of the Saints by sea carried this provocative heading: "Come On Oh Israel, It Is Time To Go."

Chapter Ten

From Nauvoo to Winter Quarters

Although the pressure exerted by the enemies of the Church had hastened the time of departure, Elder Taylor and his family were ready to leave when on February 16 they crossed the Mississippi and traveled a few miles to the first pioneer camp at Sugar Creek in Iowa. All their belongings had been carefully stowed in eight wagons, which, with the necessary teams, had been packed methodically over a period of several months. Added to these vehicles was a carriage, which would afford intermittent relief from the jolting ride aboard the freight wagons.

So diligently had Elder Taylor inculcated a sense of adventure into the move, along with a single-minded dedication to the mission of modern Israel, that his family turned its back on Nauvoo with hardly a second thought to what was being left behind or to what lay ahead. Had they been inclined to place an exaggerated emphasis on temporal things, John's wives and children might well have left with great reluctance and against their will. Behind them was a well-furnished, two-story brick home located on a quiet, tree-lined street. Next door were Elder Taylor's print shop and office, and in the rear were a garden plot and a barn for the animals. On the outskirts of the city was the Taylor farm, which included grazing and timber land and forty acres under cultivation.

The Taylors remained at Sugar Creek until March 2, making final preparations for the long trip across Iowa. Because of bad weather and muddy trails, it took over six weeks to cover the 160 miles to the west fork of the Grand River, where they arrived on April 25. At this place, called Garden Grove, Elder Taylor joined with the other brethren in plowing and planting, in making rails, and in constructing log houses for the use of the Saints who would pass that way later. Leaving there, the Taylor company traveled forty miles westward to Mt. Pisgah, which, according to John, was "beautifully situated, abundance of wood and water being convenient." (MS 8:31.)

It was June 17 when the party finally arrived at Council Bluffs on the Missouri River after an arduous yet, all in all, pleasant four-month journey.

Intermittently during the first weeks after leaving, John found it necessary to return to Nauvoo to tie together the loose ends of his private, business, and Church affairs. In a letter written to his friend Joseph Cain in Liverpool under date of May 30, John drew this derisive portrait of life in Nauvoo after the departure of the Saints: "The place has altered very much, *civilization is making rapid strides, and the people are very much improved since we left;* they have built a ten-pin alley opposite the temple, in Mulholland-street; groggeries are plentiful, at night you can hear drunkards yelling and whooping through the streets, a thing formerly unknown." (Ibid.)

In the negotiations for the sale of his Nauvoo holdings conducted from the Iowa prairie, Elder Taylor realized only about a third of their market value, a figure that approximated what other Saints received for their properties. This fact has prompted some observers to bemoan the financial losses suffered by the Mormons during the exodus. Typically, however, John Taylor viewed the episode from a more optimistic perspective. In an address to the British

Saints published in the November 15, 1846, issue of the *Millennial Star*, he recalled that when the Saints first arrived in Nauvoo, building lots sold for from three to twenty dollars an acre and farm land for from a dollar and a quarter to five dollars an acre. But when they left six years later, the price range of city land had jumped from fifty to fifteen hundred dollars an acre and farm land from five to fifty dollars an acre. In reference to these dramatic price increases, Elder Taylor told the British Saints: "Yet if we obtained even one-third of the real value, we were well paid for our labour, and in a better and richer condition than we were when we purchased . . . relatively speaking." (Ibid., p. 115.)

In the same article, Elder Taylor pictured the brighter side of pioneer travel across the Iowa prairie, despite the vagaries of the weather and the rough terrain: "We pursued our course slowly onward, encamping in several places where wood and water were convenient; . . . our cattle and horses suffered very severely from exposure, and we ourselves had frequently to endure the fury of the pitiless storm—the drifting of snow—the pelting of hail and rain—and the icy chills of storms and tempests—but we sustained no injury therefrom; our health and our lives were preserved—we outlived the trying scene—we felt contented and happy—the songs of Zion resounded from wagon to wagon—from tent to tent; the sounds reverberated through the woods, and its echo was returned from the distant hills; peace, harmony, and contentment reigned in the habitations of the Saints." (Ibid., p. 113.)

Such was the spirit that pervaded the company led by Elder Taylor, which arrived at Council Bluffs, Iowa, on June 17. As the plans then in motion contemplated an imminent departure for the great basin, John promptly sent a delegation down-river to trade horses for corn, flour, and cattle. When they returned empty-handed, the apostle received their report with an uncharacteristic sense of gloom: "I now found myself in the wilderness without the means of procuring the necessary provisions for a year and a half." The next day, however, there occurred another of the numerous incidents with which John Taylor's life abounded, showing the providential care that overshadowed him. A friend named Stewart came for counsel and, before leaving, advanced his mentor enough money to outfit his company. John Taylor noted, "I felt thankful to the Lord that He had opened my way, as He always does in time of need." (BHR, pp. 174, 175.)

Even as Elder Taylor received the loan from his friend, events were maturing that would alter the plans for an immediate departure for the mountains. These events had their origin in the instruction given by the Twelve to Jesse C. Little, president of the Eastern States Mission, to try to negotiate contracts with the U.S. government for the Saints to build bridges and forts on their westward trek. Failing in this, President Little was able to arrange for the mustering of five hundred Mormon soldiers into the U.S. Army to aid in the war with Mexico, which had erupted recently. To implement that arrangement, Colonel S. F. Kearny of Fort Leavenworth, Kansas, down-river from Council Bluffs, sent a recruiting officer, Captain James Allen, north to the temporary Mormon communities. He arrived in Council Bluffs on June 30, less than two weeks after John's arrival. When it was learned that any volunteer would receive full army pay and allowances for twelve months, would be mustered out in California, and would be allowed to retain his arms and equipment, Brigham Young, John Taylor, and the other members of the Twelve joined in Captain Allen's recruiting efforts. Shuttling back and forth between Council Bluffs, Mt. Pisgah, and Garden Grove, the Mormon leaders, emphasizing both patriotism and self-interest, generated enough support that the recruiter was able to fill his quota within a short time.

The departure of five hundred of their strongest, most active men and the lateness of the season caused the Mormon leaders to decide against traveling further west that year. So, after negotiations with the Indians who controlled the land and with representatives of the Bureau of

Indian Affairs, the Saints acquired a townsite on the Nebraska side of the river which was appropriately named Winter Quarters, thereby indicating its temporary status and purpose. With typical Mormon enterprise, the Twelve had the townsite surveyed and platted, with lots assigned to the Saints, who were organized into wards presided over by bishops. Soon a mill was constructed on one of the tributary streams feeding into the Missouri River to enable the pioneers to grind their grain into flour. It was not long before the new community began to hum with purpose and efficiency.

These vigorous efforts were interrupted by disturbing news from abroad. Word reached Winter Quarters that Reuben Hedlock, whom Wilford Woodruff had placed in charge when he left England to join the exodus, had created chaos in the British Mission. The problem had its origin in Reuben's organization of "The British and American Joint Stock Company," to which members throughout the mission had subscribed to the extent allowed by their meager resources. The ostensible purpose of the company was to finance emigration of the British Saints to the United States and to purchase and to ship to America equipment and supplies needed to plant the Camp of Israel in the wilderness. Whether through inept management or corruption, the presiding elder had squandered the resources of the company, thereby frustrating the purpose for which it was formed and destroying the confidence of those over whom he presided. Because of the importance of Great Britain to fuel the main body of the Church with new converts, the delay in the westward movement, and the large concentration of leaders in crowded Winter Quarters, the Twelve decided that three of their number, John Taylor, Parley P. Pratt, and Orson Hyde, should go to England to set the affairs of the beleaguered mission in order.

Chapter Eleven

Settling Affairs in Great Britain

The assignment to return to England came as a surprise to Elder Taylor. When he left Nauvoo, the assumption was that except for the expected layovers along the trail he would travel directly to the west, where he would help establish the Saints in their new home. Now he was faced with a major detour that, before it ended, would take him over seventeen-thousand miles, including two crossings of the Atlantic. To contemplate this required radical adjustments, especially on the part of his family, whom he would have to leave behind in less than comfortable circumstances.

John's immediate family now numbered nine, including his fourth wife, Mary Ann Oakley, whom he had married a month before the exodus, and his fifth child, Josephine, born to Elizabeth Kaighin in March during the trek across Iowa. Although the patriarch doubtless felt pangs of regret in leaving his family housed in tents and wagons, yet they were well-provisioned and were in the midst of friends who could provide comfort and assistance in times of need or emergency.

The three apostles departed from Winter Quarters on July 31 on a nondescript scow owned by a family of Presbyterian missionaries who had been living among the Pawnee Indians on the Loupe Fork of the Platte River. The owners of this flat-bottomed boat were undoubtedly overjoyed to have the three Mormons join them, not only for the modest fare they paid, but for their muscle power in helping to keep the clumsy craft in the middle of the river as it floated slowly downstream. Each evening at dusk the scow was beached to enable the passengers to prepare hot meals and to camp for the night.

When the Presbyterians reached their destination at St. Joseph, they sold the scow for a pittance to the three elders, who then continued downstream until they reached Fort Leavenworth. Here they found the men of the Mormon Battalion, who were completing preparation for the march to California and who had just received their first living and clothing allowances. Wanting to share with family and friends, these recent volunteers pooled their excess funds, which were entrusted to Elder Parley P. Pratt, who returned with them to Winter Quarters. Meanwhile, Elders Taylor and Hyde continued their meandering trip until they reached a landing where commercial transportation was available. Here they abandoned their scow and booked passage via the Mississippi and Ohio rivers into Pennsylvania and from there by stage to the coast.

Arriving on the east coast two weeks before the scheduled departure of his England-bound ship, Elder Taylor used the time to visit the branches in the area, especially those at Philadelphia and New York City. Here he found that the apostate J. J. Strang had misled many into the false belief that before his death Joseph Smith had received a revelation designating Mr. Strang as his successor. Elder Taylor was able to convince most of the Saints that these claims were spurious.

Departing from New York City on September 8 on the packet ship *Patrick Henry*, Elders Taylor and Hyde arrived at Liverpool on October 3. Joined later by Elder Pratt, they moved promptly to remedy the problems that had brought them to England. Reuben Hedlock, who had left for London on learning of the arrival of the apostles, was excommunicated. The others who were implicated with him were disfellowshipped.

An investigation revealed that Elder Hedlock was guilty of the incriminating charges that had been whispered about him. He had misappropriated large sums of Church money, had lied and misrepresented, and had consorted with lewd women. The enormity of what had happened to his friend, the forfeiture of his blessings, and the degradation to which he had sunk appalled John Taylor. "Elder Hedlock might have occupied a high and exalted situation in the church, both in time and eternity," John lamented. "But he has cast from his head the crown—he has dashed from him the cup of mercy and has bartered the hope of eternal life."

When the unpleasant task of imposing discipline had been completed, it was decided that Elder Hyde would edit the *Millennial Star* and man the mission office in Liverpool, while Elders Taylor and Pratt would circulate among the branches to calm any unrest and anxiety aroused by Elder Hedlock's misconduct. Their itinerary took the two apostles to Manchester, Birmingham, Sheffield, and Glasgow. They were pleased and not a little surprised to find that the Saints in these larger centers were "exceedingly prosperous." And in the smaller conferences they visited, the elders found the Saints to be no less "zealous, loving and affectionate." (MS 9:162.)

Parting from Elder Pratt, John visited the Isle of Man, where he was welcomed by some of his old friends; then he traveled to Edinburgh and Wales. In the latter place, he was happy to clasp hands with his old friend Dan Jones, who had commenced to publish a paper in the Welsh language and who in his missionary labors in Wales had fulfilled the prophecy of Joseph Smith spoken in the Carthage jail the night before the martyrdom. That night Joseph had asked Elder Jones, "Are you afraid to die?" Wondering about the import of the question, Dan Jones asked whether the Prophet thought death for him was near. After reflection, Joseph said, "You will yet see Wales, and fulfill the mission appointed you before you die." (HC 6:601.) John Taylor was one of the others who had shared the floor of the Carthage Jail that night and had lived to see the fulfillment of this last prophecy uttered by Joseph Smith.

Elder Taylor's meeting with another old friend during this mission to Great Britain brought sorrow instead of happiness. This friend was Martin Harris, one of the three witnesses of the Book of Mormon, who, after the martyrdom, was misled into joining the splinter group headed by J. J. Strang. Martin was traveling in England in the interests of this group when Elder Taylor met him. This pair agreed on all the basic doctrines and the early history of the Church. Their only point of difference was on succession in Church authority at the death of the Prophet. This issue was resolved for Martin a few years later when he acknowledged his error and was welcomed back into fellowship by Elder Taylor and the other leaders of the Church.

John and his brethren used this mission to Great Britain for another purpose than to straighten out the Reuben Hedlock affair. The Church leaders were anxious to obtain parliamentary support for a plan to provide subsidies to British Saints who might elect to migrate to Vancouver Island or to the territory of Oregon. Three reasons that were favorable to the government supported their proposal: First, to relieve the pressures of widespread unemployment which then existed in Britain; second, to strengthen the hand of Great Britain in its controversy with the United States over the Oregon lands; and third, to enhance the value of any crown lands there by granting alternate sections to the immigrants, whose industry in developing their lands was expected to inure to the benefit of the adjoining government-owned lands. There was, of course, a reason that was favorable to the Latter-day Saints—to reduce the cost of their migration to the North American continent and to give them a foothold there.

To stir up widespread support for this proposal, Elder Taylor had a copy of the petition published in the *Millennial*

Star, which requested the local leaders to obtain as many signatures as possible. Armed with this petition and the supporting signatures, John sought an audience with Queen Victoria to present his case. Unable to gain access to her majesty, the resourceful apostle met instead with one of her subordinates, the Earl of Dartmouth, who listened to the presentation patiently but held out no hope for it. The tenuous nature of British claims to the land and serious domestic problems that had even threatened revolution made the plan infeasible.

Having completed their work in Britain, Elders Taylor and Pratt embarked for home on the ship *America* on January 19, 1847. With them were a dozen Saints who wished to join the main body of the Church, which was poised at the Missouri River for the leap into the wilderness. John had disturbing presentiments as he boarded the returning ship in Liverpool. As it left the harbored protection of the Mersey River and plunged into the Irish Sea, the *America* encountered one of those freakish storms that intermittently harass this usually calm estuary.

For days the ship battled strong headwinds that made forward progress tediously slow. This difficulty was magnified by the incapacitation of the captain, who lay ill in his cabin during the whole ordeal with what Parley P. Pratt diagnosed as "fever on the brain." (PPP, p. 354.) Learning about the ministerial status of the two Mormon leaders, the ailing officer summoned Elders Taylor and Pratt to comfort and counsel him. Although he was delirious much of the time, the captain had interludes of lucidity, during which he yearned for his family in America and expressed the fear that he would never see them again. The two apostles tried to assure him that his fears were groundless. Momentarily they were successful, but soon the captain would lapse either into delirium or melancholy. Under these stressful circumstances, it was decided, after nine days of buffeting, to return to port. There the travelers replenished their stores and, with the first mate at the helm, departed a second time on February 7. The contrast between the second try and the first was dramatic. Elder Taylor characterized the thirty-five-day voyage from Liverpool to the mouth of the Mississippi River as "the most pleasant time that I ever experienced at sea." They never had to tack ship and, with the exception of a few hours, "never furled a sail." (MS 9:161.)

The trip was enlivened by the sighting of dolphins, porpoises, flying fish, and whales—and by a wedding feast and reception. Elder Joseph Cain, a returning missionary, was married to Elizabeth Whitaker, and John Taylor was married to Elizabeth's sister, Sophia.

The *America* was delayed two days in crossing the bar at New Orleans because of a dense fog. At last, when the weather cleared, a tug pulled her into port. Here the travelers cleared customs and immediately booked passage by steamer to St. Louis, where they arrived six days later after a leisurely trip upstream.

At St. Louis, Elders Taylor and Pratt parted again. John took a steamer up the Missouri toward Council Bluffs with the baggage while his companion, who had business to transact, purchased a horse and rode overland, going "incog" to avoid detection by his Missouri enemies.

Included in the baggage Elder Taylor carried with him were scientific instruments he had purchased in England for the use of the pioneers: two sextants, two barometers, two artificial horizons, one circular reflector, seven thermometers, and a telescope. Brigham Young, who was at the staging area of the pioneer company, thirty-five miles west of Winter Quarters when he learned of Elder Taylor's approach, delayed leaving until his associate had arrived with the priceless scientific equipment. Beyond this, President Young was anxious to hear a first-hand report from his friend about the conditions in Great Britain. And Brigham was surprised and pleased when John turned over to him the contents of a money belt that represented tithing and other donations from the faithful British Saints.

Chapter Twelve

To the Valley

The plans for the exodus, as designed following the expulsion from Nauvoo, contemplated that temporary communities like Garden Grove, Mt. Pisgah, and Winter Quarters would be established at Grand Island and Fort Laramie in 1846. The unexpectedly slow progress across Iowa and the conscription of the Mormon Battalion had modified those plans. The new blueprint had Brigham Young leading a small vanguard to the basin in the spring of 1847; this group would blaze the trail, construct bridges, and plant crops at the trail's end. Most of the vanguard would then return to Winter Quarters in the fall. Meanwhile, a larger group under Elders Taylor and Pratt would follow a few months later.

After the departure of President Young's pioneer company in April, John and Parley worked incessantly to prepare their more cumbersome company for the rigors of pioneer travel. By the end of June, they were ready to depart. There were about two thousand in the camp, divided into companies of hundreds, fifties and tens. There were 560 wagons, pulled generally by oxen from four to eight to a wagon. In addition, there were hundreds of head of livestock, which, with the ox teams, fed on the abundant grass along the route of travel.

The camp traveled on the north side of the Platte River

rather than on the more frequently traveled trail on the south side. This was a security measure to avoid contact with parties of Missouri travelers who used the south-side trail. What John's company gained in security by following this route, they lost in time because of the newness and roughness of the north-side trail.

Usually the camp was divided into companies of one hundred wagons. But when the scarcity of grass or the roughness of the trail made it necessary, these would be divided further into wagon companies of fifties or tens.

Ordinarily the camp traveled from ten to fifteen miles a day. One can imagine the discomfort and tedium of riding day after day in a springless wagon over a rough, dusty trail without the benefit of the hygenic luxuries of bathroom and laundering facilities. Yet John Taylor's account of this trip is devoid of any reference to these unpleasant conditions. Typical of his optimistic attitude is the following: "I might talk of trials, afflictions, and so forth, but what avails it? they are the common lot of man—they are momentary and pass away, and are not to be compared to the glory that is and shall be revealed, and I have not time to think, speak, or write about them." (MS 10:326.)

In the first week of September, Elder Taylor's group reached South Pass, four hundred miles east of the Salt Lake Valley. There it met the remnant of the pioneer company, led by Brigham Young, which was returning to Winter Quarters after having identified the place of settlement in the wilderness. Brigham had left part of his company in the valley to plant crops, lay out the townsite, and construct buildings. The joy of greeting each other in this lonely place was overshadowed by a gnawing uncertainty that sobered the leading brethren, an uncertainty that was deepened by a storm that day that had deposited several inches of snow on the ground. Snow in early September! Apprehension about what that portended for the Saints in the valley and for the hundreds then on their way there prompted President Young to convene a special council meeting to review the progress of the exodus, to reappraise strategy, and to implore the God of Israel for inspired direction. Perhaps sensing the need for some extraordinary event to lift the spirits of the travelers above the adversities, real or imagined, that faced them, Elder Taylor gave hurried instructions to members of his company before joining Brigham and the other leaders. Thus was set in motion a chain of events that culminated in a festivity that outshines all others celebrated by the Latter-day Saints for its originality, its spontaneity, and its scope and lavishness when viewed against the stark and austere background against which it was held. This was the genesis of the famed "Feast in the Wilderness."

As the leaders parleyed, the sisters, aided by some of the other brethren, selected a nearby grassy spot, out of the sight of the camp, where makeshift tables were set up. On these were placed snow-white linens, gleaming silverware, and treasured dishes, the remnants of gracious living in Nauvoo, which had been stored in trunks, originally intended for opening only upon reaching their destination. Meanwhile, others were busy preparing fish, game, veal, and hot biscuits and loading the tables with fruits, vegetables, jams, jellies, and condiments that had been bottled at the other end of the trail.

Fortunately, a late summer sun melted the morning snow, so that when John and his brethren were led from their council tent to the dining area in mid-afternoon, their eyes were greeted by a sight that stretched their credulity, and their appetites were satisfied by a feast they would savor and reflect upon for years afterward. In the evening, after the dishes had been cleared, washed, and put away and the camp had been made shipshape and secure, there was dancing, instrumental and vocal solos, and recitations. Of this unusual event, John Taylor, the man who had introduced a touch of class and culture into the wilderness, said merely, "We mutually felt edified and rejoiced; we praised the Lord, and blessed one another." (Ibid., p. 325.)

Encouraged and refreshed, the two companies parted the next morning to go their opposite ways. John's company, which followed by one and two days respectively companies led by Parley P. Pratt and Daniel Spencer, covered the remaining four hundred miles in a month, arriving in the Salt Lake Valley on October 5.

The scene that greeted the apostle was at once inspiring and sobering. The inspiration came from the magnificent setting of the valley, nestled between two towering, snow-capped ranges, with the blue salt lake glimmering in the distance. What sobered Elder Taylor was the tenuous foothold the pioneer company had gained in the battle with the harsh and unforgiving elements. Here was found a fort-like structure enclosing ten acres of land. Built for protection and convenience, it consisted of a series of small rooms that faced the center of the fort and whose back walls formed a barricade against unwanted animals or Indians. Within the enclosure were small garden plots in which were planted a variety of vegetables. To the southeast was a large communal farm that, in addition to duplicating the plantings in the individual gardens, included extensive acreages planted in wheat. The only harvest that had been garnered at the time of John's arrival consisted of a few bushels of potatoes ranging in size from a pea to a half-inch in diameter. Even these were not for food but for the next year's seed.

Aside from the fort and the farm, the only other evidence of civilization was a series of stakes marking the boundaries of the streets and blocks of the city-to-be. All else, as far as the eye could see in any direction, was devoid of any evidence of human husbandry or enterprise. Nature, in its most rugged and untamed aspect, reigned here. We can only surmise about the impact this stark scene had upon John Taylor, the gentlemanly apostle who had been nurtured into manhood amidst the verdant surroundings of a centuries-old civilization.

Whatever negative or questioning thoughts Elder Taylor may have had about his new home were buried in a flurry of the most intense physical activity. This was not a time for reflection and analysis. It was a time for action.

Among Elder Taylor's belongings were his valuable tools, which he had not used extensively for several years. These he unpacked and wielded in helping to build a second fort, located just south of the original structure. "About Christmas," he reported, "I had put up, enclosed and covered about ninety feet of building made of split logs, out of which was taken a four inch plank. The plank was used for partitions, etc. . . . In addition to this, I had built corrals and stables behind, and enclosed a garden spot in front, with a board-rail fence. I assisted in all this labor of sawing, building, hawling, etc.,—enough for one fall." (BHR, p. 193.)

It was into these humble quarters that John Taylor moved his families before the full brunt of winter struck the valley. By now his clan had grown to twelve with the addition of his sixth wife, Harriet Whitaker, Sophia's twin sister, whom he married on December 4, 1847, and his sixth child, Harriet Ann, Sophia's first baby, who was born three days later on December 7, 1847. The loving bond that tied these twin sisters together is suggested by the fact that when her first child was born on July 14, 1849, Harriet reciprocated by naming her Sophia.

It is doubtless true that in the minds of John Taylor's wives and children this new home in the wilderness suffered in comparison with the luxury of their beautiful Nauvoo residence. Yet it must have seemed almost palatial in contrast with the tents and wagons that had been their home since leaving Winter Quarters.

Shortly before occupying their new dwelling, Elder Taylor, and the members of his family who had reached the age of accountability engaged in a significant act of rededication and renewal. They all submitted to rebaptism in the cold, clear waters of a forked stream that entered the valley from the north, a stream later named City Creek. The family of Elder Parley P. Pratt joined with the Taylors in this cleansing ordinance that signaled for all a new beginning in what to them was a new land. And, for the two apostles, the incident would have had special significance by evoking memories of the occasion, eleven years before, when Parley led John into the waters of baptism for the first time in Toronto, and of the intervening years filled with events both trying and rewarding.

These baptisms and many others like them participated in by the early pioneers symbolize as nothing else could the spiritual foundations of the Latter-day Saints in the mountain west. This spirituality, which grew apace with the temporal development in the new land, is evidenced further by the temple site designated by Brigham Young shortly after he entered the valley the first time; the site lay in the fork of City Creek near the place where John Taylor and the others were rebaptized.

As the new year approached, there were stirrings in Elder Taylor's family for a celebration of the kind they had enjoyed in Nauvoo before the exodus. And since their new home had just been completed, there were hints that the occasion could double for a housewarming. But for John, two things stood in the way, both of which reveal salient qualities in his character. The first was the meagerness of the provisions the family had to last through the winter, whose duration and severity were a matter of pure conjecture, there being no experience or precedent on which to rely. This obstacle was removed when the family patriarch finally yielded to the entreaties of his wives that the celebration become a pot-luck dinner with each invited guest bringing part of the food. He agreed to this arrangement with great reluctance, as it seemed to him to be an affront to invite guests to dinner and then ask them to bring their own meal. "The principle itself was repugnant to me," he wrote of the incident, "but still under the circumstances, if we had a party, this must be the principle we have it on, as I could not possibly spare provisions for so large a company as we must necessarily have; and upon this plan there was one gotten up."

The other obstacle was of an even more delicate nature, involving a question of protocol and the sensitive balancing of authority between different levels of the Church hierarchy. Before returning to Winter Quarters, Brigham Young had designated Uncle John Smith as the president of the Salt Lake Stake. In that capacity, he had adopted a policy, before the arrival of Elder Taylor's company, that there would be no dancing in the valley until after the first harvest had been garnered. But Elder Taylor's wives and other wives involved in planning the affair were anxious that there be dancing. Recognizing that as a member of the stake he was subject to this policy, and not wanting to countermand it in his capacity as a member of the Twelve, which exercised world-wide authority, Elder Taylor's solution was to seek an exception to the policy. "I sent to Uncle John to see about this," Elder Taylor explained, "not because I thought there was any harm in dancing, but because I did not wish to encourage law-breaking by my example in this thing." Elder Taylor reported Uncle John's reaction: "He said if he was me he would have the dance as it had been arranged for." (BHR, p. 196.)

With this obstacle removed, John went forward with the party, where sixty-nine persons sat down to an elaborate dinner in the snug comfort of his new log cabin. After the meal, when the dishes had been cleared and the tables moved back, there was dancing interspersed with musical numbers and a comic sermon delivered by Brother Sherwood, whom the host had asked to serve as the master of ceremonies. Elder Taylor capped the evening with a few appropriate remarks on a spiritual theme.

In this extraordinary way, the Latter-day Saints ushered in their first New Year in the Salt Lake Valley. It was extraordinary because of the setting and timing of the party. It was not thought necessary to delay a celebration until more elaborate housing was available. Nor was there any apparent concern about using their precious stores for what some might have considered a frivolity without assurance they would be able to reap a good harvest the following season. After all, there had been gloomy predictions that crops would not mature in the valley because of the short growing season. Indeed, the famous Jim Bridger had been so positive about this that he had offered a sizable reward for the first bushel of corn raised in the Salt Lake Valley.

That these forebodings had no apparent effect on Elder Taylor's thinking and attitudes does not mean that he was oblivious to the uncertainties and dangers the Latter-day Saints faced. What it does mean is that he had an assurance that events would combine to enable the Saints to survive in their new home and to reach out from there to fulfill the mandate that had been given to them. A letter John wrote to his friends in Great Britain about this time conveys the feelings he had about the destiny of the Saints operating from their new mountain home. After detailing the physical improvements that had been made in the valley, he added: "And now beloved brethren, although I have been writing in a great measure on temporal things, yet my mind dwells not so much on hills, vales, brooks, lakes, houses and lands as it does on the things pertaining to the kingdom of God—the building up of Zion—the gathering together of God's elect—the fulfillment of the prophecies—the blessing, glory and exaltation of his Saints, and that I may fulfill with dignity and honor the office to which God has called me; and obtain an exaltation in the kingdom of God, for which I claim an interest in your prayers." (MS 10:326.)

It was mainly the hope of celestial reward suggested by these words of Elder Taylor, combined with an extraordinary sense of duty, that fueled the energies of the Latter-day Saints. And never were those energies more evident than they were when spring broke on the Salt Lake Valley in 1848. The pioneers had brought with them almost every variety of grain and vegetable seeds, as well as shrubs, fruits, and flowers. Two thousand bushels of wheat had been sown during the preceding fall, and at the dawn of spring in 1848 the Saints planted three thousand acres of corn and hundreds of acres in other vegetables and fruits.

After the crops had been planted, John and the other settlers were both pleased and surprised at the frequency and intensity of the spring rains. Their surprise grew from the reports they had received that the climate was extremely arid and that, therefore, they could expect little rain. But, the unexpected boon to their crops turned into a catastrophe to their houses, which, in anticipation of little rainfall, had been built with flat roofs. This caused large accumulations of water on the flat surfaces, and the resulting leakage dampened the bedding and other household articles that could not be adequately dried out while the rain continued.

Meanwhile, the steady depletion of their stores and the uncertainty about whether the crops would mature produced much anxiety among some of the settlers who lacked John Taylor's buoyant faith. These worriers even urged that mounted messengers be sent immediately to intercept Brigham Young and the large company of Saints expected later in the year and to urge them to remain at Winter Quarters until a more suitable place of settlement could be found. However, the wiser, more farsighted counsel of John Taylor and other leaders prevailed; they "struggled on, trusting in God." (PPP, p. 363.)

It was during this stressful period that the pioneers faced the most serious crisis of their first year in the valley. The crops they had planted with such care and so laboriously had just begun to thrive when they were set upon by hordes of crickets, which Parley P. Pratt likened to the locust plague that descended upon Egypt. The first defense was to beat them with shovels, brooms, sacks, rakes, or whatever else was handy. Then attempts were made to drown them by turning water from the creek into diversionary ditches. These efforts failing, the desperate Saints, who were literally fighting for their lives, turned to God for deliverance. Praying with a fervency they had seldom generated before, the pioneers sought a divine answer to an earthly problem that was beyond their power to solve. And God's response came from an earthly source the settlers had not anticipated. According to the accounts of reliable observers, soon after offering their anxious prayers, the

Mormon immigrants saw massive flocks of seagulls, which are indigenous to the Great Salt Lake, descend upon their fields, where they gorged themselves with crickets. To this point, nothing extraordinary is seen in the incident by those who have observed the tendency of gulls to be drawn, as if by some magnetic force, to newly tilled fields, where they feast upon the worms turned up by the plough. What distinguished this incident from the norm, and tinged it with a miraculous quality, was the actions of the gulls once they had eaten their fill. Instead of withdrawing to their nesting grounds, they flew to nearby streams or fields where they disgorged their prey. Then, returning to the crickets, they repeated the procedure again and again until most of them had been destroyed.

Thus, in the minds of John Taylor and the Saints, another adversity had been overcome through the human exertions of faith and prayer and the resulting show of power by an omnipotent and loving God. And in the process, Elder Taylor saw at work an eternal principle of growth, the principle of opposites, which teaches the priceless value of adversity. Elder Taylor sketched the elements of this principle a few years later in a talk delivered in the Old Tabernacle. Said he, "God is determined, if possible, to make something of us. In order to do this, he has to try us and prove us, to manifest principles unto us . . . to show us, by placing us in various positions and subjecting us to various trials, what we are,—to show us our weaknesses and follies, in order that we may be made to lean and depend upon him alone. He will try men and prove them, to see if their hearts are pure. . . . We have first to learn submission to the will of God ourselves, through various trials, persecutions, and the development of our weaknesses and imperfections, and thereby learn to appreciate the goodness and blessings that flow from him. We must see that we ourselves first learn obedience, and then teach others. But how can we teach others a lesson which we have not learned ourselves?" (JD 6:166, 167.)

Through their own industry and the blessings of God,

the Saints reaped a bounteous harvest at the end of the summer of 1848. Imitating the example of the Pilgrim Fathers, the leaders organized a gigantic public feast where the fruits of their labors burdened the long tables set up under canopies within the Old Fort. The preaching, the dancing, and, especially, the prayers on this occasion revealed both a sense of humility and gratitude for past blessings and an enterprising sense of self-confidence and enthusiasm for the future. These dual qualities of dependence and independence seem to lie at the root of the success of the Latter-day Saints and of their leaders like John Taylor. They acknowledged divine intervention in their behalf on numerous occasions, the most recent and dramatic being the seagull incident. Yet they were aware there would have been no crops to be threatened had it not been for their industry in taming the desert with their plowing, their planting, and their irrigating.

Combining practicality and spirituality in an unusual way, John Taylor moved forward in step with the other Latter-day Saints and in partnership with God to lay the foundation of a new civilization in the wilderness. To the manual chores of farming and house-building he added road and bridge construction, exploration, fishing, and hunting. He was the prime mover in the construction of the first bridge that spanned the Jordan River. Here his skills with the lathe, the saw, and the hammer, applied since his youth as a cabinet maker, served him well. With Parley P. Pratt and other brethren, he conducted several explorations into surrounding areas to map and locate suitable sites for new settlements. On one such outing, he and others constructed and launched a boat on Utah Lake; it was reported to be the first craft sailed on that lake by the Mormons. Finding an abundance of fish there, John, with the assistance of his industrious wives, fashioned a hundred-foot-long seine, which was used to catch a huge harvest of fish—an important food supplement for the Saints as they struggled to strengthen their foothold in the mountains. Apt as he was in the use of analogies, we might easily infer that as John Taylor, a modern apostle, seined for fish on Utah Lake, the American Galilee connected with a dead sea by the means of the Jordan River, he was reminded of the first apostles whom Jesus summoned from their nets to become fishers of men.

Elder Taylor had no difficulty in reconciling the heavy physical labors he performed during his first few months in the Salt Lake Valley with his predominate role as an apostle of Jesus Christ. To him, the various tasks of life were all of one piece as long as they were directed to a common end. And to him, that end was self-perfection through obedience to the laws of God and the preparation of a people ready and worthy to receive the Lord at his second coming. This preparation entailed a variety of tasks, all of which Elder Taylor accepted with enthusiasm and discharged with competence. An assignment he received from President Young in August 1849 took him away from his physical exertions and introduced him again into the realm of politics and diplomacy, a realm from which he had been absent since his management of Joseph Smith's abortive presidential campaign and his parleys with Governor Ford before and with Major Warren after the martyrdom.

Along with Charles C. Rich and Daniel Spencer, Elder Taylor was assigned to confer with General John Wilson, President Zachary Taylor's personal emissary, about the creation of an exceedingly large new state that was to include the territories of California and Deseret. The expectation in Washington was that this new state would enter the union as a non-slave state, thereby counterbalancing the recent annexation of Texas. Elder Taylor and his associates finally reached an accord with General Wilson, an accord ratified by the Twelve, that the Saints would cooperate in the formation of the proposed new state with the understanding that at some appropriate time in the future, steps would be taken to spin off Deseret as a separate state. With that agreement in his pocket, the general left Salt Lake for the west coast to confer with another presidential emissary who had been meeting with leaders in California to formulate a joint report and recommendation to the president. Bad weather over the Sierras caused a lengthy delay of General Wilson's party, so that by the time it arrived on the coast, the other representative, tired of waiting, had left by ship for the east. For this reason, the joint proposal was never made, which nullified the efforts of Elder Taylor and his committee. However, one benefit to the Church came out of these labors as the result of a complimentary report General Wilson made about the Latter-day Saints. Excerpts from this report were read by Senator Truman Smith during a speech he delivered on the floor of the Senate on July 8, 1850. "A more orderly, earnest, industrious and civil people, I have never been among than these," read the report, "and it is incredible how much they have done here in the wilderness in so short a time. In this city which contains about from four to five thousand inhabitants, I have not met in a citizen a single idler, or any person who looks like a loafer. Their prospects for crops are fair, and there is a spirit and energy in all that you see that cannot be equaled in any city of any size that I have ever been in, and I will add, not even in old Connecticut." (BHR, p. 202.)

Chapter Thirteen

Mission to France

Few things dramatize the evangelical fervor of John Taylor and his fellow apostles more than the extraordinary event that occurred only a few weeks after General Wilson left Salt Lake City. It took place at the 1849 October conference of the church. At that time, only two scant years after the arrival of the pioneer company, while the Saints were still struggling to secure their tenuous foothold in the mountains, the Twelve decided on a major proselyting effort abroad. So, during the conference, it was announced that four members of the Twelve would leave soon for missionary service overseas, John Taylor to France and Germany, Franklin D. Richards to Great Britain, Lorenzo Snow to Italy, and Erastus Snow to Denmark. Within two weeks after the announcement, these four, with ten missionary companions and several brethren who were going east on business, were ready to go.

The party left the valley on October 19, making its way slowly up Emigration Canyon along a trail that by now had been well defined by the thousands of wagons, walkers, and animals that had traversed it during the previous two years. Although John and his friends had embarked on a journey that would take them thousands of miles across the sea and back, they had undertaken it with a degree of unconcern one might expect of a planned trip from Salt Lake City to Provo, Utah. Nothing is more striking about the labors of these early apostles than is their extraordinary mobility, especially when seen against the background of the wild terrain through which they often traveled and the comparatively crude nature of the modes of transportation they used.

This company had the usual experience of those who traveled on the western plains during this period—the tedious hours on the trail, the occasional excitement of encounters with friendly but fearsome looking Indians, the singing and conversation around the campfire at night, and the astonishing sight of herds of thousands of buffalo, which were so dense and extensive as to make the distant landscape appear to be alive and undulating. Because of its late start, this company also encountered the early winter storms that often sweep the high country with intermittent sleet, snow, and blustering winds. But the group was fortunate in its makeup, being comprised of young, vigorous men who were traveling light and who had the endurance to travel long distances each day. So, although the journey was a long one, judged even by today's standards, it was made much shorter by the speed of travel and by the buoyancy, the joviality, and the cooperation of those who comprised the company.

But for John Taylor—and doubtless for others who were going to non–English-speaking countries—there was another factor that made the days and the journey pass quickly. This was Elder Taylor's intense absorption in studying the history and language of a foreign land—in this case, France. Because of his aptitude for scholarship and reflection and his cosmopolitan perceptions of the world, gained through his extensive travels, Elder Taylor acquired a good grasp of French culture and history and the rudiments of the language before arriving at his new field of labor. His studies were greatly accelerated by three-week layovers in both Kanesville and St. Louis, where he spent most of his leisure hours in study, although he devoted considerable time to counseling and admonishing local members and leaders and to writing letters.

A message written to his family from St. Louis gives us insight into his studious habits, his ministerial activities en route to Europe, and his love for family. "I have been going leisurely along for the purpose of studying French," he explained, "that I might be the better prepared to enter on my mission on my arrival in France. I have made some progress in the language and hope to be able to speak it on my arrival there." As to speaking and counseling demands imposed by his apostolic rank, he observed, "On my arrival both here and in Kanesville, the Saints flocked around me like bees: and the greatest trouble I have is that of not being able to fulfill the many engagements that have pressed themselves upon me." He was impressed with the attitudes and activities of the Saints in St. Louis, commenting on them with a hint of combined surprise and pleasure. "Here the Saints have a magnificent hall and a splendid band and do things up in good style." Finally, the letter writer got around to the theme that dominated his thoughts more than any other: "But, say you, 'do you think of us and home? And do you ever think of me, and of me?' This is what I have been wanting to get at for some time, and this long, tedious preface has become wearisome to me—let me tell you my feelings if I can. Home! Home! Home! What shall I say? Can I tell it? No, a thousand times no. Your forms, your countenances, your bodies and your spirits are all portrayed before me as in living characters. . . . Oceans, seas, mountains, deserts and plains may separate us—but in my heart you dwell." (BHR, pp. 207, 208.)

Lest his family might wrongly interpret the meaning of his words, John hastened to add that he was not complaining or murmuring about their separation which, he reminded them, was inherent in the position he occupied.

Before leaving St. Louis, Elder Taylor purchased a wagonload of supplies, which his friend Brother Hoagland took to the Taylor families in Salt Lake City with the apostle's instruction to sell them for their sustenance while he was gone.

Traveling to New York City without incident, Elder Taylor embarked on the packet ship *Westwelt* in company with Curtis E. Bolton and John Pack. They touched shore at Liverpool on May 27, 1850, and were met by elders from the mission office.

After spending a few weeks in his native country renewing acquaintances and regaining his land legs, John Taylor was ready at last to make his proselyting assault upon ancient Gaul, which for centuries had lain in the grip of orthodox Catholicism. For this effort, he had added Elder William Howell to his meager corps; this elder was a diligent missionary from Wales who seems to have been imbued with some of the enthusiasm generated there by Elder Taylor's friend Dan Jones. Since Elder Howell had done some work already across the English channel and had baptized a few converts, it was decided to visit the places where he had given the Church a foothold, however tenuous it was.

This decision took the Elders first to Jersey in the Channel Islands, west of the Cherbourg peninsula. After visiting briefly, it was decided to leave Elder Pack in Jersey temporarily while Elder Taylor and his other two companions sailed up the channel to Boulogne sur Mer, southwest of Calais and across the channel from Hastings and Eastbourne. Here Elder Taylor was introduced to the time-worn civilization of continental Europe with the encrustations of the centuries layered gloomily on its gabled buildings and cobbled streets. Here in Boulogne sur Mer the apostle found the remnants of military fortifications set up defiantly by Napoleon; these faced the English coast, which could be seen across the channel on a clear day. And, more provocatively, he found the crumbling remnants of some of the battlements thrown up by the Caesars almost two thousand years before, the last physical vestige of Roman power and dominion.

The Roman influence was not as evident in these ancient structures, however, as it was in the pervasive presence of the Catholic Church, which the dominance of the Holy Roman Empire after Charlemagne had imposed upon France. That influence was evident not only in the religious beliefs and practices of the people, but in their social and political institutions as well. So, it was the political power of the Catholic Church in France with which Elder Taylor first had to contend. Knowing that the dominant sect had influenced the passage of ordinances that tightly restricted public religious gatherings, Elder Taylor sought approval to hold Mormon services by going to the one who had the ultimate power of decision in such matters—Monsieur le Maire, Boulogne sur Mer's mayor. Whatever prejudices the mayor may have had toward the Church were soon dissolved by the geniality and adroitness of the Englishman turned Yankee who, in presenting his credentials—a letter from the governor of Deseret—charmed and honored his grace by conversing in French. Not to be outdone, the mayor reciprocated by trying his equally limited English on the visitor. At John's elbow was Elder Bolton, who was quite fluent in French, and who safely piloted the conversation over the rough shoals of this pair's linguistic deficiencies.

The result of this interview was blanket authority for Elder Taylor and his companions to hold meetings in consecrated church buildings and limited authority to speak elsewhere, conditioned only on prior notice to the mayor's office of the time and place of such a meeting and a general statement of the subject matter to be discussed. While this arrangement hardly met the apostle's high standard of free speech, formulated during years of unfettered proselyting in Great Britain and America, it was acceptable; indeed, it was extraordinary, given the repressive religious climate that existed in France at the time.

Soon after this interview with the mayor, Elder Pack arrived from Jersey, and that evening, June 26, 1850, Elder Taylor and his three companions went through a ritual that is customarily followed when a new country is opened to the preaching of the gospel by Mormon elders. They sought a place of seclusion where they would not be interrupted. There being no mountaintops nearby, a favorite place for such ceremonies, they found an isolated spot on the beach. There, with the sounds of the sea as a backdrop, and after the usual preliminaries of singing, praying, and testimony bearing, Elder Taylor offered a moving dedicatory prayer. It was a prayer of both thanksgiving and invocation—thanks for past blessings and direction, and an imploring cry for wisdom, judgment, and revelation as they sought to establish a Mormon beachhead on what to them was a foreign and formidable shore.

The next steps followed a familiar pattern set by Elder Taylor on his other missions. He first rented a hall and then sought to publicize his lectures by writing a series of letters to the editor of the *Boulogne Interpreter*. These were duly published in both English and French and outlined the basic history and doctrines of the Church.

The results were disappointing. Instead of the large crowds such publicity had drawn in Great Britain, here only a small handful turned out. And among these was a knot of volatile and vocal protestant preachers who seemed intent on embarrassing and thwarting Elder Taylor's work in its very inception. During the first lecture, the Reverend James Robertson, an independent minister, arose to ask questions of the speaker, who, forwarned that he was a troublemaker, put him off. In doing so, Elder Taylor had two concerns; that his lectures would be interrupted, diverting him from presenting his message; and that in the process of answering provocative questions, a disturbance might erupt that could jeopardize the elders' speaking license. So, John ignored the man, as far as his boisterous conduct would allow, and completed his lecture. Afterward, Mr. Robertson, joined by another minister who, the apostle said, "was also very officious," followed, or, as John put it, "dogged" the elders home. On the way, the hecklers made insulting remarks about the Prophet Joseph Smith, calling him an impostor. Elder Taylor merely responded that they could entertain any opinion about Joseph Smith they wished, however false, that having been personally acquainted with the man, he knew them to be false, and that he wished no further conversation with them. Despite this rebuff, "they still dogged after" the elders, but John "answered them no further." (See *Three Nights' Public Discussion*, published in Liverpool in 1850 by John Taylor, p. 1.)

A few days later, Elder Taylor and his companions received a letter from C. W. Cleeve, James Robertson, and Philip Cates, challenging them to a public debate where the "extraordinary nature of your pretensions and announcements" could be inquired into. Specifically, the challenging ministers sought to debate three issues: Joseph Smith, the Book of Mormon, and the elders. As to the last issue, the challengers asked to debate "The pretended facts of your Direct Appointment by God to preach what you call the Gospel." (Ibid., p. 2.)

Aware that debate is a notoriously inefficient and often self-defeating method of proselyting, Elder Taylor was understandably reluctant to accept this challenge. However, under the circumstances, there appeared to be no graceful way to decline, given the openness with which he had been challenged and the vigorous way in which the ministers had been pressing their attack. So, the invitation was accepted, and through negotiations the ground rules for the debate were worked out. It was agreed that in addition to debating the three issues posed by the ministers, Elder Taylor would have the privilege of discussing the validity of the faith and calling of his opponents. It was also agreed that an admission fee of half a franc would be charged, out of which the expenses would be paid first, with the remainder to be divided evenly between the mayor and the English consul for the benefit of the poor.

Elder Taylor entered the debate under severe handicaps. He was in a foreign land surrounded by determined foes. He had no library facilities. And he had only a few days in which to prepare for a lengthy confrontation that would extend over three nights of arduous argument. Reading the transcript of the proceedings against this background arouses a sense of admiration, bordering on awe, for the analytical and linguistic ability of forty-two-year-old John Taylor, whose opportunity for formal education had been severely limited. This defect had been compensated for by years of reading, writing, editing, and extemporaneous speaking. These exercises, carefully and prayerfully performed, had indelibly imprinted good sentence structure, word usage, and literary cadence on his mind. And overlying all these qualities and skills was an extraordinary spiritual sensitivity that illuminated and dramatized his words so as to bring understanding of his message and, in some instances, conviction of its truthfulness. One need only read the report of this debate to find confirmation of this appraisal.

The Reverend C. W. Cleeve led off for the challenging ministers. As to the issue of Joseph Smith's character, he read lengthy excerpts from the writings of several anti-Mormon authors, including the Rev. Henry Caswell, an angry Protestant minister, and John C. Bennett, a bitter excommunicant from the Church. Elder Taylor first answered the charge affirmatively, giving personal, first-hand evidence of Joseph Smith's character. He then impugned the motives and objectivity of Caswell and Bennett: "I have heard a great deal said about Joseph Smith and his character," the apostle began. "I was intimately acquainted with the late Joseph Smith, and know that the statements made by Mr. Cleeve were untrue. I have been with Mr. Smith for years; I have traveled with him; I have been with him in public and in private, at home and abroad; I was with him living, and when he died—when he was murdered in Carthage gaol, and I can testify that he was a virtuous, moral, high-minded man—a Christian and a philanthropist." (Ibid., p. 5.)

As to Mr. Caswell, the apostle observed, "I was at Nauvoo during the time of his visit. He came for the purpose of looking for evil. He was a wicked man, and associated with reprobates, mobocrats, and murderers." Elder Taylor went on to assert, in essence, that the reverend's ministerial vestments could not hide his devious malignant character, and he cited an instance, of which he had personal knowledge, when Mr. Caswell had lied.

As to John C. Bennett, the American missionary told his French audience, "I was well acquainted with him. At one time he was a good man, but fell into adultery, and was cut off from the church for his iniquity; and so bad was his conduct, that he was also expelled [from] the Municipal Court, of which he was a member." (Ibid., p. 6.)

After reciting how Bennett and Caswell had made a career of slandering and libeling the Latter-day Saints through their lectures and writings, the speaker made what to some in the audience must have been an uncomfortable comparison: "These infamous lies and obscene stories, however, had been found very palatable to a certain class of society, and in times of our persecutions multitudes were pleased with them." Having laid this foundation, John Taylor then turned the full force of his not inconsiderable power of derision upon those whom his opponents in the debate had chiefly relied upon: "This Gospel does not agree with the systems of men, which are conflicting and various; and instead of acknowledging, as honest men, the truths contained in the Bible, which they profess to believe, but, in reality do not, they seek to cover over their tottering systems and unscriptural theories, to wrap themselves in their cloak of self-righteousness. . . . And instead of meeting what they call error with the scriptures, and testing it with the touchstone of truth, like the persecutors of the Prophets, they substitute vituperation, scandal, persecution and abuse; and as they know that error cannot combat the truth, they tread in the steps of their venerable predecessors, the Pharisees, who called Jesus an impostor; and that he cast out devils through Beelzebub, the prince of devils; declared that he was born of fornication, and accused him of blasphemy." With that before the audience, the speaker drew another uncomfortable analogy: "So the same kind of persons, in these days, in the absence of truth, seek to undermine the character of a good, honorable, and virtuous man. Hence, we have the hue-and-cry of false prophet, impostor, deceiver, blasphemer, adulterer." But Elder Taylor then brought the matter closer to home, to the very doorstep of the ministers in Boulogne sur Mer: "Ministers in America join with the drunkard, profligate, and murderer, to hatch up stories against the Saints, and we have an importation to this country, circulated by pious people, revived and reprinted by ministers for the same purpose." Having thus brought the bird home to roost on the shoulders of the ministers who opposed him in the debate, John said to them reprovingly, "Gentlemen, men of your calling ought to use other weapons. What do you gain by this system? All honorable men are ashamed of it." The Mormon apostle also reminded his opponents that even if the scurrilous things they said about the Prophet Joseph Smith were true, that could not lend credence or support to their own unscriptural claims. (Ibid., pp. 6-7.)

Elder Taylor's personal knowledge of most of the facts relating to the history of the Church and his sure grasp of the scriptures gave him a decided edge over his opponents. And from the record that has come down to us, he seems to have dominated the debate as a whole. But he was not unassailable. His weakest position was on the issue of polygamy. Typically, his opponents relied on the fulminations of John C. Bennett and other such critics of the Church who had manufactured mythical stories about polygamy and the sisters of the "White Veil" and the "Black Veil." Elder Taylor gave the issue short shrift, contenting himself merely to poke fun at these nonsensical stories and to read the Church's policy on marriage that was then in the Doctrine and Covenants. Included in it was the following: "Inasmuch as this Church of Jesus Christ has been reproached with the crime of fornication and polygamy, we declare that we believe that one man should have one wife, and one woman but one husband, except in case of death, when either is at liberty to marry again." (Ibid., p. 8.)

This statement was adopted as Church policy in August 1835 (See HC 2:247), several years before Joseph Smith and a few of the inner circle of Church leaders had begun to take plural wives. It had never been changed officially nor would it be for a while after the Boulogne debates. Therefore, Elder Taylor was correct in quoting the statement as Church policy. And as far as his personal status was concerned, he was on solid ground as he had entered into the practice reluctantly because of a mandate from one whom he sustained as a prophet of God. But although John could rationally reconcile this variance between official Church policy and his own conduct, he was intelligent enough to realize that had this been known to his opponents and the audience, his credibility would have been shattered and the debate ended. Then the mass mind would have been led to believe as true all of the vile and false charges that had been circulated about the Church and its members. There can be little doubt that the open endorsement of polygamy given by the Church not long after was influenced strongly by the compromising position in which missionaries like Elder Taylor had been placed by this difference between policy and practice.

None of the elders in John Taylor's group seemed to feel that the debate had advanced their cause appreciably. Indeed, Elder Bolton recorded pessimistically, "I feel in my own bosom that we were most signally defeated." (Curtis E. Bolton diary, Collection of Mormon Diaries, Brigham Young University.)

The forensic outcome apart, it seems that the Mormon elders were defeated in the minds of the audience, as only two listeners turned out to hear them when the debates had ended. Thereupon, Elder Taylor relinquished the hall and afterward held meetings in his quarters. With a seeming I-told-you-so attitude, Elder Bolton recorded a few days later, "Bro. Taylor preached in his own room to three persons. Mormonism is dead here." (Ibid.)

Any seeming failure of the proselyting effort in Boulogne sur Mer must be laid as much at the door of the listeners and the dominant church as to any other cause. In a report to the editor of the *Millennial Star*, John characterized the French of that day as "gay, careless, and volatile." (MS 12:270.) And the deadening influence of the Catholic Church on Mormon proselyting is implicit in the fact that the Latter-day Saints would gain no substantial foothold in a Catholic-dominated country until many decades after John Taylor's initial work in France.

But the success or failure of an enterprise cannot be reckoned merely in terms of the outcome of a single episode. However ineffective the debates may have been, Elder Taylor gathered them up and made good use of them. Of the record of the debates prepared from Elder Bolton's extensive notes, John wrote to the editor of the *Millennial Star*, "I will publish it in pamphlet form, and the proceeds may help a little on our mission." (MS 12:270.) Aside from its monetary value, the published debates provided an important historical record of the beginning of the work in France; it aided future missionaries to that land in understanding some of the attitudes and obstacles they would encounter; and it served as a caution to the elders about the futility of debate as a tool of conversion and about the points of Church doctrine and practice on which they were most vulnerable. Finally, to the student of human character and achievement, the record provides an index to some of John Taylor's salient qualities of mind and spirit. It shows him to have been capable of precise, cogent reasoning while speaking extemporaneously and under pressure. It demonstrated the depth and accuracy of his knowledge of the scriptures and of Church history and doctrine. It reflects a quality of poise and courtliness, even while under attack by able, determined opponents. And it mirrors an extraordinary power of will and combativeness. Moreover, the highly intellectual tone of his arguments and responses seem, in retrospect, to have foreshadowed the composition while in France of his most enduring philosophical work, *The Government of God*, of which the historian Bancroft wrote, "As a dissertation on a general and abstract subject, it probably has not its equal in point of ability within the range of Mormon literature." With all that, the record reveals perhaps the only real failure of John Taylor as a missionary.

The kind of abstraction referred to by Mr. Bancroft is more often referred to as philosophy. And in the complimentary sense used by the historian, Elder Taylor most likely would have accepted the title with appreciation. However, he doubtless would have rejected it out of hand had it been intended thereby to classify him with the philosophers he found in Paris, the French city to which he went after leaving Boulogne sur Mer.

French philosophy at that day was an intellectual game that brainy people played with each other, substituting catchy words and nebulous phrases for meaningful ideas and concepts. Elder Taylor had not been in the nation's capital long before he had been exposed to the airy theories of these highly intellectual but impractical men. Knowing of John Taylor's intelligence and his sense of dignity and self-esteem, one might easily have predicted his reaction to their condescending ways. His views on the subject surfaced one day as he walked through the ornate grounds of the Jardin des Plantes with a few friends. One of them purchased a thin, fragile cake, almost wholly lacking in substance, and, ignorant of its name, asked John to identify it. Answering that he did not know its real name, he offered to give it one: "I will call it French philosophy, or fried froth, which ever you like."

While it is mere conjecture to suggest it, it is not unlikely that Elder Taylor undertook to write *The Government of God* during his stay in France as a result of his negative reaction to the ideas of the Parisian philosophers.

Among the more rational of this group the apostle met in Paris was M. Krolokoski, a disciple of Charles Fourier, the French social philosopher who had died about the time John Taylor had joined the Church and who had expounded the idea of a utopian society based upon the voluntary association of producers formed into units called *phalanxes*. It was the influence of this philosophy that prompted William Ellery Channing and others to organize the famed phalanx at Brook Farm near Boston. And of more interest to Elder Taylor, it was the influence of these ideas that had prompted M. Cabet and the Icarians to acquire many of the former holdings of the Latter-day Saints in Nauvoo, where they had hoped to operate a successful phalanx. But although the Icarians had acquired their Nauvoo farms and buildings at exceedingly low prices and in a condition that would have allowed for a prompt and efficient execution of their plans, the project appeared to be failing.

As these two intelligent men discussed their alternate plans for solving the aggravated social problems of the day, John referred to the Icarian phalanx in Nauvoo and said, "Rich farms were deserted, and thousands of us had left our houses and furniture in them, and almost everything calculated to promote the happiness of man was there. Never could a person go to a place under more happy circumstances. Besides all the advantages of having everything made ready to his hand, M. Cabet had a select company of colonists. He and his company went to Nauvoo—what is the result? I read in all your reports from there—published in your own paper here, in Paris, a continued cry for help. The cry is money, money! We want money to help us carry out our designs." The apostle then underscored the dependent status of the Icarians, who lived in an already developed community they had inherited, and the independence of the Latter-day Saints, who toiled alone and without aid to reclaim a desert from nature's grasp. "While your colony in Nauvoo with all the advantages of our deserted fields and homes . . . have been dragging out a miserable existence, the Latter-day Saints, though stripped of their all and banished from civilized society . . . have built houses, enclosed lands, cultivated gardens, built school-houses . . . and are prospering in all the blessings of civilized life." (BHR, pp. 226-27.) Since Mr. Krolokoski had previously questioned John Taylor's claim that the solution to the world's social problems lay in following the first principles of the gospel, the Mormon elder asked pointedly, "Now, which is the best, our religion, or your philosophy?" Seemingly nonplussed by the weight of the unfavorable comparison his questioner had made, the Parisian could only respond, "Well, Mr. Taylor, I can say nothing." (Ibid., p. 27.)

Realizing that proselyting success could not be founded upon cogent and convincing arguments such as those used in confounding Mr. Krolokoski, Elder Taylor searched for a key that would unlock the door for the Mormon elders in France. A first step was suggested in a letter John wrote to the editor of the *Millennial Star* on July 21, 1850: "We find we are very much embarrassed for the want of books in the French language. I purpose writing some immediately on the first principles of the Gospel, so that we can circulate them among the French." (MS 12:270.) The major project in pursuing this goal was the publication of the Book of Mormon in French. The cost of printing was borne by some well-to-do and anonymous members in England who responded willingly and promptly to Elder Taylor's request for financial aid. This source of funds was also called upon to finance the publication of a monthly Church periodical that Elder Taylor founded and edited. Meanwhile, John worked intermittently but diligently on his masterpiece, *The Government of God*. Because of the press of other affairs, he was never able to devote long, uninterrupted periods of time to this undertaking, and so he worked at it now and then as opportunity allowed, picking up the task and then laying it down when other more urgent work made its demands. We see in this a methodology used by other great and accomplished men and women who regard time as their most valuable commodity, never to be wasted or frittered away.

To an extent, the timing of Elder John Taylor's call to France made him a victim of circumstance. Only a few months before, in 1848, Louis Philippe had been forced from the throne room by a revolution that had created enormous upheavals, not only in the realm of government, but in every aspect of French society. The provisional government set up by the revolutionaries was soon supplanted by the republic headed by Louis Napoleon, Bonaparte's nephew, as president. The ink was hardly dry on Louis Napoleon's election certificate before he began to agitate for a ten-year presidential term rather than the four-year term to which he had been elected. Through connivance, intimidation, and deception, he achieved this end, and, having done so, moved resolutely toward his ultimate goal of dictatorship. This he achieved by coercing the senate into enacting a decree that made him a hereditary emperor with the title of Napoleon III. All of these political shenanigans were accompanied by extraordinary civil disorders, street fighting, riots, and labor revolts. Adding to the confusion were interminable rumors, threats, false arrests, and public punishments, all of which were calculated to keep the nation in constant turmoil. Amidst such chaotic conditions, which were aggravated by the volatile character of the French and the awesome opposition of the Catholic Church, Elder Taylor and his companions had difficulty in securing a foothold in the French capital. But they had staying power, so that little by little the Latter-day Saint community in Paris grew through a steady trickle of conversions. Compared with the flood of converts being gathered in Great Britain, the French results were nominal and disappointing. But the disparity disappears or is greatly minimized when one considers that Elder Taylor and his brethren were fighting their way upstream against odds and obstacles that their counterparts across the channel never had to confront.

Undoubtedly the most significant achievement of Elder Taylor's mission in France was the publication of the Book of Mormon in the French language. In a talk delivered in the Old Salt Lake Tabernacle on August 22, 1852, he referred to this accomplishment, saying that the translation was "as good a one as it is possible for anybody to make." (JD 1:21.) He buttressed this by saying that "some of the best educated men in France" had examined the book and had affirmed his appraisal. (Ibid.) His statement, however, fails even to suggest the difficulty through which he had to pass in order to achieve the goal. Aside from the linguistic problems, the difficulty lay chiefly with Elder Bolton, who had begun the translation but who lacked the technical competence to complete the work satisfactorily. When others who had the requisite skills were brought into the picture, Elder Bolton bridled and then turned bitter, especially when it was decided he would not be shown as the translator. Elder Taylor was not insensitive to his friend's feelings, as the apostle's later solicitude toward Elder Bolton demonstrates, but he was determined that personal feelings had to be subordinated to the good of the work.

Another solid achievement of the French Mission was Elder Taylor's publication of *L'Etoile du Deseret* (The Star of Deseret), in which the editor reviewed the history and doctrines of the Church and the accomplishments of the Latter-day Saints in the western American desert. Because of severe restrictions imposed by the government on active proselyting, the deficiencies of the elders in speaking French, and the flippant, condescending attitude of many of those whom they met toward religion, it was the latter aspect of the Church that most attracted and intrigued the French people. "It is the organization in this place," Elder Taylor later told a Tabernacle audience, "the wise policy of the Governor who presides here, in the extension of this infant state, by building up new colonies, making such extensive improvements that preach louder among the courts of Europe, at the present time." (JD 1:19.)

Although it was slow, tedious work, Elder Taylor and his small force, which had been augmented by the addition of Elders Piercy and Stayner, were able to raise up branches in Paris, Calais, and Le Havre, in addition to the one at Boulogne sur Mer. However, the refusal of the central government to grant permission for the Mormon elders to preach openly was a great impediment to the growth of the work in France. Elder Taylor seems to have been more annoyed and irked by the restraint on freedom of speech than by the frivolities of French philosophy. His ire led him into this condemnation of the restrictive government policy: "'Liberty,' 'Equality,' 'Fraternity,' were written upon almost every door. You had liberty to speak, but might be put in prison for doing so. You had liberty to print, but they might burn what you had printed, and put you in confinement for it." (BHR, p. 232.)

Whatever the successes or failures of the work in France, it is apparent that the experience was of incalculable personal benefit to Elder John Taylor as it honed and illuminated qualities of character that had been evident before but not to the extent shown during this mission. The apostle's faith in God and His purposes, always a key characteristic, never shone brighter than in this statement made during the report of his mission: "Some people have said to me, sometimes, Are you not afraid to cross over the seas, and deserts, where there are wolves and bears, and other ferocious animals. . . . Are you not afraid that you will drop by the way, and leave your body on the desert track, or beneath the ocean's wave? No. Who cares anything about it? What of it, if we should happen to drop by the way? . . . These things don't trouble me, but I have felt to rejoice all the day long, that God has revealed the principle of eternal life . . . and that I am counted worthy to engage in the work of the Lord." (JD 1:17.) With that kind of faith, which was tinged with a certain fatalism, came a will and determination to succeed despite great obstacles. "We found many difficulties to combat," he told his audience, "for it is not an easy thing to go into France and learn to talk French well; but at the same time, if a man sets to work in good earnest, he can do it. I have scratched the word "can't" out of my vocabulary long since, and I have not got it in my French one." (Ibid., p. 21.)

Closely related to the qualities of faith and willpower that these statements imply was an innate sense of destiny and self-worth that existed in John Taylor and that was manifested in an unusual way while he was in France. The incident occurred one day in Paris as he and some of the brethren visited the Palace Vendome, where they climbed Napoleon's Column of Victory. There the others, having inscribed their names on the monument as countless others had done to immortalize themselves, invited Elder Taylor to do likewise. Presumably they were not so much surprised by his refusal as by his explanation for not doing so. "No," he said, "I will not write my name there; but I will yet write it in living, imperishable characters!" (BHR, p. 228.) At the time, the remark may have seemed presumptuous and elitist to some of those who heard it. In the present, however, one is impressed mostly by the prophetic accuracy of the comment, viewed in the light of Elder Taylor's subsequent career and the knowledge that his name will be held in honored remembrance by the members of The Church of Jesus Christ of Latter-day Saints through the ages.

It is a mere speculation, but not beyond the realm of possibility, that John Taylor's startling remark was prompted in part by the satisfaction of having completed his major literary work, *The Government of God*. With that he had placed himself in the front rank of the moral philosophers. In this scholarly work he defined the character, power, and beneficience of God; the contrasting impotence and imperfection of men and their works; and the eternal relationships between God and man, holding out the prospect of man's ultimate redemption and exaltation conditioned on his faithfulness and obedience to divine law.

As the summer of 1851 drew to a close, Elder Taylor felt that his mission in France had been completed, and he began to make arrangements to go home. These plans were suspended, however, when he received a letter from the First Presidency suggesting that he remain in Europe until the following year. "I, therefore, thought I would alter my course immediately," he later reported, "and follow the directions of the Spirit of God—for I wished all the time, as Paul says, to be obedient to the heavenly calling." (JD 1:24.) It was then that the decision was made to go to Germany, an undertaking that was not previously contemplated. "I made a plan before I got up in the morning," he said, "for thought flows quickly, you know." (Ibid.)

At the heart of this new plan was the intention to publish the Book of Mormon in the German language. His first move was to write to Elder Orson Hyde to request that he send an elder who knew German. At that time, Elder Hyde was the only one of the leaders of the Church who had any first-hand knowledge of Germany, he having spent several months there in connection with his mission to dedicate the Holy Land. Indeed, Orson Hyde had written and published a Mormon tract in Frankfurt in 1842, *Ein Ruf Aus Der Wueste (A Cry from the Wilderness).*

Unable to make immediate contact with Elder Hyde, John went to England to try to find a qualified companion. There he met Elder George P. Dykes, who had labored under Elder Erastus Snow in German-speaking Schleswig-Holstein, which was then under Danish rule. Agreeing to assist the apostle, Brother Dykes went directly to Hamburg, where Elder Taylor and Elder Viet, a German-speaking schoolteacher who had been converted in Paris, joined him in October 1851. (Ibid.; Gilbert W. Scharffs, *Mormonism in Germany* [Salt Lake City: Deseret Book Co., 1970], pp. 6-7.)

Once in Germany, Elder Taylor and his associates moved with alacrity. Elders Dykes and Viet, both of whom were competent in the German language, began the translation of the Book of Mormon under the apostle's direction. Meanwhile, the brethren engaged in conventional proselyting activities, harvesting a number of converts, including Charles Miller, an able man who rendered significant service in the translation. And John, ever imbued with the need for an official Latter-day Saint organ, established and began to publish still another Church periodical, this one named *Zions Panier* (Zion's Banner), the first issue of which came off the press November 1.

In an apparent attempt both to obtain an expert opinion as to its literary quality and to widen the circle of his acquaintances in the city, Elder Taylor submitted a copy of *Zions Panier* to a Hamburg professor who gave it high marks, stating that had he not been so informed, he would not have known that it was written first in English and then translated.

By mid-December, the work in Hamburg was well underway on all fronts, and, leaving Elder Dykes in temporary charge, John returned to Paris, knowing that the first German Mission President, Daniel Carn, had already left Utah for Europe, having been recruited by Elder Orson Hyde.

Arriving at Paris on December 19, Elder Taylor found the french capital in chaos. Less than three weeks before, Louis Napoleon had overthrown the first republic with his bloody coup d'etat. Evidence of the savagery that had elevated another Napoleon to dictatorship was all around. Fully armed and intimidating soldiers patrolled the streets. Buildings blackened by fire or gutted by bombings could be seen along the main thoroughfares. And here and there were the telltale bloodstains of those who had given their lives in a useless defense of the republic, whose promises of liberty and equality were now only a distant dream.

It was into this maelstrom that converts from all over France streamed in the latter part of December for a mission-wide conference called by Elder Taylor. That approximately four hundred assembled for this purpose attests to the proselyting success of Elder Taylor and his associates, achieved against heavy odds, and of the relative unconcern with which the French regarded a major upheaval in their political institutions.

By coincidence, the LDS conference in Paris fell on the same day that the French people were going through the charade of voting for Louis Napoleon. Taking note of this, Elder Taylor prophesied that "our cause would stand when theirs is crushed to pieces; and the kingdom of God will roll on and spread from nation to nation, and from kingdom to kingdom." (BHR, p. 233.)

As the gathering of such a large congregation in Paris

technically violated the restrictions that had been placed on the missionaries, a police officer who had been told about the conference sought to question John the following day. Arriving at the home of M. Ducloux, where the apostle had been staying as a guest, the officer found that the foreigner had already left. Indeed, Elder Taylor had taken a cab for the railway station only ten minutes before. Aware of the complex legal snarl in which his friend could have become enmeshed were he to have been detained by a dictatorial regime suspicious of every organization or individual it did not fully control, M. Ducloux delayed the officer for almost two hours on one pretext or another. This enabled Elder Taylor, who was unaware of the attempt to arrest him, to leave Paris unmolested. Had John known about the officer's pursuit and about the extensive dossier on his movements the police had compiled, the week he spent in a quiet French seaside town doubtless would not have provided the untroubled interlude of reflective review and planning that he in fact enjoyed. It was learned later that the local police had a detailed record of all of Elder Taylor's movements to and from England and Germany and within France. It seems apparent, therefore, that the French police suspected the Mormon apostle was a political subversive rather than an evangelist.

Chapter Fourteen

The Missionary Turned Entrepreneur

Part of Elder Taylor's week spent at his seaside retreat was devoted to mundane affairs. Like his associates among the general authorities, the apostle combined his preaching of heavenly things with a keen interest in the development of the temporal resources and capacities of the Saints. This dual thrust of the Mormon leaders was, in a sense, a reflection of their understanding of man's status and purpose, a being whom they considered to be both spiritual and temporal in his makeup, who aspired to perfection and Godhood by obedience to Christ's teachings and by controlling the earthly elements within himself and his environment. For this reason it is not surprising that while John Taylor was heavily involved in laying the spiritual foundations of the Church in France, he was at the same time exercising his talents and energies to promote the prosperity and temporal well-being of the Latter-day Saints.

This propensity and thrust, coupled with urgings from President Young to be on the lookout for projects to better the living conditions of the Saints, caused Elder Taylor to be alert constantly for economic opportunities. By the spring of 1851, he had two specific enterprises in mind, a woolen mill and a sugar manufacturing plant. These were organized under the umbrella of the Deseret Manufacturing Company, which, it was originally intended, would later include other manufacturies. In March, John shared with President Young his projections about the woolen mill, whose machinery was to be manufactured in England; the wool would come from merino sheep to be transported from western England. At the same time he was investigating the possibility of establishing a beet sugar manufacturing plant in Utah, patterned after similar plants that were then operating successfully in France and whose origin there traced to an English embargo during the Napoleonic Wars on cane sugar shipped to France. To obtain information and insights into the manufacturing process, Elder Taylor spent some time in Arras inspecting the Crespel-Delisse refinery there, reported to be the oldest beet sugar refining plant in France. Later in Paris, he conferred with M. Crespel, the managing partner, who willingly provided him with a copy of the plans for the plant machinery at Arras. Armed with this material and satisfied from investigations that the growth of sugar beets in Utah was compatible with its soil and climate, the new entrepreneur went forward with his organizational plans.

Capital being the first need at this point, John found several investors to subscribe to stock in the Deseret Manufacturing Company: Captain Joseph H. Russell, a shipbuilder who had constructed the *Brooklyn*, the craft that had carried Sam Brannan and his company around Cape Horn to California; Philip de la Mare, a moneyed convert from Jersey who had contributed toward the publication of the French translation of the Book of Mormon; John W. Coward, a salt dealer; and W. Collinson, a boot manufacturer.

With capital either paid in or promised, Elder Taylor had contracted with Fawcett-Preston & Co. in Liverpool for the manufacture of the machinery for the sugar plant and woolen mill; he had purchased twelve hundred pounds of choice beet seed in France; and he had begun to assemble the staff necessary to construct buildings, to transport and install the machinery, and to operate the completed plant. Young Elias Morris, the progenitor of a long line of successful Utah businessmen, was his builder. John Vernon, who had worked with Fawcett-Preston in the manufacture of the machinery, would install it. M. Mollenhauer, John's brother-in-law, who was a skilled sugar refiner, was slated to operate the plant; he would be assisted by John Bollwinkel and a Mr. Conner who had worked in a sugar factory in Liverpool. John Nuttall, who would later become John Taylor's son-in-law as well as his personal secretary, was being groomed as an administrative assistant. And finally, Captain Russell, aided by Philip de la Mare (who would be responsible to purchase the necessary teams), was appointed to construct the numerous wagons that would be necessary to freight the bulky machinery the twelve hundred miles from Fort Leavenworth to the Salt Lake Valley. (See *The Beet Sugar Story*, U.S. Beet Sugar Association; and the *Genealogical Magazine* 21:88.)

Most of the planning and arrangements for this ambitious undertaking had been finalized by the time Elder Taylor crossed the channel to England after completing his mission in France and Germany. For the most part, he left to John Nuttall and Elias Morris the task of pulling the loose ends together and of seeing that the machinery was properly stowed aboard the *Rockaway*, a freighter scheduled to depart from Liverpool. Among the cargo were three zinc-lined caskets marked "machinery" that contained the bodies of three Mormon elders who had died in the mission field.

While his associates were busy with the *Rockaway*'s cargo, Elder Taylor was involved in making final arrangements for the publication of *The Government of God* and obtaining from an artist named Gahagan busts of the Prophet Joseph Smith and his brother Hyrum, which had been sculptured at John's request. As an apparent means of honoring and memorializing the famous brothers who had been murdered in his presence, John had brought with him from Salt Lake City casts molded from the faces of the martyrs shortly after they were killed. At that time, there were not among the Latter-day Saints artists who had the technical competence to do a job that would measure up to Elder Taylor's high artistic standards.

It was on March 6, 1852, that both the *Rockaway* and the steamer *Niagara* departed from the Mersey Pierhead at Liverpool, both destined for America. The freighter's port of call was New Orleans, while Elder Taylor's steamer, with a company of twenty Latter-day Saints aboard, was aimed toward Boston.

A seasoned sea traveler by now, Elder Taylor enjoyed the twelve-day voyage to Boston except, perhaps, for a slight by the *Niagara*'s captain, who refused permission for him to preach on Sunday, even though some non-member passengers had requested him to do so.

From Boston, the apostle traveled to Philadelphia, where he preached to the Saints and visited his old friend Colonel Thomas L. Kane, who was ill. He then went to Washington, D.C., where he counseled with Dr. John Bernhisel, Deseret's congressional representative, who introduced him to several capitol dignitaries, including Senator Stephen A. Douglas. John then proceeded to St. Louis where, by prearrangement, he rendezvoused with those who had accompanied the machinery on the *Rockaway*. He was appalled to learn that custom officials at New Orleans had imposed a duty on the incoming machinery of over four thousand dollars, representing 40 percent of its cost. This seemed particularly inconsistent to John because of the government's efforts to promote industry and the severe sugar shortage that then existed in the United States.

As it turned out, this was only the first drop in a torrential outpouring of misfortune that descended upon Elder Taylor's company. Soon after, as the steamer carrying the machinery chugged upstream, the boiler on one of them, the *Saluta*, exploded, killing several passengers and sending the cargo to the bottom of the river. After extensive dredging, the heavy boxes loaded with machinery were located in the murky stream and were winched out of the water to other craft. At length all of the machinery reached Fort Leavenworth, where it was warehoused pending the completion of the wagons being constructed under the supervision of Captain Russell. Here the entrepreneur found more woe. His practiced eye convinced John that the wagons were being shabbily built. And sharing that appraisal with the doughty captain only served to create a rift with the company's principal stockholder. Meanwhile, Philip de la Mare was having trouble finding suitable animals for the long trek west. It was only after much travail that everything was in readiness to begin the long, arduous trip from Fort Leavenworth to Salt Lake City.

In reflecting on the matter, Elder Taylor apparently became convinced that a conspiracy lurked behind the otherwise unaccountable action of the New Orleans customs officials in levying such a high duty on his machinery. So, as the wagons carrying the DMC's heavy equipment lumbered westward, the entrepreneur headed east for the nation's capital. There, with the aid of Dr. Bernhisel and Colonel Kane, recently risen from his sickbed, he made what turned out to be a futile attempt to uncover the reason for the New Orleans conspiracy. Not being a novice in his understanding of the vagaries of government, John was probably not wholly surprised by the resistance he encountered in Washington. On the surface, everyone seemed concerned about his plight and anxious to help. But the plentiful platitudes offered were never translated into concrete assistance, so the Mormon apostle left the city with nothing other than the satisfaction that he had tried.

Because of the slow pace imposed on the DMC wagon train by the cumbersome machinery, fragile wagons, recalcitrant animals, and inexperienced teamsters, Elder Taylor overtook it on the prairie. Seeing that help from the valley would be needed if the wagon train were to arrive safely, he pushed on to Salt Lake City and made arrangements for relief wagons to be sent back with much-needed supplies.

It was not until November that the wagons carrying the embryonic sugar plant struggled into the valley.

It may have been providential that Elder Taylor did not foresee the final outcome of his cherished enterprise. It was to fail ultimately through circumstances beyond his control. But, on August 22, 1852, when he addressed an audience in the Old Tabernacle, he exuded nothing but confidence and optimism. Indeed, he even showed an uncharacteristic joviality when he told the Saints, "The sugar factory will be here soon. If you will only provide us with beets and wood, we will make you sugar enough to preserve yourselves with." He then went on to indulge in a little boasting, which also was uncharacteristic, and which perhaps he later regretted: "We can have as good sugar in this country as anywhere else; we have as good machinery as is in the world. . . . Nor [are there] better men to make sugar than those who are coming." (JD 1:25.)

Despite the problems in transporting the machinery to Salt Lake City, there appeared to be good grounds for the optimism Elder Taylor manifested. It seemed he had the capital, the equipment, and the expertise necessary for success. But his plans for a burgeoning sugar industry in Utah soon began to sour. At the administrative level was a conflict with his principal stockholder, Captain Russell, who apparently had taken umbrage at John's criticism of his wagons. The captain, in turn, had shared his negative views of Elder Taylor with Brigham Young and others. These seeds of doubt apparently took root and grew when John opposed President Young's suggestion that the sugar plant be set up in conjunction with the blacksmith shop near Temple Square. Instead, Elder Taylor felt it should be established at Provo. Because his friend had conceived and developed the enterprise, Brigham deferred to John's wishes. Later, however, when the drumbeat of criticism against the embattled apostle by DMC's largest stockholder continued, the Church president reversed himself and, having acquired the control of a majority of the company's stock, directed that the machinery be returned to Salt Lake City and set up in the blacksmith shop near Temple Square on the banks of City Creek. At that time, Orson Hyde, president of the Twelve, who was characterized by President Young as a "snug businessman," was placed in charge. Even though the sugar maker and the engineer selected by Elder Taylor, Brothers Mollenhauer and Vernon, remained on the job, the plant did not produce sugar. Later the plant was moved to a Church farm southeast of town. Appropriately called "Sugar House," this plant also was at a temporary site, for the factory was never able to produce sugar there—or anywhere else, for that matter.

Ultimately, the plant was dismantled, and parts of it were used in a bookbindery, a woolen mill, and a paper mill. The only evidence that remains of this enterprise that was begun with such high hopes and ended so dismally is the Salt Lake City suburb Sugar House, which stands in the minds of some as a symbol of John Taylor's failure as an entrepreneur. Yet the judgment seems unduly harsh. An expert in the field has concluded that with a few mechanical and chemical adjustments, John's sugar plant would have ended as a frontier success story. (See Fred G. Taylor, *A Saga of Sugar* [Salt Lake City: Utah-Idaho Sugar Co., 1944].) Could it be that the French manufacturers omitted key elements from the plans and formulas given to Elder Taylor to protect their world markets? And the apostle's personnel problems could as easily be attributed to the pique of some of his associates as to his own shortcomings.

Regardless of how one might explain or rationalize the outcome, John's removal from DMC and the ultimate failure of the enterprise likely stands as one of the great disappointments of his life. He had devoted long hours to the project and confidently expected it would succeed, thereby providing his people with a much-needed commodity, rewarding his associates with a good return on their investment, and offering employment opportunities to many Latter-day Saints. So the mere failure of itself would have been most stressful to someone like Elder Taylor, who was accustomed to success and seemed to expect success in any enterprise with which he became associated. But to add to failure the hint of personal incompetence, implied by President Young's action in removing him from the project, would have been a bitter pill indeed. But the disappointed apostle took his medicine like a man. He had exercised priesthood authority long enough and had often enough found it necessary to make unpleasant decisions affecting those under him to make him amenable to the direction of his presiding officer. Such submissiveness grew both from a conviction that Brigham Young was God's mouthpiece on earth and from a determination to subvert his own personal desires in the interest of the work. This is not to say that John Taylor accepted this rebuff without feelings of upset. Nor does it mean that he necessarily agreed with Brigham's appraisal of his business acumen—or lack of it. It is to be inferred that one possessing the self-esteem of a John Taylor would, in his own mind, have questioned his leader's appraisal, while, at the same time, accepting it and yielding to it.

Whether Orson Hyde was a more "snug businessman" than John Taylor must forever remain a matter of conjecture, as the sugar plant fared no better under him than it had under his predecessor. Brigham Young's appraisal, therefore, must be regarded as a purely subjective one, yielding to no objective test. Nevertheless, one must give some credence to President Young's undoubted skill in judging men and their abilities. It was precisely this skill that accounted in large measure for his success as a colonizer. He had the knack of matching men with responsibilities in such a way as to produce good results.

Conceding this aptitude in Brother Brigham and that it operated appropriately in John Taylor's release from DMC, what are we to say about the action he took in June 1875? At that time President Young rearranged the order of seniority in the Twelve, making John Taylor senior to Orson Hyde, thereby ensuring that Elder Taylor would become the third president of the Church. One might logically say of these two unrelated events, separated in time by a period of twenty-three years, that while Brigham Young considered Orson Hyde to be a better businessman than John Taylor, he felt the latter had skills and aptitudes that better equipped him to be the president of the Church.

Even had Elder Taylor made such an analysis in retrospect, it is questionable that it would have erased completely the disappointment he undoubtedly felt upon being severed from the sugar project. But other duties soon sprung up to absorb his interest and claim his abilities.

Chapter Fifteen

Preacher, Politician, Editor

Having completed a mission abroad where, in turn, he was proselyter, philosopher, and entrepreneur, John Taylor turned first to a duty that was in some ways reminiscent of his duties long before as a Methodist exhorter. At the general conference in April 1853, in connection with which the cornerstone of the Salt Lake Temple was laid, he and other general authorities were called by Brigham Young to preach the gospel in the "valleys of the mountains." In this role, unlike the one he played as a proselyter in Europe, his purpose was to instruct and inspire members of the Church to live their religion, rather than to bring new converts into the fold. In modern parlance, this was an attempt at reactivation found necessary by the Church leaders because in their mammoth pioneering and colonizing efforts, many Latter-day Saints had begun to lay too much emphasis on temporal things, often to the detriment of their spiritual well-being. So, John and the brethren who had received similar calls traveled throughout the mountainous west, instructing, cajoling, and motivating the Saints to live on a higher plane of spirituality. This effort was, in reality, the opening phase of what has since been called the Mormon reformation. As a sign of their commitment to better living, many members of the Church were rebaptized as were John and members of his family upon first entering the Salt Lake Valley.

The following year, 1854, marked Elder Taylor's successful entry into the Utah political arena when he was elected a member of the territorial legislature. However, another special call from President Young made it necessary to resign his new office before he ever undertook its duties. The prophet's call directed John to go to New York City to organize and publish a newspaper whose purpose would be to present the doctrines and practices of the Church in such a way as to neutralize a groundswell of anti-Mormon feeling that had been mounting for over a year. As a part of this public relations effort was the appointment of additional brethren to organize and publish Latter-day Saint newspapers in other key cities—Orson Pratt being assigned to Washington, D.C.; Erastus Snow and Orson Spencer to St. Louis; and Elder Taylor's nephew and future counselor, George Q. Cannon, to San Francisco.

From its inception, the Mormon Church and its leaders had been the object of derision, ridicule, and abuse. Seldom had they received kindly treatment at the hands of the public or the press. The antagonisms toward them had been generated in large part by the militancy of the Mormons in denouncing other religious sects and by the astonishing inroads the new church had made into the memberships of the old, established denominations. Moreover, some saw in the monolithic structure of the new religion an awesome political threat they were anxious to thwart. For these and other reasons, diverse, powerful groups and individuals never lost an opportunity to attack the Church or its members.

On August 29, 1852, there came to light an aspect of Mormonism that all of its enemies and detractors could join in enthusiastic and unrestrained denunciation. It was on that date that Orson Pratt, at the direction of Brigham Young, made the first public address on the revelation given to Joseph Smith explaining and sanctioning the doctrine of plural marriage. Later, on January 1, 1853, the revelation was first published in the *Millennial Star*. Thereafter, it was reprinted, reviewed, and rehashed in dozens of publications, both at home and abroad, often with lurid stories or implications that portrayed the Mormon Church as a nest of moral depravity. It was the vilification and slander emanating from the critics of plural marriage that had produced the groundswell of anti-Mormon feeling the Latter-day Saint publications in San Francisco, St. Louis, Washington, D.C., and New York City were intended to neutralize.

Elder Taylor was given broad discretion in the organization and editing of the new publication in New York—but he received no financing with which to establish and operate it. So, using proven procedures he had followed abroad in establishing *Etoile du Deseret* and *Zion's Panier* in France and Germany, he called upon members of the Church in the eastern United States for monetary assistance. Despite the attrition in Church membership caused by the plural marriage bombshell and the cautious, defensive attitude created in many Latter-day Saints by its powerful public aftershocks, John was able to obtain sufficient money to establish the new periodical.

Any observer of that day who thought this new publisher-editor from the wastelands of the west would confront the giants of the eastern press with trepidation did not reckon with the audacity of the Mormon hierarchy or with the boldness and intellectual force of the agent it had sent into their midst.

The novelty of what the Church leaders had undertaken in establishing regional publications across the nation was explained by Elder Taylor in a letter he addressed to the *Millennial Star* under date of November 15, 1854. Wrote he, "In relation to our present mission, it is indeed a new phase in the history of "Mormonism;" hitherto, with the exception of home officers, we have not meddled in politics; our missions have been strictly religious, in the view of the world; but as our religion embraces everything that pertains to the happiness of the human family, whether it relates to this life or the life to come . . . [so] we are now entered fairly into the political arena, and it remains yet to be shown whether we can or cannot teach a better order of things than exists in the world at the present, an order which shall be more conducive to the wants of a degenerated world, for, politically speaking, there is as great development of old dame Babylon's confusion in the political as there is in the religious, world." (MS 16:811.)

Few things in his career show more clearly the aggressiveness and drive of John Taylor than does his establishment and publication of the new Church periodical in New York City. Although by then it was an opprobrium to many New Yorkers because of the recent disclosures about plural marriage, the editor selected the name *The Mormon* for his new paper. Moreover, the masthead, prepared by John's twenty-one-year-old son, George J., who had accompanied his father to New York, was a study in flamboyance. It pictured a huge American eagle with outstretched wings perched on a beehive, with two large American flags unfurled behind. On and below the beehive, in huge letters, was the name *The Mormon*, and on and above the flags were various symbols (including an all-seeing eye) and quotations (including one from Brigham Young—"Mind Your Own Business"—and one from Heber C. Kimball—"Truth Will Prevail"). Below all was the motto of the new weekly: "IT IS BETTER TO REPRESENT OURSELVES, THAN TO BE REPRESENTED BY OTHERS."

Nor was the apostle content to locate *The Mormon* in an out-of-the-way place. Rather, he established headquarters on the corner of Nassau and Ann Streets, between the offices of the city's media goliaths, the *Herald* and the *Tribune*. From the beginning, this spunky David of the New York press hurled his defiance and his reasoned editorials at the news giants that surrounded him and at the reading public. The first issue of this extraordinary little paper established its tone and announced its policy: "We are Mormons inside and outside, at home and abroad, in public and private, everywhere. We are so, however, from principle. We are such, not because we believe it to be the most popular, lucrative, or honorable, (as the world has it); but because we believe it to be more true, more reasonable and scriptural, moral and philosophic; because we conscientiously believe that it is more calculated to promote the happiness and well being of humanity, in time, and throughout all eternity, than any other system which we have met with."

This opening message, mild as it was, called forth abuse and criticism from almost every quarter. It was open season on the Mormons, and most of the editors in New York City denounced them at one time or another on the pages of their newspapers. And most of the ministers took occasion to do the same from their pulpits. The embattled editor of *The Mormon* did not wilt before the attack. Indeed, he responded with a boldness that approached truculence, challenging his critics to prove their defamatory charges: "We have said before, and say now, that we defy all the editors and writers in the United States to prove that 'Mormonism' is less moral, scriptural, philosophical; or that there is less patriotism in Utah than in any other part of the United States. We call for proof; bring on your reasons, gentlemen, if you have any; we shrink not from the investigation and dare you to the encounter." (CHC 4:63.) Apparently smarting over some of the more abusive attacks made upon him and the Church, John added this scorching postscript: "If you don't do it and you publish any more of your stuff, we shall brand you as poor, mean, cowardly liars, as men publishing falsehoods, knowing them to be so, and shrinking from the light of truth and investigation."

The New York tabloids responded, but not in the way Elder Taylor had hoped. Instead of a reasoned analysis of issues and claims, they pursued a deliberate campaign of vilification and abuse. The *New York Mirror* was the most explicit in its denunciation, characterizing Mormonism as a "hideous system" and as "an immoral excrescence." It urged its readers to vigilance to confront and defeat what it considered to be a national peril. "The evil has become a notorious fact," the *Mirror*'s editor intoned. "Its existence cannot be any longer ignored, and it is not therefor prudent that the eyes of the public should be closed to its effect." The *Herald* called on the ministers of the city to join in a concerted campaign to discredit the Mormon Church and its teachings. This effort backfired when Elder Taylor picked up on the suggestion and offered to debate the ministers one and all—a challenge that was never accepted. The *New York Sun* offered a variation of the *Herald*'s proposal when it urged missionaries of other churches to descend upon Utah en masse in an all-out campaign to convert the Mormons from their ways. When Elder Taylor applauded the idea in the pages of *The Mormon* and assured the *Sun* that these visitors would be accorded a friendly welcome, the plan seemed to lose its appeal.

Later the *Herald* turned to lewdness when it suggested that the answer to the Mormon "problem" was to send handsome, virile soldiers to Utah to seduce and win away the wives of the Mormon polygamists. This decadent idea was inspired by a report that several Mormon women were seduced by soldiers in a U. S. detachment that wintered in Salt Lake while en route to California and that they left their families to follow.

This vile suggestion, made with apparent seriousness, seems charitable compared with the reaction of the eastern press to a disaster that confronted the Saints in 1855. In that year, drought and crickets combined to bring them face to face with famine. Instead of a sympathetic response to this threatened tragedy, John's journalistic opponents in Manhattan implied that death of the Mormons by starvation might be the best solution to a troublesome problem. Only one voice of sympathy was heard. That came from the *Woman's Advocate*, whose editorial on the subject was reprinted in *The Mormon* on September 22, 1855. After alluding to the threat of famine to the Saints and the expectation that their plight would evoke a charitable response from the New York press, the *Advocate*'s editorial noted accusingly, "But not one word is spoken anywhere of regret or sympathy; on the contrary, there are frequent manifestations of satisfaction that the problem of Mormonism and its destiny is likely to be settled by the grasshoppers. What little comment we have noticed here and there has a tone of delighted chuckle that chills the blood. There is a spirit of murder in it, a suppressed shout of triumph of the persecutor over his victim, that is suppressed only because the triumph is not yet sure."

The *New York Sun* defended against this tongue-lashing on the ground that the Mormons had not asked for help and that if they did the American people would respond charitably despite the "degrading and disgusting doctrines of Brigham Young." This facade of charity was too much for the editor of *The Mormon*, who, in his October 6, 1855, issue, lashed out in understandable anger: "We have been robbed of millions and driven from our own firesides into the cold, wintry blasts of the desert, to starve by your charitable institutions, and shall we now crave your paltry sixpences? Talk to us with your hypocritical cant about charity! Pshaw! It's nauseating to every one not eaten up with your corrupt humbuggery and pharisaical egotism." After reminding the *Sun* that it wasn't speaking of the dependent inmates of almshouses, but of independent, intelligent, and enterprising Americans accustomed to making their own way, the aroused editor figuratively shouted his defiance: "The 'Mormons' neither need your sympathy nor your cankered gold. Your malicious slanders only excite contempt for those base enough to utter them. Your contemptible falsehoods fail to ruffle a feather in our caps." With these maledictions out of his system, Elder Taylor then lectured the *Sun* about the source to which the Latter-day Saints looked for assistance: "The God of Jacob in whom the 'Mormons' trust—he who brought up Israel out of Egypt—he it is who sustained the 'Mormons' in their tedious journeyings over the barren deserts and wild mountain passes of this continent. In the dark hour of trial . . . God upheld and sustained them; he sustains them still, and will cause them to shine forth . . . long after their malicious slanderers shall have sunk to oblivion."

If the *Sun's* editor did not know it beforehand, he learned after reading this response to his insulting little piece that he had taken on a man of mental stature with a will and spirit to match. This was no doctrinaire country bumpkin who could be intimidated or bamboozled. This was, instead, a cosmopolitan, erudite scholar, skilled in composition and debate, who refused to be pushed around.

While these few excerpts make it clear that John Taylor was not averse to intellectual combat and confrontation, they should not mislead one into the false belief that he was always at war. Indeed, such passages, while more intriguing and provocative than moderate prose, comprised only a small part of *The Mormon's* literary content. Its pages were devoted mostly to an affirmative exposition of the doctrines and objectives of The Church of Jesus Christ of Latter-day Saints and the character of its members.

Of the church he represented, John Taylor affirmed boldly: "The omnipotent power of eternal truth will stand unscathed in the view of gathering hosts, and the nations will know that God rules in the heavens, and that Mormonism is not a vague phantasy and wild chimera, but the greatest boon that could be conferred upon man, the offspring of heaven, the gift of the Gods, a celestial treasure, an earthly, heavenly inheritance, a living, abiding, and eternal reality." (*The Mormon*, July 28, 1855, p. 2.) In the same issue, he also sketched for his readers the salient characteristics of the converted Mormon. Wrote he, "He grasps at all truths, human and divine; he has no darling dogma to sustain or favorite creed to uphold; he has nothing to lose but error; nothing to gain but truth. He digs, labors, and searches for it as for hidden treasure; and while others are content with chaff and husks of straw, he seizes on the kernel, substance, the gist of all that's good, and clings to all that will ennoble and exalt the human family." (Ibid.)

In a later issue, John undertook to consider the philosophical foundations of Mormonism. He explained that a Latter-day Saint understood certain basic principles of philosophy or truth without being able to define the supporting reasons. "The Mormons know by obedience," he said. "They may not be all philosophers, but they know it by inspiration through obedience." He cited examples of persons who know certain things or phenomena without being able to explain the underlying reasons that account for them, for example, the woman who knows how to make bread without understanding how wheat is raised. Then referring to the knowledge acquired by Christ's servants through spiritual means that they could not objectively explain or demonstrate, he concluded, "They had the gift of the Holy Ghost that brought things past to their remembrance, led them into all truth, and showed them things to come. They had a principle of living revelation, or a living fountain of true eternal principles. Those principles would always overturn the puerile principles of a corrupt philosophy and the ridiculous fantasies of a false religion and vanquish them; they might not always understand why—it was the gift of God to them; but it was philosophical; such is Mormonism." (*The Mormon,* March 8, 1856, p. 2.)

In addition to his frequent articles defining the doctrines of the Church and explaining the character and objectives of its members, Elder Taylor spoke out affirmatively on public issues. During a period when there was much national dissension, *The Mormon* spoke out strongly in favor of unity and accommodation. It also was a strong advocate of a transcontinental railroad, thereby answering the false claims of enemies who had asserted that the Mormon leaders opposed the railroad as a means of slowing the influx of non-members into the Western basin.

While handling the duties of editing and publishing *The Mormon,* Elder Taylor also discharged heavy ecclesiastical responsibilities as the president of the Eastern States Mission. In this role, he directed the activities of the missionaries assigned to labor there, oversaw the work of the numerous branches within the mission, and coordinated the immigration of the many converts from the mission fields abroad who streamed through New York City.

In March 1856, an additional burden was laid on the busy apostle when he was appointed by the Territorial Constitutional Convention as a delegate to lobby for statehood in Washington. Appointed at the same time as a co-delegate was fellow apostle George A. Smith. This pair went to Washington, D.C., in the summer of 1856 on what proved to be a wholly fruitless assignment. All ears were closed to their pleas for statehood for Deseret. Indeed, it would seem that no one there even wanted to get within earshot of these Mormon representatives who to Washington officialdom were political pariahs. The problem, of course, traced to the national furor that had been stirred up over polygamy. And the likelihood that John and his companion would receive a sympathetic hearing was worsened by the fact that a presidential campaign was then gearing up. The Republican Party had put as much distance as possible between it and the Mormon Church by adopting a plank that condemned slavery and polygamy as the twin relics of barbarism. And the Democrats, anxious not to have the political albatross of Mormon friendship hung around their necks, treated the two lobbyists with cold disdain. Even President Franklin Pierce, who had previously received Elder Taylor with graciousness, was distant despite the fact that he was a lame-duck president and had nothing to lose politically by befriending the Mormons. This handsome man, who at the time was the youngest president to occupy the White House, had earlier consulted with Elder Taylor about the appointment of a territorial governor for Deseret. He was intensely interested in the development of the West and, with John Taylor, shared the dream of a transcontinental railroad. But his advocacy of the Kansas-Nebraska bill, whose chief object was to accelerate western development, sealed his political doom, as it nullified the Missouri Compromise by leaving the question of slavery to popular vote in the new states. This aroused bitter antagonisms toward him by Democrats in the south and paved the way for the candidacy and ultimate election of James Buchanan, whose misguided politics were to result in the untimely death of *The Mormon* and the termination of Elder John Taylor's mission in New York.

While all this lay in the future, the seeds of the unfolding drama had all been planted at the time of the abortive lobbying effort by Elder Taylor and his associate in the summer of 1856. Returning to New York City, John continued with his numerous activities connected with *The Mormon,* expounding and defending the faith, and his duties with the Eastern States Mission. These continued until the spring of the following year, when a series of unfortunate events dictated John's return to the West.

Although there were numerous subsidiary and contributing events, the most significant one that influenced Elder Taylor's departure from New York was the departure of three non-Mormon judges from Salt Lake City. W. W. Drummond, George P. Stiles, and John F. King fled to the nation's capital in the spring of 1857 following James Buchanan's inauguration. These erstwhile judges bore tales of alleged disloyalty on the part of Brigham Young and other Mormon leaders. Specifically, they charged Brigham and the others with the destruction of court records, an accusation that was later proven false. This charge, when added to numerous others made by frustrated federal administrators who had returned from Utah, having failed to bend the Latter-day Saints to their will, stirred President Buchanan into a hasty action he would later regret. That was to organize a well-equipped and heavily manned expeditionary force whose main purpose was to quell the alleged Mormon sedition. An ancillary purpose seems to have been to send a cautionary message to the prospective new states in the West not to read too much self-determinism into the Kansas-Nebraska bill.

Being aware of these stirrings in Washington, and conscious of the ominous implications they held for his people, John Taylor departed from New York in May 1857, leaving William I. Appelby and T.B.H. Stenhouse in charge of publishing and editing *The Mormon*, tasks they would perform only until mid-September of that year, when the paper was dissolved because of the crisis brought on by the so-called Mormon War.

It was on August 9 that Elder Taylor made a public report of his recent mission. For those assembled in the bowery, he drew a sharp contrast between the spirit of the Saints and the spirit of the world. Of the latter, he said, "I have been for some length of time past associated with the gentiles. I have been engaged in battling corruption, iniquity, and the foul spirits that seem to fill the atmosphere of what you may term the lower regions." Having made that general indictment, he went on to particularize by selecting certain editors, politicians, and apostates for special denunciation. He was especially explicit about Horace Greeley, the editor of the New York *Tribune*, who popularized the slogan "Go west, young man, go west." Of this gadfly, Elder Taylor observed, "I have examined his articles, watched his course, read his paper daily, and have formerly conversed with him a little; but latterly, I would not be seen in his company." The apostle faulted the *Tribune's* editor for both personal and professional reasons, noting that he was the "principal supporter" of one of the free-love societies in the east, and that in writing for his paper he wrote "what suits his clandestine plans, and leaves the rest untold."

After sharing other details about his experience in editing *The Mormon*, John told of the abortive attempt of his committee to influence Congress to approve statehood for Utah, noting, "I have never yet inquired what the First Presidency thought about our proceedings there." (JD 5:122.) In responding, President Young, who followed John Taylor at the pulpit, commended his friend and the others for their work in Washington and then added this unsolicited compliment about Elder Taylor's work in editing and publishing *The Mormon:* "I have heard many remarks concerning the editorials in that paper, not only from Saints, but from those who do not profess to believe the religion we have embraced; and it is probably one of the strongest edited papers that is now published. . . . I have never read one sentence in them but what my heart could bid success to it and beat a happy response to every sentence that I have read or heard read." Then turning to the man whom he had just honored with one of the lengthiest eulogies he ever delivered, the Lion of the Lord, who was known for his economy with words, added, "Brother Taylor, that is for you; and I believe that these are the feelings and the sentiments of all in this community who have perused that paper." (Ibid., p. 123.)

While the editor of *The Mormon* obviously was not one whose self-esteem depended on the accolades of others, there can be little doubt that he was built up in his confidence by this praise from his leader. And one might logically infer that Brigham's remarks were doubly meaningful to John because of his embarrassment resulting from the Deseret Manufacturing Company fiasco.

Chapter Sixteen

The Saints under Siege

The mood Elder Taylor found in Salt Lake City on his return from New York was an amalgam of excitement and apprehension. But there was no sense of hopelessness or despair in it. That the Saints had not only survived but had prospered in the wilderness, despite the gloomy predictions of onlookers to the contrary, had given them a resilient self-confidence in their ability to cope with any adversity. And a benign fatalism taught them that they would find triumph even in death. It was precisely this sentiment that the lyricist William Clayton captured in his song of the Exodus, "Come, Come Ye Saints": "And should we die before our journey's through, Happy day! all is well." (*Hymns*, no. 13.) But, while the Saints were prepared, though not anxious, to die at the hands of President Buchanan's approaching army, they were preparing vigorously for life and victory. Like a tortoise guarding against attack by withdrawing its exposed parts into its shell, the Mormon chieftans recalled their leading men from around the world to return to the protective sanctuary of the Salt Lake Valley. In addition to John's return from New York, Amasa M. Lyman and Charles C. Rich were summoned from San Bernardino; Orson Hyde from Carson Valley, Nevada; and the missionaries and their leaders from throughout the United States and Europe. Meanwhile, the

Nauvoo Legion had been mustered and armed and stood ready to act on command.

Immediately upon returning from the East, John Taylor became deeply involved in the leading Mormon councils, where the strategy to meet the threat of invasion was devised. It was decided to use guerilla tactics of harassment as the army approached, rear-guard defensive action as the heavily armed federal troops drew nearer, and, if necessary, a scorched earth policy in the event the valley was overrun, so as to rob the invaders of the spoils of war. This strategy, which would have seemed impractical if not suicidal to some, was wholly reasonable to the Mormon leaders, who were confident that the Saints, who had survived a mass migration into the wilderness, were capable of fleeing and surviving again. While not stated in that terminology, it was implicit in their planning that the God of ancient Israel would come to the rescue of modern Israel and would, if necessary, lead it with a shadow by day and a pillar by night and feed it with manna in the desert.

Elder Taylor hinted at these sentiments in the same address in which he reported on his mission to New York. Said he, "So far as I am concerned, I say, let everything come as God has ordained it. I do not desire trials; I do not desire affliction. . . . But if the earthquake bellows, the lightnings flash, the thunders roll, and the powers of darkness are let loose, and the spirit of evil is permitted to rage, and an evil influence is brought to bear on the Saints, and my life, with theirs, is put to the test; let it come, for we are the Saints of the most High God, and all is well, all is peace, all is right, and will be, both in time and in eternity." (JD 5:114, 115.)

Elder Taylor, Brigham Young, and other high leaders of the Church repeated these sentiments over and over again, sentiments that found affirmation in the minds and hearts of the rank and file of the Church. This had the effect of welding the Latter-day Saints together in an extraordinary way and of producing a community will implacably opposed to yielding to the invaders. The U. S. Army had no conception of what it faced in terms of community resistance until September, when it sent a quartermaster officer, Captain Stewart Van Vliet, to Salt Lake City. Ostensibly, the captain was merely to negotiate for supplies, although the inference is that he was to test the waters for a negotiated settlement and to appraise the temper of the people. There can be little doubt that the Captain was surprised at what he found. There was no evidence of dismay or fear among this relatively defenseless people faced with the prospect of invasion by a well-trained, professional army. Instead, there was a uniform attitude of defiance, even truculence, among them.

As might be expected, the visitor's first insight into the defenders' resolve came from the Mormon chieftan, Brigham Young. When reminded that the Saints could not hope to withstand forever the military might of the United States, Brigham conceded the point but assured the surprised officer that when the victorious troops entered the valley, they would find a desert wasteland: "Every house will be burned to the ground, every tree cut down, and every field laid to waste." The Lion of the Lord then advised the quartermaster that the Saints had a three-year supply of provisions and that if pushed to it, they would "take to the mountains and bid defiance to all the powers of the government." In talking around, he found that these sentiments of the Mormon leader were shared by all. Convincing confirmation of this came from a mild-mannered Mormon mother who agreed with what Brigham had said and who added, "I would not only consent to it, but I would set fire to my house with my own hands, cut down every tree and root up every plant."

The clinching evidence of the inflexible determination of the Mormons to resist the U.S. Army came on Sunday, September 13, as Captain Van Vliet sat in the Bowery listening to Elder John Taylor preach a sermon whose main thrust was to compare the principles and fruits of the restored gospel with communism and sectarianism. In discussing the cohesion and sense of loyalty that existed among the Latter-day Saints, he asked rhetorically, using the words of the apostle Paul, "Can anything separate us from the love of God?" Answering the question, he said, "No, brethren; we are cemented together by eternal ties that the world does not know, nor can it comprehend." Then, apparently reminded by this statement of the threat of invasion that hung over the community, he veered from the principal theme of his discourse to say with obvious fervor, "Talk to us of bowing to the Gentile yoke! Nonsense. What would be your feeling if the United States wanted to have the honour of driving us from our homes and bringing us subject to their depraved standard of moral and religious truth? Would you, if necessary, brethren, put the torch to your buildings, and lay them in ashes, and wander houseless into the mountains? I know what you would say and what you would do." At that, President Young spoke up from his seat behind the pulpit to say, "Try the vote." Acting on that direction, John said to the vast audience, "All you that are willing to set fire to your property and lay it in ashes, rather than submit to their military rule and oppression, manifest it by raising your hands." There then occurred a demonstration of unity and defiance that doubtless had its impact on the visiting army quartermaster, when every hand in the audience was raised. Obviously pleased with that show of unity, the speaker added this postscript: "I know what your feelings are. We have been persecuted and robbed long enough; and, in the name of Israel's God, we will be free!" At that, the audience broke into a spontaneous "Amen" to which Brother Brigham added his benediction, "I say amen all the time to that." (JD 5:247.)

Soon after this electrifying incident, Captain Van Vliet returned to the encamped army to report the results of his mission. The insights into the Mormon character and goals it had provided radically altered his views about the expedition and caused him to declare that if the United States made war on the Latter-day Saints, "he would withdraw from the army." (Hubert Howe Bancroft, *History of Utah*,

p. 509.) His report, which was sympathetic to the Mormon view, is credited as a chief factor in altering some of the misconceptions in Washington that had produced President Buchanan's misadventure.

The day after the captain's departure, President Young, acting in his role as territorial governor, declared martial law and later dispatched part of the militia to keep the approaching army under surveillance and to conduct raids of diversion and harassment. Elder Taylor accompanied this arm of the militia to the front, where he served for several months on the staff of Lieutenant-General Daniel H. Wells. In mid-December, he left this assignment to return to Salt Lake City to attend the territorial legislature, which convened the latter part of the month. There he was chosen as speaker of the house. In this role, he steered through the legislature a memorial to the president and Congress, pleading for a wiser policy in the appointment of territorial officials, for a recognition of the rights of the Saints as U. S. citizens, and for a withdrawal of the army.

The impact of this memorial, added to the favorable report of Captain Van Vliet and the intercession of the Saints' friend Colonel Thomas L. Kane, began to effect a change in official thought in Washington about the solution of "the Mormon problem." President Buchanan was particularly anxious by now to find a way out of his embarrassment, as public sentiment had begun to shift toward the embattled Saints.

A first overt step toward peace was taken when Colonel Kane, with the blessing of the Buchanan administration, traveled to Utah by way of Panama and California to parley with Brigham Young, John Taylor, and other Mormon leaders. It was then agreed that President Young would yield the territorial governship to his designated successor, Alfred Cumming, who was with the invading army. The colonel then traveled to the military encampment in Wyoming, where he convinced Mr. Cumming of the bona fide intentions of the Mormon leaders to seek peace. Receiving assurances for his safety, the new governor accompanied the roving diplomat, who served without official title, to the Mormon stronghold in the Salt Lake Valley where, on April 15, 1858, Brigham Young turned over the reins of government to his successor. As a tangible token of peace, President Buchanan, nine days earlier on the twenty-eighth anniversary of the organization of the Mormon Church, signed a proclamation pardoning all the Latter-day Saints for their alleged treason. While they resented the insulting implication of the proclamation's language, the residents of Deseret accepted it as a means of restoring some semblance of normalcy to their lives.

One would have thought that these dramatic actions spelled the end of the Mormon war. And, in retrospect, they did. But a spectator viewing the scene in Salt Lake City at the time would hardly have identified it as a peace celebration. Instead of flags, parades, fireworks, and optimistic speeches, an onlooker would have seen a somber, silent, business-like preparation for another exodus. After carefully packing and loading their belongings, the Mormon families would have been seen placing straw in their homes and other buildings ready for the incendiary's torch and then fleeing south. This incongruity, a negotiated peace coupled with hurried plans for exodus and a scorched earth left behind, was dictated by distrust of the invading army and its masters in Washington. The Saints had little faith in the federal government. Too often had they relied upon its promises to their detriment. So, they had retained leverage to ensure that the army would comply with the negotiated peace by threatening to burn their cities and destroy their fields. The Saints seemed confident this was an eventuality the invaders feared, both because of the army's need for food and the possibility of a backlash against the administration by an aroused public that seemed more and more sympathetic to the plight of the Saints.

It was not a simple task for Elder Taylor to prepare his family for still another exodus. By now he had seven wives, including his most recent one, Margaret Young, whom he had married in September 1856. And there were eighteen children, most of whom were under the age of ten and who, therefore, had been born in the wilderness after the flight from Nauvoo. Moreover, Sophia was expecting her fourth child, who turned out to be a fine, healthy boy; he was born in Provo, Utah, on May 15, 1858, a few weeks after the family left Salt Lake City. This child of promise, John Whitaker Taylor, would grow into a handsome, articulate, intelligent man who years later would follow his father into the apostleship as a member of the Quorum of the Twelve Apostles.

After boarding up the family homes along "Taylor Row," packing their belongings in large schooner wagons and placing dry straw throughout their buildings, the Taylor family, led by its fifty-year-old patriarch, traveled south toward an uncertain destination with their domestic animals trailing behind, herded by the older sons.

At Provo, where the family stopped after the forty-five mile trip that took over two days to negotiate, John found cramped, temporary housing for his family in a shantytown encampment, west of Provo in the bottom lands toward Utah Lake. Jammed with refugees from the north and descriptively called "Shanghai" because of the overcrowding, the nondescript appearance of the buildings, and the hive-like activity of the residents, this was the place where the Mormons awaited the outcome of President Buchanan's war.

By now the government was backed into a corner because of the shift of public opinion in favor of the Saints. As President Young, John Taylor, and the other Church leaders parleyed in Provo, they were aware of the strength of their strategic position despite a hopeless vulnerability from a military point of view. In this posture, the defenseless Saints were able to dictate the terms of the peace that followed—full amnesty for the defenders and agreement that the army would leave the Mormon communities and their inhabitants unmolested and would bivouac a long distance from Salt Lake City.

Obtaining these concessions from the government negotiators, the Mormon leaders made one face-saving concession to an army that had been robbed of the laurels—and the spoils—of victory. That was to allow it to march through Salt Lake City in an empty show of triumph. This charade was carried out on June 26, 1858, when the army, under the command of Colonel Albert Sidney Johnston—later of Civil War fame—rode through the town's empty streets, across the Jordan River, and on to Cedar Valley, some forty miles from the city. There it bivouacked and later established a garrison named Camp Floyd. Derisively called Frog Town by the Mormons, this military post was later to be a thorn in the side of the Saints. But, in the summer of 1858, they were scarcely aware of its existence as the refugees returned to Salt Lake City from their temporary, self-imposed exile in nearby Provo.

There can be little doubt that as Elder Taylor and the other Mormon leaders resumed their duties after returning home, they were conscious of an achievement almost without parallel in the annals of military history. This was their dominance over a vastly superior force, accomplished without direct confrontation, with negligible damage to property, and with no loss of life. The brethren credited this extraordinary result to the intervention of God in their behalf. Elder Taylor gave voice to this sentiment in a fiery talk delivered to the Saints assembled in the Old Tabernacle in Salt Lake City. Said he, "I do not remember having read in any history, or had related to me any circumstance where an army has been subjugated so easily, and their power wasted away so effectually without bloodshed, as this in our borders. If this is not the manifestation of the power of God to us, I do not know what is. Has any man's life been lost in it? No—not one. It is true our brethren have been fired upon; but their balls failed of doing the injury that was expected. Our brethren were told not to retaliate, and they did not do it. Where is there such a manifestation of the power of God?" (JD 6:112.) And as far as Elder Taylor was concerned, the affair also magnified the leadership genius of President Brigham Young. "Suppose you or I had had the dictation of this matter," he asked the audience. "We should have been firing clear away on the Sweetwater, and killed a lot of them before they got here. It was not we, then, that directed this matter. No. Who was it? Why, it was those who are placed over us; and those very things that seemed hard for us to do at that time have really accomplished one of the greatest things that history has yet developed." (Ibid., pp. 112-113.)

Chapter Seventeen

Caesar, the Gentiles, and Polygamy

The peaceful subjugation of Johnston's army did not end the running controversy between the Saints, the federal government, and the Gentile population in Utah and the United States. It was merely a transitional interlude during which the controversy shifted from the battlefield back to the arenas of politics, economics, and religion.

Before and after the exodus, the Mormon leaders had envisioned a governmental structure in which civil and ecclesiastical authority would be intermingled under one head. In a vague way, never clearly defined, the council of fifty was intended to be an instrument to help bring about this merger and thereby to lay the groundwork for the ultimate dominance of the kingdom of God on earth in which Christ would be the reigning monarch. This goal and concept, coupled with the experience during a short period after the Exodus when both civil and ecclesiastical authority were vested in Brigham Young as territorial governor and Church president, had created erroneous ideas in the minds of some Latter-day Saints about the relationship between the Church and the state. There can be little doubt that these erroneous ideas contributed significantly to the misunderstandings that existed between the Saints and the federal government for several decades. It also seems plain, however, that within a few years after the Exodus, Brigham Young, John Taylor, and other leaders of the Church had abandoned any idea of a combined civil-ecclesiastical government and had reconciled themselves to exerting their influence on the civil side, either through the ballot box or by other legitimate means.

In order that Mormon views would be adequately expressed in the councils of civil government, able leaders of the Church were encouraged to stand for election to territorial offices. Consistent with that policy, Elder Taylor energetically took up his duties as the speaker of the house in the territorial legislature upon becoming resettled in Salt Lake City after the Johnston War. He would continue to serve in the house until 1876, completing five full terms, during each of which he was elected as speaker. His service in the house was followed by a term as the territorial superintendent of district schools, to which he was elected in 1877. And from 1868 to 1870, he served as the probate judge of Utah County. At that time, territorial probate courts wielded extensive power as they exercised original jurisdiction in both civil and criminal matters, as well in chancery as in common law. Meanwhile, John continued to exert important influence in ecclesiastical affairs in his role as a ranking member of the Twelve. And his background as a proselyter, a publisher, and a confidant of Joseph Smith added to his eloquence, his forcefulness, and his style gave this defender of the faith an eminence and status among the Saints second only to President Young. And, in some respects, this urbane, learned, and dignified apostle outshone even the Lion of the Lord in the estimation and affection of the Saints.

Acting in these diverse roles and given his experience and skill, the apostle was in a unique position to observe and influence major issues of policy and preference affecting the Latter-day Saints. Preeminent among these was the issue of polygamy, which, in one way or another, would dominate the thinking and the activities of John Taylor throughout the remainder of his life.

It was not possible for John Taylor to look upon polygamy with the same detachment with which we view it today. He was too much caught up in it to see it as anything other than a principle upon which salvation depended. It was in that spirit that he had acceded to the urgent demands of the Prophet Joseph Smith and had taken his first plural wife, Elizabeth Kaighin, in 1843, and thereafter had taken other plural wives. Having done that, he had not only fulfilled the mandate of the Prophet, but he had also assumed solemn covenants running to these women and their children that made him morally responsible for their care and protection. John Taylor, therefore, was irrevocably committed to this principle, both theologically and practically. Any suggestion that it was other than a holy principle sanctioned and, in his case, mandated by God was an affront to him. And any suggestion that the government might attempt to prevent him from living this principle was rejected as an unwarranted invasion of his right to religious freedom.

John's vigorous and skillful defense of both the theory and practice of polygamy in the pages of *The Mormon* affirm these views. And, in the process of defending polygamy in New York City, he had been exposed personally to the wrath, vindictiveness, and single-mindedness of those bent on eradicating it. The efforts of these enemies were not abated by the temporary wave of sympathy for the Saints generated by the Mormon War. After that conflict ended, John Taylor, as the speaker of the territorial house of representatives, as a professional editor, and as a leading Mormon polygamist carefully monitored the press reports from New York and Washington pertaining to this volatile issue. From these it was obvious that prohibitive legislation aimed at the practice of polygamy was being pushed in Congress by enemies of the Church. The theme seemed to be that the Civil War was aimed at the first relic of barbarism—slavery; and that the second alleged relic—

polygamy—should be attacked through repressive legislation.

By 1862 the forces in Congress arrayed against the Saints were able to pass the Morrill Anti-Bigamy Act, which applied specifically to the Territory of Utah. It disincorporated the Church, limited to $50,000 in value the real estate it could own, and imposed sanctions on polygamists. The act was signed by President Abraham Lincoln on July 8, 1862. Preoccupation with the Civil War and a relaxed attitude on the part of the chief executive toward the Mormons forestalled any immediate effort to enforce the law. President Lincoln likened the Saints to a heavy log in a field that was plowed around because it was "too hard to split, too wet to burn and too heavy to move." When asked what he intended to do about the Mormons, he is reported to have said, "You go back and tell Brigham Young that if he will let me alone, I will let him alone." (See George U. Hubbard, "Abraham Lincoln as Seen by the Mormons," *Utah Historical Quarterly* 31:91-108.)

As far as John Taylor and the other brethren were concerned, the act was unconstitutional because it infringed their religious freedom. This view inevitably carried over into the elective probate courts, which had criminal jurisdiction and which were officered by Latter-day Saints, thereby creating an even greater inertia than existed in the nation's chief executive toward enforcement of the new law. For these reasons, the Morrill Act lay practically dormant for several years. But its apparent lifelessness was misleading. Like a time bomb, it contained the explosive ingredients that in a few years would be detonated by increasingly stressful events, rocking the Church to its very foundations.

Only three months after signing the Morrill Act, President Abraham Lincoln sent to Utah a man who was to add another volatile element to the Mormon-Gentile controversy. This was Colonel Patrick Edward Connor, the commander of a corps of 750 volunteers from California, whose unit had been assigned to guard the telegraph and stage lines from attack by the Confederate army. The Saints assumed the new commander and his troops would occupy Camp Floyd, which only recently had been evacuated by the remnants of Johnston's army. Instead, the Colonel and his men marched menacingly through the streets of Salt Lake City with fixed bayonets and loaded rifles to a camp on the east bench of the Salt Lake Valley, where the Mormon headquarters were within the range of their cannon. This flamboyant entry into the heart of Mormondom, and other events that followed soon after, demonstrated to the Saints that guarding the telegraph and stage lines was not Mr. Connor's first priority. A letter written to a fellow officer in San Francisco revealed his main purpose: "My policy in this territory," he confided to his friend, "has been to invite hither a large gentile and loyal population . . . numerous enough to put a check on the Mormon authorities and give countenance to those who are striving to loose the bonds with which they have been so long oppressed." The zealous Colonel made no attempt to conceal the way in which he intended to attain this goal: "With this in view, I have bent every energy and means of which I was possessed, both personal and official, towards the discovery and development of the mining resources of the territory, using without stint the soldiers at my command, whenever and wherever it could be done without detriment to the public service." To advance this purpose, the commander spearheaded the organization of the first daily newspaper in the territory, the *Union Vedette*, whose pages trumpeted news about mining prospects and bristled with articles critical of the Church and its leaders.

Meanwhile, the representatives of other religious groups began to descend upon Utah in ever-increasing numbers, bent on "rescuing" the Saints. These ministers joined with Colonel Connor and the *Union Vedette* in denouncing Brigham Young, John Taylor, and the other Church leaders in condemning the practice of polygamy and in exhorting the Saints to turn away from Mormonism.

In the midst of this turmoil, a rift opened within the

Church when a group of dissident members began to oppose the economic policies of their leaders, who encouraged home manufactories. These dissidents, who included Elder Taylor's former associate on *The Mormon,* T.B.H. Stenhouse, who later became the editor and proprietor of the *Salt Lake Telegram,* urged that Utah turn its energies toward the development of the area's mineral resources. It was their thesis that with the coming of the transcontinental railroad, goods manufactured in the East or on the West Coast would be cheaper and better made than home-manufactured goods. Therefore, the argument went, it would be more rational and productive for the Saints to devote themselves to the work (mining exploration and development) that could be more efficiently and economically performed by local residents. This logic received the enthusiastic endorsement of Patrick Connor because he was confident the discovery of rich mineral deposits by Utah prospectors, whether Mormon or non-Mormon, would bring a flood of immigrants similar to the hordes that had swarmed to California during the gold rush.

Following the Civil War, the three branches of the federal government added their weight to the increasing pressure being exerted upon the Mormons to abandon polygamy. The first to act was Congress, which made three unsuccessful but, to the Saints, frightening attempts to dilute if not eradicate the influence of the Latter-day Saints on territorial government. The first two attempts, the Wade and Cragin bills, sought to give the 1862 anti-bigamy bill some teeth. The Wade bill, among other things, would have empowered the territorial governor to appoint probate judges and the U.S. marshall to impanel juries. The Cragin bill went further by eliminating trial by jury in polygamy cases. A third measure, the Ashley bill, would have dissolved the territory of Utah and divided its area among surrounding states or territories. The Saints lost their fear of this measure, and its proponents lost their enthusiasm for it, when it was discovered that the division suggested by the genius who drafted the bill possibly would have given the Latter-day Saints political control in four jurisdictions instead of one.

The federal executive pressure on the Mormons began to be felt as soon as Ulysses S. Grant took office in early 1869. This president promptly abandoned the relaxed attitude toward his Utah constituents that had been adopted by both Abraham Lincoln and Andrew Johnson. The tough Union general who had crushed the Confederate army with his remorseless tenacity and drive sought to destroy Mormonism through the force of his presidential appointments and the voice of his vice-president, Schuyler Colfax, holding in reserve the threat of further military action.

The most noteworthy of President Grant's appointments was that of General J. Wilson Shaffer, who had contributed significantly in yoking the South after the Civil War as the radicals in Washington tamed the rebel slaveholders with an army of carpetbaggers. Moving into another arena where he confidently expected to stamp out the remaining "relic of barbarism," polygamy, General Shaffer was heard to boast, "Never after me shall it be said that Brigham Young is governor of Utah." It was through the influence of General Shaffer that Judge Charles C. Wilson was removed from office, thereby clearing the way for President Grant's appointment of Judge James B. McKean as the chief justice. Judge McKean was one of the prime movers who had influenced the Republican Party to adopt the plank condemning the "twin relics of barbarism." He brought to his new appointment an uncommon zeal not for the law, but for the destruction of polygamy and the Mormon Church. Indeed, the chief justice was determined to ignore the law or to take it into his own hands should that be necessary to reach his objective. His intent was plainly expressed to Judge Louis Dent, President Grant's brother-in-law. Said he, "Judge Dent, the mission which God has called upon me to perform in Utah, is as much above the duties of other courts and judges as the heavens are above the earth, and whenever or wherever I may find the Local or Federal laws obstructing or interfering therewith, by

God's blessing I shall trample them under my feet." (Edward W. Tullidge, *Life of Brigham Young* [New York, 1876], pp. 420-21.)

These extreme views were shared by associate justices O. F. Strickland and C. M. Hawley, who in 1869, the year before Judge McKean's appointment, began a "judicial crusade" whose object was to deprive the local probate courts of criminal jurisdiction. The timing of this crusade seems to have marked a coalesence of several forces that had been set in motion whose object or effect was, in part, to destroy polygamy and to reduce the influence of the Church. It was in May of this year that the transcontinental railroad was linked up at Promontory Point, thereby bypassing Salt Lake City. With that, Colonel Connor's dream seemed to be on the threshhold of fulfillment.

And at this time the voices of the apostates had reached their most strident pitch and the Grant administration was gearing up for its administrative and judicial onslaught against the Mormons. It was in these circumstances that Vice-President Schuyler Colfax made an official visit to Salt Lake City in October 1869. This forty-six-year-old former speaker of the house had first claimed public attention as the founder and editor of the *St. Joseph Valley Register* in Indiana. He had been a pillar of the radical wing of the Republican Party during the reconstruction era and had advocated disenfranchising the confederate leaders while extending the vote to all negroes. The apparent purpose of his visit was to survey the scene in Utah for President Grant to determine what degree of coercion against the Mormons, not excluding another war, would be necessary to bring them into line. In a conversation with fellow editor T.B.H. Stenhouse, who by now was irrevocably in the apostate camp, he had asked, "Will Brigham Young fight?" He was warned by the proprietor of the *Salt Lake Telegram* to keep the United States off: "You will . . . drive the thousands back into the arms of Brigham Young who are ready to rebel against one man power." (H. H. Bancroft, *History of Utah*, p. 656.)

Mr. Colfax apparently decided that under the circumstances the best way to attack the Mormon Prophet and polygamy was through rhetoric and reasoning, however faulty. So, departing from his investigative chores, the vice-president scheduled a talk on October 5, 1869, during the course of the Church's semiannual conference, where he proceeded to lecture the Mormons. Mr. Bancroft's appraisal of the impact of this speech on the Latter-day Saints may not be far off the mark. Wrote the historian, "The sentence most acceptable to the Mormons was the concluding line, 'I bid you all good night and good by.'" (Ibid.)

Even a cursory review of the talk shows why it was so offensive to the Saints. At the outset, he assumed the very points at issue: the constitutionality and binding effect of the anti-bigamy statute and the invalidity of the revelation on the plurality of wives: "I have no strictures to utter as to your creed," began Mr. Colfax, "on any really religious question. Our land is a land of civil and religious liberty, and the faith of every man is a matter between himself and God alone. You have as much right to worship the Creator through a president and twelve apostles of your church organization as I have through the ministers and elders and creed of mine. And this right I would defend for you with as much zeal as the right of every other denomination throughout the land. But our country is governed by law, and no assumed revelation justifies anyone in trampling on the law." (See *The Mormon Question* [Salt Lake City, 1870], pp. 3-4.)

His next point (that the Morrill Act should be observed until struck down, regardless of the issue of constitutionality), while persuasive from a narrow, legalistic point of view, hardly set well with the people for whom the law had been specially and malignantly tailored.

The vice-president then clucked at the Saints because the revelation countered the prohibition against polygamy found in the Book of Mormon. Moving to the most offensive part of his speech, he argued, "You would not yourselves tolerate others in assuming rights for themselves under revelation they might claim to have received, or under religions they might profess." (Ibid., p. 4.) By way of illustration, the speaker cited the practice of the Hindus to burn widows with the dead bodies of their husbands.

Following that, Mr. Colfax likened the Morrill Act to local ordinances regulating gambling and liquor sales, admonished the Saints to encourage foreign investments and competition in trade, and, as a parting shot, again enjoined upon them "obedience to law." (Ibid., p. 5.)

The negative reaction of the Saints to this condescending speech was prompt and pervasive. While the rank and file seethed with resentment, their leaders mounted a massive counterattack. Two days later, on assignment from the First Presidency, Orson Pratt delivered a lengthy sermon on celestial marriage in the Tabernacle, where he advanced the thesis that under the protection of the constitution guaranteeing religious freedom, the Latter-day Saints had the right "to believe in the Patriarchal, in the Mosaic, or in the Christian order of things; for the God of the patriarchs, and the God of Moses is also the Christian's God." (JD 13:184.)

On the following day, October 8, George A. Smith, a counselor in the First Presidency, took up the theme again, covering much of the ground Elder Pratt had covered and, in addition, focusing on New Testament scriptures. Specifically, he interpreted Paul's injunction to Timothy "A bishop then must be blameless, the husband of one wife" (1 Timothy 3:2) to mean that a bishop should be the husband of one wife *at least*. And he interpreted Paul's laudatory remarks about the ancient patriarchs in the eleventh chapter of Hebrews as implying an endorsement of their polygamy. (JD 13:39.)

And on October 9, for the third day running, the Saints were treated to still another discourse on the subject, this one by John Taylor's nephew George Q. Cannon. Elder Cannon, while endorsing what his brethren had said, put the practice of polygamy in a modern context. Said he, "If there were no record of its practice to be found, and if the

Bible, Book of Mormon and Book of Doctrine and Covenants were totally silent in respect to this doctrine, it would nevertheless be binding upon us as a people, God Himself having given a revelation for us to practice it at the present time." (JD 13:197.)

However, it was left to Elder John Taylor to prepare a detailed and analytical answer to the vice-president's remarks. It seemed appropriate that John would pull the laboring oar in this controversy. After all, he had been battling newspaper editors for years, and behind the facade of this government dignitary stood a knowledgeable and tough newspaper editor of the kind the apostle had jousted with in the urban canyons of New York City. Moreover, his status as an incumbent probate judge in Utah, whose role had been impliedly scored by Mr. Colfax, and his apostolic status in the Church the vice-president had openly condemned, added other convincing credentials supporting Elder Taylor's role as the principal Mormon spokesman in this debate.

At the time this controversial issue was stirred up in Salt Lake City, John was in Boston on Church and personal business. Judged by the response it evoked from him, the Colfax talk registered in the upper ranges of Elder Taylor's annoyance scale. He promptly prepared an answer and, using his professional contacts in Manhattan and his skills in publicity and propaganda honed over the years, he arranged to have it published in the *New York Tribune*. It was later republished in the *Deseret News*. To make certain his readers grasped the full import of his argument, the author repeated and then commented on the exact words of the vice-president.

On the basic issue of the conflict between law and religious belief and practice, the Mormon leader observed, "That our country is governed by law we all admit; but when it is said that 'no assumed revelation justifies anyone in trampling on the law' I should respectfully ask, 'What! not if it interferes with my religious faith, which you state 'is a matter between God and myself alone?'" As to the vice-president's demeaning use of the words "assumed revelation," Elder Taylor referred to the revelation as "one of the most vital parts of our religious faith; it emanated from God and cannot be legislated away." And in justifying the Saints' efforts to stonewall the application of the Morrill Act, he asked whether Joseph and Mary were justified in seeking to avoid Herod's decree in order to protect the life of Jesus. "But Herod was a tyrant," he declared rhetorically, and then responded in the same vein, "That makes no difference; it was the law of the land." Clinching the analogy, he added, "I have yet to learn the difference between a tyrannical king and a tyrannical congress. When we talk of executing law in either case, that means force—force means an army, and an army means death. Now I am not sufficiently versed in metaphysics to discover the difference in its effects, between the asp of Cleopatra, the dagger of Brutus, the chalice of Lucretia Borgia, or the bullet or sabre of an American soldier."

Answering the criticism that the Book of Mormon speaks against polygamy, John merely noted the embarrassing fact that Mr. Colfax had not quoted the whole scripture. "Had he read a little further he would have found it stated: 'For if I will, saith the Lord of Hosts, raise up seed unto me I will command my people; otherwise they shall hearken unto these things.'"

As to the burning of Hindu widows, Elder Taylor observed that the British administrators in India had countenanced both polygamy and suttee (the burning of widows), but he assured the vice-president that if the Hindus were converted to Mormonism, they would no longer burn them.

He gave the issue of competition short shrift, advising the speaker, "We think we have a right, as well as others, to buy or sell of and to whom we please."

John reserved his sharpest words to answer Mr. Colfax's flat assertion that polygamy was not a religious issue. "Are we to understand by this that Mr. Colfax is created an umpire to decide upon what is religion and what is not, upon what is true religion and what is false? If so, by whom and what authority is he created judge?" The apostle then suggested that had the speaker given the matter more careful thought, he would not have made such an incriminating statement. "According to this theory, no persons ever were persecuted for their religion. Could anybody suppose that that erudite . . . body of men, the great Sanhedrin . . . would persecute anybody for his religion? Jesus was put to death—not for his religion—but because he was a blasphemer; because he had a devil and cast out devils, through Beelzebub the prince of devils."

Having addressed the issues raised by the vice-president, Elder Taylor proceeded to address words of condemnation and counsel to the federal government. He focused first on Congress, which he condemned for singling out the Mormon Church for special, punitive treatment. Responding to those congressmen who assumed a stance of wounded innocence toward this charge, John asserted, "If a law had been passed making it a penal offense for communities or churches, to forbid marriage, who would not have understood that it referred to the Shaking Quakers, and to the Priories, Nunneries and Priesthood of the Catholic church?" Therefore, he concluded, "This law, in its inception, progress and passage, was intended to bring us into collision with the United States, that a pretext might be found for our ruin." To the rejoinder that the Saints had recourse to the courts to remedy any injustice, Elder Taylor answered with a sarcastic litany, "But we are graciously told that we have our appeal. True, we have an appeal. So had the Hebrew mothers to Pharaoh; so had Daniel to Nebuchadnezzar; so had Jesus to Herod; so had Caesar to Brutus; so had those sufferers on the rack to Loyola; so had the Waldenses and Albigenses to the Pope; so had the Quakers and Baptists of New England to the Puritans."

Elaborating on these analogies, the aroused apostle continued, "Pharaoh's exterminating order about the Hebrew infants was one of acknowledged policy—they grew, they increased too fast. When Jesus was plotted against by

Herod and the infants put to death, who could complain? *It was law:* we must submit to *law.* The lord Jehovah, or Jesus the Savior of the world, has no right to interfere with *law.* Jesus was crucified *according to law.* Who can complain?"

With that foundation, the author moved toward what for Mr. Colfax was an uncomfortable analogy: "We are told we are living in a more enlightened age. Our morals are more pure, our ideas more refined and enlarged, our institutions more liberal. . . . We won't persecute, very far be that from us; but we will make our platforms [the twin relics plank], pass congressional laws [the Morrill act] and make you submit to them." Then rising to the height of his sarcastic denunciation, John added, "We may, it is true, have to send out an army and shed the blood of many; but what of that. It is so much more pleasant to be proscribed and killed according to the laws of the Great Republic, in the 'asylum for the oppressed' than to perish ignobly by the decrees of kings, through their miserable minions in the barbaric ages."

In conclusion, the writer reviewed the bitter persecutions the Saints had endured before they began to practice polygamy and offered the opinion that the ultimate issue was not polygamy but Mormonism. "It was our religion then, it is our religion now. Monogamy or polygamy, it makes no difference."

The publication of this scathing answer to the speech of the vice-president ended the first round of what turned out to be the only national debate of any consequence on the issues of polygamy and Mormonism. The more extensive scope of Elder Taylor's answer and the telling points he had made guaranteed a response from Mr. Colfax. It came soon in a lengthy article he published in the *New York Independent*. It was an oblique counterattack, as Elder Taylor's answer to the Salt Lake City speech was not even mentioned until well along in the piece. This seemed to reflect a feeling that it would offend protocol were the number-two man in the national government to engage in a face-to-face confrontation with one of twelve men who comprised the second level of authority in a small religious denomination centered in the western desert.

So the vice-president chose as his point of reference for the *Independent* article a recent Utah application for statehood. This, he said, compelled the nation "to meet face to face, a question it has apparently endeavored to ignore." He proposed, therefore, to canvass the Mormon question "in the light of history" and, in the process, to treat "the favorite themes of the Mormon leaders." He identified these as their fertilizing of the desert, their persecutions, and their polygamy.

As to the first theme, he conceded that the Saints had made large portions of the desert "fruitful and productive" and that they had prospered economically. However, his explanation for all this practically ignored Mormon intelligence and industry. He saw only two factors in Utah's formula of success—water and markets. "But the solution of it all," he explained "is in one word—WATER." Having made that astonishing revelation, he added, "What seemed to the eye a desert became fruitful when irrigated; and the mountains whose crests are clothed in perpetual snow, furnished, in the unfailing supplies of their ravines, the necessary fertilizer." As to the markets for their products, which had brought prosperity, he referred to "the almost continuous procession of teams crossing the continent which stopped there naturally for supplies."

His avowed purpose under the head of persecution was to show that the Saints "were not driven from any region on account of hostility to their religion, as they so persistently assert." He ascribed the Kirtland persecution to antagonism growing out of alleged fraud in the management of the Kirtland bank in connection with which "Smith and Rigdon were tarred and feathered in 1832." He blamed the Saints for the Missouri difficulties, citing the alleged depredations by the Mormon Danites (a myth given unfortunate credence by the apostate Thomas B. Marsh and by Orson Hyde) and the charge of Missouri's governor that the Saints had "violated the laws of the land by open and armed resistance" and had "driven the inhabitants of an entire county from their homes, ravaged their crops and destroyed their dwellings." He saw the cause of the Nauvoo expulsion in the destruction of the *Expositor*'s press, and the Buchanan invasion and other federal harassments in Utah as justified by the alleged mistreatment of federal officers by the Mormons. Mr. Colfax ended his critique of Mormon persecution with this self-serving comment: "This sketch is not colored by any views of my own. I have simply drawn it from history, nothing extenuating nor setting down aught in malice. But the reader will fail to find in it that any of what they call persecution sprang from their peculiar religious beliefs."

Having belittled the achievements of the Saints in settling the West, and having heaped the blame for their persecutions on their own shoulders, the vice-president was prepared to answer Elder Taylor. As to the modifying provision in the Book of Mormon that sanctions polygamy where God commands it, he merely cited the argument of the apostate anti-polygamy Mormons, that in light of the positive statement quoted by the vice-president in his Salt Lake speech denouncing the actions of the polygamists David and Solomon, God "could not make a revelation afterward commanding it." He also quoted a policy statement, originally published in the 1830s, denying that the Church taught or practiced polygamy; the statement had found its way into an 1845 reprinting of the Doctrine and Covenants.

Aside from some minor skirmishing on extraneous points, Mr. Colfax then focused chiefly on the Hindu practice of suttee, as to which Elder Taylor had said, "It is difficult to say what we should do about our permitting the Hindus to burn their widows." Jumping on that opening, Mr. Colfax went to great length to explain how the British government had ultimately abolished the practice. However, he maintained silence about the fact they never attempted to prevent the Hindus from practicing polygamy.

Soon after the vice-president's article was published,

John prepared and circulated a reply that turned out to be the last chapter of this well-publicized debate. It is apparent that Elder Taylor took up his task with relish. He openly ridiculed, perhaps to excess, Mr. Colfax's explanation that Mormon colonizing success was assignable to water. After twitting him about a "wonderful little water nymph" that played with the clouds and frolicked with the snow, he asked seriously and pointedly: "Did water tunnel through our mountains, construct dams, canals and ditches, lay out our cities and towns, import and plant choice fruit trees, shrubs and flowers, cultivate the land and cover it with the cattle on a thousand hills, erect churches, school houses and factories and transform a howling wilderness into a fruitful field and garden?" He then added to the impact of this many-pronged question with the obvious corollary: "If so, why does not the Green River, the Snake River, Bear River, Colorado, the Platte and other rivers perform the same prodigies?" He hardly needed to add the conclusion: "Unfortunately for Mr. Colfax, it was 'Mormon' polygamists who did it."

His reply to the charges about the reasons underlying Mormon persecution was direct and sharp. He called the vice-president's comments about the Kirtland bank failure "a gross perversion," pointing out, in support, that Joseph Smith and Sidney Rigdon could not have been tarred and feathered for their involvement in the bank failure because they were tarred and feathered in March 1832 in Hiram, Ohio, but the bank was not organized in Kirtland until December 1836.

John countered the charge about the Danites by asserting, "It is not true that these things existed, for I was there and knew to the contrary; and so did the people of Missouri, and so did the Governor of Missouri." He had no explanation for the conduct of Thomas B. Marsh and Orson Hyde other than "the weakness of our common humanity," adding, as if in their defense, "We were living in troublous times, and all men's nerves are not proof against such shocks as we then had to endure." He likened Elder Hyde to the repentant Peter who wept bitterly after thrice denying the Christ: "So did Orson Hyde repent sincerely and weep bitterly, and was restored and has since been to Palestine, Germany and other nations." As to Thomas B. Marsh, Elder Taylor lamented that he "returned a poor, broken-down man, and begged to live with us. . . . He was a poor wreck of a man, a helpless drivelling child and he is since dead."

The apostle was outraged at the quotation from Governor Boggs's statement that accused the Mormons of persecuting the Missourians: "Mr. Governor, it was your bull that gored our ox. We were robbed, pillaged and exiled, were you? Our men, women and children were murdered without redress; driven from their homes in an inclement season of the year, and died by hundreds, in the state of Illinois, in consequence of hardship and exposure."

Elder Taylor then sketched the events surrounding the *Expositor* affair in Nauvoo, showing that its destruction was precipitated by religiously motivated attacks on the Saints and was carried out pursuant to a deliberate order of the city to abate a nuisance, not by a mob as Mr. Colfax had suggested. Similarly, he detailed the background of the invasion of Johnston's army, indicating that it occurred not to quell Mormon rebellion, but to destroy Mormon polygamy as the Republican Party had committed itself to do.

And as to polygamy, John here gave the issue the light touch, noting that the vice-president's comments about the subject were merely "a rehash of his former arguments."

Mr. Colfax made no effort to respond to this convincing reply. And thus the national debate about Mormonism and polygamy ended. It is doubtful that it changed the minds of anyone who already had strong opinions on the subject. But to those whose minds were not yet closed and who viewed the matter objectively, the arguments doubtless had an impact. Moreover, the perceptive readers who looked beyond the words to the authors and to their style, their stance, and their abilities would have found much food for thought. Such readers, who were previously unacquainted with John Taylor's work in editing *The Mormon* were probably surprised to find a Mormon polygamist from the western desert at least holding his own, from an intellectual and literary point of view, with one of the most noted writers, speakers, and politicians then on the national scene. And though they may not have agreed with his conclusions, and though they may have been critical of his hyperbole in ridiculing the vice-president's argument about the extraordinary properties of water, it would have been difficult for them to fault his writing and analytical abilities or his grasp and handling of historical facts, qualities as to which Mr. Colfax may have suffered by comparison.

Chapter Eighteen

John Taylor and His Pen

Soon after the dust from the Colfax-Taylor debate had settled, the focus of the federal vendetta against the Mormons shifted from the executive to the judiciary. In the spotlight glare of this new drama of duress stood the imposing and intimidating figure of Judge James B. McKean. This son of a Methodist minister, noted for intellectual brilliance and a mercurial temper, had come to Utah with an unprecedented presidential mandate. President Ulysses S. Grant had told him, "Go there and make the laws respected. If your associates do not sustain you, I will choose men who will; and if civil process will not restrain lawlessness, I will support you with the army of the United States." (CHC 5:320.) The mark of this man's faulted vision is that he attempted to gain respect for the law by ignoring or mutilating it.

The new judge soon decided that the chief obstacle to attaining his objective was the lack of original jurisdiction in the federal courts to try criminal cases. He quickly removed this impediment merely by decreeing, without authority or precedent, that when the United States became a party to a suit, his federal court, not the territorial probate court, had jurisdiction. With that roadblock out of the way, in September 1871 Judge McKean promptly impaneled a grand jury from which all Latter-day Saints had been systematically excluded. With the guidance of the Gentile United States district attorney, who was in league with the judge, the jury took aim on the head of the Mormon Church, handing down a sixteen-count indictment against President Brigham Young for "lewdly and lasciviously associating and cohabiting with women, not being married to them." (CHC 5:395.)

President Young's attorneys filed a motion to quash the indictment because the jury was illegally impaneled. For want of a better or more appropriate site, the judge established his chambers over Faust's stable in downtown Salt Lake City. There, in October, he summoned the aging prophet before him to rule on the defense motion and on whether the defendant should be bound over for trial on the indictment. In the audience sat John Taylor, who, out of concern for his friend, and with an editor's feel for a significant event and story, was there to observe and to take notes. The literary output that followed suggests the depth and intensity of the feelings the incident aroused in the apostle.

The drama began with a demonstration of judicial one-upsmanship, obviously intended to impress all in attendance with the dominance of civil over ecclesiastical authority. Even though the judge had summoned President Young to the hearing as he was en route to his winter home in St. George, necessitating a long trip over rough roads—an agonizing ordeal for a seventy-year-old man wracked with rheumatic pains—he kept President Young waiting for the hearing to commence. The reaction of the Prophet to this indignity was impressive, especially to the dour editor of the *Salt Lake Tribune*, who wrote that Brigham's "quietude, and an altogether seeming absence of a spirit chafing with rage at being brought to trial, evidently made a good impression." (CHC 5:397.) But Elder Taylor, who had witnessed and who had been impressed by this demeanor in his leader on numerous occasions over the years, was most impressed, at this time, and was aroused by the words of James B. McKean. In lecturing the defendant and those in the courtroom, including press representatives from outside Utah, the judge made this astonishing statement: "While this case at the bar is called *The People versus Brigham Young*, its other and real title is *Federal Authority versus Polygamic Theocracy*. The government of the United States, founded upon a written Constitution, finds within its jurisdiction another government—claiming to come from God—*imperium in imperio*—whose policy and practice in grave particulars, are at variance with its own. The one government arrests the other in the person of its chief, and arraigns it at his bar. *A system is on trial in the person of Brigham Young*. Let all concerned keep this fact steadily in view; and let that government rule without a rival which shall prove to be in the right." (*Deseret News*, October 18, 1871.)

John Taylor heeded the admonition to keep this fact in view but not for the purpose intended by the judge. He promptly wrote a letter to the editor of the *Deseret News* in order to put the matter into perspective: "He has not so stated it;" John wrote, "but by a very fair inference we must conclude that the United States has, if not openly, covertly . . . proclaimed war against Utah and the 'Mormons.'" (MS 33:722.) To make certain that his readers understood what this meant to the defendant, Brigham Young, he explained that "he has been accused of one thing and is being tried for another, and furthermore he is already prejudged of guilt." (Ibid., p. 724.)

That Elder Taylor was not alone in his condemnation of Mr. McKean, and that the judge was on a collision course, is shown by the comments of non-Mormon reporters who were present: "It is our judiciary and not polygamy that is being tried, and sorely tried," wrote a reporter from the *Washington Capitol*. (Ibid.) And the *Indianapolis Journal* editorialized, "It is unfortunate for the nation that it is in the power of such men as Judge McKean and the deputy district attorneys, Maxwell and Baskin, to precipitate a collision between the federal authorities and the Mormons, in a contest in which the government occupies a false and untenable position. . . . We are convinced that the pending prosecutions are conceived in folly, conducted in violation of law, and with an utter recklessness as to the grave results that must necessarily ensue." (CHC 5:400.)

Elder Taylor added to the media pressure being exerted on Judge McKean by writing a second lengthy letter to the editor of the *Deseret News*. This one was in the nature of a tract on political science, tracing the "immemorial" struggle between the "governors and the governed" and the accommodations made from time to time to bring harmony into this stressful relationship. He lauded the framers of the United States Constitution, declaring them to have been raised up by God and inspired to surround all citizens with safeguards and immunities from government encroachments. And he traced the ultimate authority of government to the voice and will of the people, ending with these provocative statements and questions: "There is said to be a hundred thousand inhabitants in this Territory. How many of them had a voice in the selection of the present Federal officers? Not one." And again: "There is a grand jury here—out of one hundred thousand 'Mormons,' how many of them sat on this grand jury? Not one." (MS 33:741.)

In retrospect, these questions may be seen as a prophetic portent of an event that would nullify Mr. McKean's judicial usurpations and lead to his downfall. Soon after, the United States Supreme Court reversed the judge in a case (Englebrecht) where a jury had been unlawfully drawn. The effect of this decision was to void all criminal proceedings in the territorial courts of Utah during the previous year, including the proceedings involving Brigham Young.

Although Mr. McKean weathered this storm and remained on the bench until his dismissal was forced by the furor stirred up over the Ann Eliza Webb divorce suit against President Young, his effectiveness and influence in fighting the Church was largely destroyed at this time.

When these events made it apparent that the key in fighting Mormon polygamy did not lie with the judiciary or, for that matter, with the executive, the scene shifted again to Congress, where another massive effort was made to shore up the Anti-Bigamy Act of 1862. Several bills seeking to accomplish this were introduced in 1873. But they suffered the same fate as the earlier Cragin, Cullam, and Ashley bills and were all defeated. However, in 1874 the efforts of the anti-Mormon forces in Congress were rewarded with success when the Poland Act passed both houses of Congress and was signed by the president. This bill, which was aimed patently at Utah and the Latter-day Saints, deprived territorial probate courts of the exclusive original jurisdiction in criminal and civil matters they had previously exercised and abolished the offices of territorial marshal and attorney general.

This legislation was passed despite the determined opposition of many influential Latter-day Saints, including Elder John Taylor, who fought it with his powerful and persuasive pen, and Elder George Q. Cannon, who fought it with his eloquence and forensic skills within the halls of Congress, where he served as Utah's representative.

When John became aware of the energetic efforts of Congress in 1873 and 1874 to enact additional legislation to repress the Saints in their religious practices, he reacted in a way that by now had become habitual with him. He took up his pen to write incisive articles designed to influence public opinion and to solidify the views and objectives of the Latter-day Saints.

"As time rolls on, and Congress is again in session," John wrote on March 17, 1874, "it seems necessary, in the common routine of events, that Utah and the 'Mormons' should be dragged into the political arena and receive their usual quantums of knocks, kicks and upheavals, from the battledore of public opinion, aided by the press . . ." (MS 36: 161.) He expressed the sense of frustration and annoyance shared by all Latter-day Saints at the unremitting pressure exerted upon them by the various branches of government:

"We are getting tired of special legislation, packed juries, and mission jurists." (Ibid., p. 162.) And he repeated the charges made in previous articles that these actions represented gross violations of sacred rights presumably protected by constitutional safeguards: "These bills are a direct attack upon the rights, immunities and freedom of the citizens of a whole Territory; guilty or innocent, unheard and uncondemned." (Ibid.) Then in a flight of literary imagery, he condemned the perpetrators of these attacks on the Latter-day Saints and painted a gloomy picture of the possible consequences of their actions: "Has it indeed become necessary to trample under foot every vestige of republican institutions to destroy 'Mormonism?' " he wrote accusingly. "Hateful as it may be to us, can we not find some plausible excuse, some legal outlet, to wreak our vengeance on their devoted heads, without rending into fragments our own institutions, recklessly grasping the pillars of the State, like Sampson, pulling down the house on our doomed foes, though we ourselves perish in the overthrow?" (Ibid.)

Elder Taylor then went on to repeat and embellish the charges he had previously made against government usurpations and encroachments against the Saints, pleaded for a return to principles of justice and moderation, and ended with another verbal volley at the judicial shenanigans of Judge McKean.

In quick succession there followed five other letters to the editors of either the *Deseret News* or the *Salt Lake Herald* that were republished in the *Millennial Star* between March 24, 1874, and May 12, 1874. Building on the foundation laid in the preceding letter or letters, each one of them elaborated on either the injustice or the lack of necessity of the proposed legislation. The first two (*Millennial Star* 36:177-181 and 36:193-197) included a section-by-section analysis of the offending bills, portrayed them as an effort to foment religious persecution, and characterized their sponsors as members of an odious class. "It is right to call things by their proper names," noted the author. "Despotism is not confined alone to emperors or autocrats; there is the despotism of a mob, judicial despotism, military, civil, and religious despotism, manifested by generals, legislatures and religious dictators, as well as a variety of other forms in public and private life." (MS 36:178.)

The third letter, which is worthy of the emulation of the most exacting lawyer, contained a detailed analysis of the work of the territorial probate courts and was designed to show a lack of need for remedial legislation. The author reported that a review of eighty-four civil cases in the Salt Lake County probate court had revealed that the plaintiffs in sixty-two of them were either "non-Mormons" or "dissenters" and that fifty-nine of the cases were decided against "Mormons," thus demonstrating "that the administration of justice in this court is not affected by the religious status of the parties litigant." (MS 36:225.) John proceeded to discuss some of these cases in detail, ending with the comment, "I feel proud to see a record like the above; for while it gives the lie flatly to our defamers, it proves that our courts and juries act justly, and are not influenced by any religious bias." (Ibid., p. 226.)

Having lauded the performance of the territorial probate courts, Elder Taylor condemned the federal district courts, referring to a study of their records as opening the "Black Book." He cited 127 cases involving convictions in the Salt Lake City Police Court for selling liquor without a license that were subsequently discharged by the Third Judicial District court. The lost fines in these cases, according to John's calculations, totalled $12,450. He also referred to other police court criminal convictions that were reversed by the district court and cited a long list of criminal actions pending in the district court that had lain dormant for want of prosecution. These included felony charges of seduction and rape, assault, grand larceny, and murder. "It is a sorry thing to have to present such a record of any of our Federal courts," wrote John, "and individually I would rather it had slept in eternal oblivion; but it is time the veil was lifted, that men may be seen in their true light." (Ibid., p. 229.)

In the fourth letter, Elder Taylor continued with an extensive catalog of items from the "Black Book," chiefly cases where convicted felons had been released from custody on what he considered to be questionable writs of habeus corpus. And the apostle's last letter in this series contained an explanation or defense as to various doctrines of the Church, or incidents involving members of the Church, that had received wide publicity, including blood atonement and the Mountain Meadows massacre.

While John was busy with his pen in Salt Lake City stirring up opposition to the proposed legislation, his nephew George Q. Cannon was busy contesting personally with the sponsors of these bills in the halls of Congress. There Congressman Cannon was the beneficiary of his uncle's exhaustive research into the Utah court records and used the same factual data in his work on capitol hill.

But, as indicated, this doughty pair fought a losing battle, the outcome being the passage of the Poland Act, which removed the last procedural barrier that had protected John and the other Mormon polygamists from an all-out federal legal assault under the 1862 Anti-Bigamy Act.

Chapter Nineteen

Changing the Guard

The three years following the enactment of the Poland bill brought about revolutionary changes in the hierarchy of the Church and in the life and status of John Taylor. For several decades, John had been shown in the Church rosters as being junior to Orson Hyde, Orson Pratt, and Wilford Woodruff. This fact reflected a vague ambiguity that then existed in the minds of the brethren about the criterion to be applied in determining the order of seniority in that quorum. At first, shortly after the latter-day organization of the Twelve in 1835, its members were listed in the order in which they were ordained and set apart. Not long after, however, this order was changed at the direction of Joseph Smith so as to list the brethren according to age. Thus, the seniority of some of the brethren was based on ordination while the seniority of others in the quorum was based on age.

Joseph Smith's change of policy elevated Brigham Young to the number-three position, junior only to Thomas B. Marsh and David W. Patten. And the intervening apostasy of Elder Marsh and the death of Elder Patten had elevated Brigham Young to the senior position at the martyrdom of Joseph Smith. From this position Elder Young succeeded to the prophetic office.

The confusion created by these two methods of determining seniority is graphically shown by the situation that existed at the beginning of 1875. At that time, Orson Pratt, who was younger than John Taylor, was listed as senior in the quorum to John because Orson had been ordained first. And Wilford Woodruff, who was older than John Taylor, was senior to John even though Elder Woodruff had been ordained after Elder Taylor. This anomalous situation had been discussed intermittently by the brethren over the years. But a resolution had been deferred because of preoccupation with more urgent issues and because the likelihood of a change in the presidency—the situation in which the question of seniority is most vital—seemed remote, given the robust health and comparative youth of Brigham Young.

However, as 1875 dawned, the seventy-three-year-old Lion of the Lord, afflicted with rheumatism and other ailments, had become painfully aware of his mortality and, foreseeing the possibility of an early demise, had decided to unsnarl the tangled issue of seniority among the Twelve. He took the critical step at a meeting held in Sanpete, Utah, in June 1875. At that time, President Young affirmed the concept that seniority in the Twelve is based on the date of induction into the quorum, not on age. And he made this policy apply to all members of the quorum. This automatically gave Elder Taylor precedence over Wilford Woodruff. President Young also declared that John took precedence over both Elders Hyde and Pratt because their seniority was to be measured from dates after Elder Taylor's induction into the Twelve, not from 1835 when they were called as original members of that body. This unprecedented action resulted from a hiatus in the continuity of their service in the quorum. The hiatus occurred with Orson Hyde between May 4, 1839, and June 27, 1839, when his membership in the quorum was in suspension because of an unjustified attack he had made on the Prophet Joseph Smith. Orson Pratt was out of the quorum from August 20, 1842, until January 20, 1843, because of excommunication. With this action, Elder Taylor became the senior member of the Twelve with authority and responsibility to direct its activities, although he was not formally sustained as president of the quorum until 1877.

President Young likely selected Sanpete to make the announcement because Elder Hyde had lived and presided in this area for many years, and the prophet would have wanted to explain the reasons for the change in person, thereby softening the blow to the extent possible. And there can be little question that it was a blow to Elder Hyde—and to Elder Pratt—as Elder Hyde had served as president of the Twelve for over two decades, and in that position he stood next to President Young in seniority with the prospect of becoming the president of the Church at Brigham's death.

Elder Taylor later wrote about this extraordinary meeting, explaining, "President Young brought up the subject of seniority, and stated that John Taylor was the man that stood next to him; and that where he was not, John Taylor presided." (John Taylor, *Succession in the Priesthood*, pamphlet, Church Archives, p. 17.)

Thus was effected a revolution in Church organization that would profoundly affect the Church through the generations, as also Elder John Taylor throughout the remaining years of his life. But it was a quiet revolution that hardly made a ripple on the placid surface of the Latter-day Saint hierarchy. These men, taken as a group, approached closely to the ideal of selfless service. Therefore, while there may have been momentary feelings of disappointment or embarrassment, these quickly healed over, and they moved forward under the new order of things with hardly a break in stride.

This unexpected change in John's role was perhaps the most significant and far reaching one of his career, overshadowing in some respects his later elevation to the presidency. It placed him in charge of the second governing body of the Church, responsible for its world-wide proselyting efforts. These efforts included not only the training and supervision of an international missionary force, but also the emigration and settlement of the thousands of converts who were the fruits of Latter-day Saint evangelism. And the role of the Twelve was soon to be magnified with the release of some of its members who had been serving as stake presidents in outlying areas; this release would make them available for the broader service of supervising the Church's global interests.

Thus was Elder Taylor presented with his first major challenge as a Church administrator. It is true he had served briefly and intermittently in other administrative roles—as the presiding elder in Upper Canada and as mission president in France and Germany and in the Eastern United States. But these were relatively minor, localized roles compared with the one he now faced. Moreover, knowing of President Young's frail health and understanding the procedure for succession in the presidency, he took office as the senior member of the Twelve knowing he might soon be elevated to the pinnacle of Latter-day Saint leadership. Given the weight of his present responsibilities and the awesome prospect of what lay ahead, one might have expected a reaction of some nervousness or uncertainty. If these existed, there is no evidence of their presence in either Elder Taylor's words or actions. On the contrary, he moved into this new role as quietly, easily, and confidently as an honored parent takes his accustomed place at the head of the family table.

One need not look far for reasons to explain such a smooth transfer of authority and power. Such a change in most other organizations, whether secular or religious, would have resulted in major, convulsive upheavals. First was the character, the training, and the discipline found among John's hierarchal associates. These were men who had been tried and tested in the crucible of persecution, deprivation, and extraordinary personal exertions. In the process, they had been stripped of egotism and the desire for self aggrandizement and had subordinated personal goals to the interests of the Church. Moreover, they shared the common conviction that the man who had decreed the change was God's earthly spokesman and that therefore the realignment had divine sanction. Equally important were the qualities and experience of the man who now stood at the head of the Twelve and who was only a stride away from the presidency. John Taylor was now a mature sixty-seven, having served with distinction as a member of the Twelve for thirty-seven years. He had shown courage and skill in defending the Church, its doctrines, and its leaders; had been dependable and loyal in times of crisis; and had been prompt and effective in fulfilling all assignments. Underlying these important qualities was a vast reservoir of spirituality that colored and gave life to the outward forms and achievements. This spirituality, which was inherent and evident from his youth, had been fed and nurtured by the ministrations of the Holy Ghost, received as a gift after joining The Church of Jesus Christ of Latter-day Saints, and by his exposure to men and women who had learned to wield the tools of spiritual enlightenment, especially the Prophet Joseph Smith. It was Joseph who had given Elder Taylor an important key to revelatory guidance. "Brother Taylor," the Prophet once said to him, "you watch the impressions of the Spirit of God; you watch the whisperings of that Spirit to you; you carry them out in your life, and it will become a principle of revelation in you, and you will know and understand this Spirit and power." (MS 53:642.) It was this principle, and John Taylor's faithful adherence to it, that had set him apart in an exclusive circle of discipleship. It had been an anchor to his life and the sure guide that had led him unerringly through the maze of human existence, untroubled, serene, secure. And it was this quality in the apostle's many-sided character more than any other that equipped him to fill this new role and ultimately his role as president of the church.

Elder Taylor's apprenticeship as the senior member of the Twelve under the direct tutelage of President Young was to last only a little more than two years. During that time, in addition to supervising the Church's far-flung missionary and emigration enterprises, he helped publicize and support President Young's "United Order of Enoch" and helped reorganize the stakes in which members of the Twelve had presided. He also helped complete and dedicate the St. George Temple, finalize the language of the temple ordinances, and dedicate the temple sites in Manti and Logan.

As Elder Taylor sat in the St. George Temple on April 6, 1877, listening to President Brigham Young deliver what turned out to be the last major address of his distinguished career, he may have detected a note of nostalgic farewell in these words of his leader: "As to my health I feel many times that I could not live an hour longer, but I mean to live just as long as I can. I know not how soon the messenger will call for me, but I calculate to die in the harness." (JD 18:357.)

The messenger made his call on Brother Brigham at 4:00 P.M. on Wednesday, August 29, 1877. In the interval between then and his last address, President Young had kept his pledge to remain at his task and to die in the harness. He had worked hard and consistently through August 23, only six days before his death. At the instant of his passing, John Taylor, in his role as the senior member of the Twelve, automatically became the de facto head of the Church since President Young's death dissolved the First Presidency and relegated those who had served as his counselors to the positions they had occupied before their calls. So, Elders Lorenzo Snow, Brigham Young, Jr., Albert Carrington, and George Q. Cannon, who had served as counselors, took their places of seniority in the Quorum of the Twelve Apostles, all subordinate to Elder Taylor. And Daniel H. Wells and John W. Young, who also had served as counselors to President Young but who had never been inducted into the Twelve, were left without a place among the general authorities, although they were later appointed as counselors to the Quorum of the Twelve.

It was a solemn yet serene assemblage that gathered in the Salt Lake Tabernacle on Sunday, September 2, 1877, to pay tribute to the departed leader. On the stand, which was banked with beautiful late summer flowers, were the general authorities of the Church, presided over by Elder John Taylor. Behind them was the Tabernacle Choir, which had been a vast favorite with the musically inclined prophet and which rendered some of his favorite hymns. Most of the speaking came from others, but Elder Taylor capped the services with brief, moving remarks. He began by contrasting the bitter, tragic circumstances that surrounded Joseph Smith's death with the peace and serenity that accompanied Brigham's passing. Joseph, the speaker pointed out, was "immured in prison, surrounded with enemies who sought his life, and attacked by a ruthless mob, savage and relentless," while Brigham had "lain down to sleep in the midst of a loving and affectionate family and surrounded by faithful and tried friends; with hosts of associates that were loving, sympathetic and interesting, who breathed nothing but condolence, kindness and blessings, and throughout the Territory the people as with one voice offered up their prayers to the Most High in behalf of their suffering, dying President." (*Woman's Exponent* 6:78.) The speaker then lauded the life and works of his departed friend, observing that "his name and fame are known among all people, and a knowledge of these events has spread to the uttermost bounds of the everlasting hills." (Ibid.) He also extended his personal condolences and love to the family of the deceased: "To the family of President Young I say 'God bless you! The God of heaven comfort your hearts! May peace flow unto you, and may you be led in the paths of life, and imitate the example of your departed husband, father and friend.'" (Ibid., p. 79.)

Being acutely aware of the significance of Brigham's passing, both to himself and to the Church, Elder Taylor used the occasion not only to commend the departed and to comfort his family, but also to remind the listeners of the cause to which President Young had devoted his life, and to strengthen his own hand as the new leader and spokesman of that cause: "Although we mourn the loss of our departed friend, a brother and a president," John told the audience, "and although the feelings of our hearts sympathize with his family and friends, yet at the same time there are principles greater and grander than any personal interest, or any individuality associated with these matters. It is a heavenly interest, the building up of Zion, the establishment of the Kingdom of God and the rolling forth of his purposes upon the earth." (Ibid., pp. 78-79.)

Elder Taylor and his brethren in the Twelve had only a month to prepare for the October general conference. Following the precedent established after the death of the Prophet Joseph Smith, it was decided not to reorganize the First Presidency immediately. Instead, the action taken by President Young at Sanpete in 1875 was formalized, and Elder Taylor was sustained by his brethren as the president of the Twelve. He was also sustained as the Church's trustee-in-trust, which gave him control over the financial and other temporal affairs of the Church.

To assist John in directing the international affairs of the Church were his eleven brethren in the Twelve, whose broad experience, abilities, and dedication would lighten his load and ensure that President Young's death would not cause any pause in the work. Next to him in seniority stood Wilford Woodruff, a missionary without peer, who ultimately succeeded Elder Taylor in the presidency and whose faith, spirituality, and diligence had earned the confidence of all. Then came Orson Hyde, whose work as a colonizer and whose missionary labors abroad in Great Britain, Germany, and Jerusalem, where he dedicated the Holy Land for the return of the Jews, had already assured him of a place of honor in Latter-day Saint history. The other Orson—Orson Pratt—filled the number-four spot in the quorum, bringing to that body an extraordinary distinction as a scientist, theologian, analyst, speaker, historian, and author. Charles C. Rich, next in line, who was a prime exemplar of the Mormon pioneering spirit, had provided solid, disciplined leadership in Mt. Pisgah during the exodus and afterward in San Bernardino, California, and the Bear Lake country in Northern Utah. The erect posture and stoical demeanor of this splendid man coincided perfectly with his role as a general in the Nauvoo Legion. Lorenzo Snow, sixth in line, whose celestial countenance and bearing would distinguish him as Church president in later years, was then chiefly known for his creativity and skillful administration in founding the Brigham City cooperatives and as a counselor in the First Presidency. The other Snow—Erastus—followed Lorenzo. It was he who had opened the missionary work in Scandinavia and who, with Elder George A. Smith, had pioneered in Southern Utah's Dixie. Franklin D. Richards, number eight, then noted as a missionary, an administrator, and a leader of the Saints in Ogden, Utah, would later become the president of the Twelve. George Q. Cannon, John Taylor's nephew and a future counselor in the First Presidency came next. This able man was acknowledged and respected as a superior editor, author, businessman, and statesman. Joseph F. Smith, another future president of the Church, as well as a future counselor to three other presidents, was number ten in line. Few of his generation exceeded this distinguished man in eloquence, diligence, and patriarchal concern for his family and the Church. President Young's namesake, Brigham Young, Jr., occupied the eleventh place in the quorum. While he hardly grew to the heroic proportions of his illustrious sire, this apostle was an accomplished man in his own right, achieving recognition as a missionary, a businessman, a counselor in the First Presidency, and later as president of the Twelve. The junior member of the quorum was Elder Albert Carrington, a graduate of Dartmouth College, who was a former editor of the *Deseret News*, a legislator, a mission president, a personal secretary to President Young, and a counselor in the First Presidency. This brilliant man, who was one of President Young's sons-in-law, served as one of the executors of the deceased prophet's will. Regrettably, he later fell into transgression and was excommunicated.

This was the group of men, presided over by John

Taylor, that was sustained as the Quorum of the Twelve Apostles at the general conference that convened in Salt Lake City in the first week of October 1877. This action formalized Elder Taylor's status as the presiding officer of The Church of Jesus Christ of Latter-day Saints and set him on the road toward which his whole life had been trending since those early days in England when the impressionable boy had often heard soft, melodious music, ostensibly performed by angelic and supernatural beings, and had received spiritual impressions that he was to go to America "to preach the gospel."

Chapter Twenty

President of the Twelve

The first sermon of the newly sustained president of the Twelve was delivered on October 6, 1877, to an appreciative audience packed into every seat of the dome-roofed tabernacle on temple square and standing around the periphery of the building on both the main floor and the balcony. Although John Taylor was only a few days short of his sixty-ninth birthday, and although his hair was almost pure white, he presented a striking image of strength and virility both physically and spiritually. At an age when most men of his generation were either in the grave or retired, this man was alert and vigorous and ready to assume the grueling responsibilities of a vibrant, global organization. Shortly before President Taylor walked to the pulpit, the vast audience had unanimously sustained the Twelve as prophets, seers, and revelators and as the governing body of the Church. Obviously intent on teaching a lesson, and differentiating between civil and Church government, the speaker emphasized that the action by the audience was not a vote to "elect" the twelve but rather an approval or affirmation of what had already been accomplished through divine mandate and priesthood authority. Likening this to the practices of ancient Israel, the speaker said, "Then it was the voice of God and the voice of the people; or, in other words, the voice of the people assenting to the voice of God." (JD 19:120.) But though President Taylor and his brethren did not look to the people as the source of their authority and power, he was quick to recognize their desire and need for public endorsement. "Unless we had the sanction of the people," he said, "we would be unwilling to assume them [the responsibilities of the apostleship], and, were it not that these things are plainly laid down in the law of God, we would not have accepted the situation that we find ourselves placed in today." (Ibid.) After expressing appreciation for the support of the Saints and after commending President Young for his years of inspired leadership, John called upon Elder George Q. Cannon to read excerpts from a letter dated March 20, 1839, and written by the Prophet Joseph Smith from Liberty Jail. (See D&C 121.)

The sentiments of this letter, being repeated as they were during the first address President Taylor delivered after officially assuming the principal leadership of the Church, seem to represent the keystone of President John Taylor's administration. He gave special emphasis to the reason why many are called but few are chosen—because they fail to learn "that the rights of the priesthood are inseparably connected with the powers of heaven, and that the powers of heaven cannot be controlled nor handled only upon the principles of righteousness." (D&C 121:36.) The restatement of this basic concept placed President Taylor's administration on the most solid foundation possible. It was an announcement that his administration would be rooted in heavenly influences and that his earthly stewardship would be ruled by righteous principles.

Another significant aspect of President Taylor's keynote address was his use of Elder George Q. Cannon to read these excerpts, something he could as easily have done himself. Viewing it with hindsight, this seems to have been a signal to the Church that Elder Cannon, one of the fruits of John's missionary labors and a nephew by marriage, would be the right hand of his administration. This pair was bound together not only by family ties and the proselyter-convert relationship, but by common interests and competence in editing, writing, statesmanship, and, above all, spiritual sensitivity.

The lengthy talk President Taylor delivered the next day did not carry the philosophical tone of his keynote, and it could be accurately described as a review of his administrative agenda. First on the list was an audit "of the accounts of the Trustee-in-Trust," a matter any person assuming executive responsibilities would want to have clarified at the outset of his administration. Because of restrictions the 1862 Anti-Bigamy Act had placed on the property the Church could hold, it was a common practice thereafter for Brigham Young and other leaders to acquire property in their own names, the equitable interest of which belonged to the Church. So when the Lion of the Lord passed away, there was extensive intermingling of his own assets and the assets of the Church. Because of this, Elder Taylor was aware of the potential for conflict between the Church and the deceased prophet's heirs. He therefore moved promptly, proposing that Elders Wilford Woodruff, Erastus Snow, and Joseph F. Smith of the Twelve serve as the audit committee. In this capacity, they would work closely with the three executors of President Young's will, apostles George Q. Cannon, Brigham Young, Jr., and Albert Carrington, in ironing out the complex problems this intermingling had created, problems compounded by the crude or careless accounting procedures used by some of the prophet's bookkeepers.

Elder Taylor then opened up a question the general authorities had been reluctant to broach for obvious reasons: the need for some remuneration to the brethren whose church duties prevented them from devoting any significant time to their private affairs. "My proposition," said the speaker, "and I know it will meet with the hearty response of the brethren generally, is that they have a reasonable recompense for their services." This proposition was unanimously approved, and Elder Taylor as the trustee-in-trust was authorized to "arrange" the matter. (JD 19:122.)

The speaker then turned to subjects of more substantive importance, addressing himself first to priesthood organization and responsibility. In this he commended President Young for steps he had taken in the twilight of his administration to perfect the structure of quorum, stake, and ward units and to train and to motivate their leaders: "As was remarked this morning," said President Taylor, "the Church never since the day of its organization was so perfectly organized as it is to-day." He made it plain that calls to serve were intended to yoke leaders with heavy responsibility, not to cloak them with honor and distinction: "It is expected that these Presidents of Stakes be full of the Holy Ghost and the power of God," Elder Taylor told his audience. "It is necessary also that the High Councils and the Bishops act in the same way, together with the High Priests, Seventies, Elders, and all those of the Aaronic Priesthood, and that all operate together in the fear of God, for his eye is over you, and he expects you to work righteousness and purge the church from iniquity, and teach the people correct principles and lead them in the paths of life. This is what God requires at your hands." (Ibid., pp. 124-25.) The speaker then reviewed the accomplishments and aims of the Church in the construction and operation of temples, in the conduct of missionary work, and in pursuing the goals of the United Order which had been so sedulously promoted by Brigham Young.

Apparently recognizing that the heavy work agenda he had cataloged for the Church might intimidate or discourage some, John, aware of the past responsiveness of the Saints to trial and tribulation, put the matter to them in a way that was hard to resist: "Some of our brethren feel sometimes that these things draw heavily upon them," he began. "Of course they do; and God expects to try us, to see what we are made of, and see whether the right ring of metal is in us or not, and whether we are prepared to stand up to the rack and walk forth in the name of Israel's God." (Ibid., p. 128.)

This talk, and particularly the last quoted statement in

it, in a sense marks a watershed in the leadership career of John Taylor. It marks a significant transition from the intellectual-spiritual leadership that had characterized most of the apostle's earlier ministry to the more practical, work-a-day duties necessary to keep the Church running smoothly. Indeed, if one were to read the last quotation without knowing its author, he might well attribute it to Brigham Young rather than John Taylor. The talk reflects more than anything else the apparent sense of immediacy and urgency that dominated the thinking of one called to such a position of high administrative responsibility. There was then no time or any apparent inclination to dwell on broad theological or philosophical themes. There were too many things of a current and urgent nature calling for his attention to allow the luxury of a leisurely survey of the past or a too-detailed scan of the future.

The situation that faced Elder Taylor in 1877 when he assumed the leadership of the Church was not unlike the one that confronted Moses as he led the children of Israel toward the Promised Land when the daily manna and the constant need to watch the shadow by day and the pillar by night completely absorbed his attention and claimed his energies. Ordinarily the pattern of almost frenetic activity that confronts a newly called leader will moderate with time as procedures are formalized and as experience in carrying the burden enlarges the capacity to cope. Then the leader has more opportunity to survey the future and to chart a clear course harmonious with the past and calculated to fill the present and future needs of his followers.

Regrettably, John Taylor was never allowed such a respite from the heavy burdens of his prophetic office. During the decade of his leadership, he moved from crisis to crisis, ending with the several depressing years on the underground when he attempted to administer the affairs of the Church and to motivate the Saints while in hiding and while moving surreptitiously from place to place.

But these dark scenes seem to have been blessedly withheld from President Taylor's view as he commenced his service as the third chief leader of The Church of Jesus Christ of Latter-day Saints. It was doubtless something of a cultural shock for a man of his literary tastes and skills to trade his pen and editor's eyeshade for the executive chair and the reins of authority and influence that were transferred to his hands as the leading Latter-day Saint. But he quickly adjusted to the new order of things and began to wield the authority of his presidential office with wisdom and a sure hand. While the new leader was immediately confronted with numerous questions and projects vying for his response or attention, he discovered that there were many heads and hands to help him. Aside from the members of the Twelve, who were always ready and willing to assist, he found an experienced staff that was thoroughly acquainted with the policies and procedures of his predecessors and that helped to smooth the transition to a new administration. Included among this group were men of ability and dedication who, except for distinctions they attained in other capacities, were for the most part practically anonymous as far as the general membership of the Church was concerned. The patriarch of this faithful cadre of clerks was William Clayton, who had served as the personal secretary to both Joseph Smith and Brigham Young, and who by this time saw only limited service on the presidential staff. This man was privy to most of the important and confidential happenings in the latter part of Joseph's administration, was a principal historian of the exodus, and was frequently used by President Young in the handling of sensitive matters. It is ironic, in a way, that this man's reputation among later generations of Latter-day Saints traces mainly to his composition of the lyrics for the song of the exodus, "Come, Come Ye Saints."

Also serving as a member of the staff was George Reynolds, who would later receive national attention as the defendant in the famous supreme court case *U.S. v. Reynolds*, in which the high court upheld the constitutionality of the 1862 Anti-Bigamy Act. Among the saints, Elder Reynolds later attained reputation as a member of the First

Council of the Seventy and as the author of several scholarly works, including a complete concordance of the Book of Mormon. George F. Gibbs was the member of the staff who reported most of the general conference talks. In this he was assisted by a number of other reporters, including Rudger Clawson, who was later called as a member of the Twelve and was sustained as a member of the First Presidency, although he was never set apart to that office, as President Lorenzo Snow, who had called him, passed away only a few days after Elder Clawson was sustained. Later, others were called to assist Elder Taylor in a staff capacity, including L. John Nuttall, another fruit of John's proselyting efforts in England, who was a president of the Kanab, Utah, stake and one of the president's sons-in-law.

And in addition to the members of his quorum and staff, the president of the Twelve found numerous others to counsel and assist him in matters beyond his ecclesiastical responsibilities. These were the officers and directors of the several companies in which the Church had an interest and to the boards of which he was elected following President Young's death. So, the new leader soon found himself involved in a wide variety of businesses, wisely counseled by trustworthy Latter-day Saints who devoted themselves full time to their management and who looked to John Taylor only for the special insights and spiritual perceptions he brought to their corporate counsels. Consequently, John soon became intimately acquainted with the operations of Zions Cooperative Mercantile Institution, Zions Savings Bank, the Salt Lake City Railway Company, the Provo Manufacturing Company, and the Deseret Telegraph Company, whose board meetings he regularly attended.

Meanwhile, in his role as the superintendent of district schools, Elder Taylor was deeply immersed in the first few months following President Young's death in preparing a report and recommendations to the territorial legislature. This was completed in time for presentation on February 5, 1878.

During this dizzying round of activities, John, like the skilled juggler who manages to keep many balls in the air with seeming ease, continued with a full schedule of strictly ecclesiastical activities. He held weekly council meetings each Wednesday with the members of his quorum. Ordinarily, these were held in the Endowment House on Temple Square, although occasionally they were held in the First Presidency's office in the annex between the Lion House and Beehive House, or in the Historian's Office, which was in a separate building on South Temple across the street and a little west of the Lion House. In 1879, President Taylor, a man of simple tastes, was finally persuaded to occupy the ornate Gardo House on South Temple across from the street from the Beehive House, and thereafter some of the council meetings of the Twelve were held there.

Under delegations from the Twelve made at these council meetings, John Taylor directed the overall ecclesiastical affairs of the Church as if he were its president. And in his role as the trustee-in-trust, he directed its temporal affairs. The matters he handled were as varied and as extensive in scope as was the Church membership. In a sense, he was at once legislator, executive, and judge for an international church whose membership then numbered approximately one hundred fifty thousand. He donned his legislative hat when policies and procedures were adopted, usually in consultation with the Twelve. The implementation of these policies and procedures led him into his executive realm. And he put on his judicial robes as he decided appeals made from judgments of high council courts or directly from members.

Being relatively unacquainted with legalisms and legal procedures and, in fact, being somewhat antagonistic toward them, Elder Taylor brought a refreshing unorthodoxy to his judgmental tasks. A prime example of this quality involved two Latter-day Saint veterans of Nauvoo and the exodus who were at odds and who had refused to submit to the counsel of their local leaders. Being personally acquainted with them, John had agreed to hear and to try to resolve their grievances. After the pair had entered his office and were comfortably seated, John said that with their approval he would like to sing one of the songs of Zion to them. They agreed, of course, whereupon the host proceeded to sing a familiar Mormon hymn in his melodious baritone voice. We might logically infer that these listeners were not a littled awed by this rendition, coming from the head of the Church, who, they would not have failed to recall, had similarly serenaded the Prophet Joseph Smith during his last hours in the Carthage jail. Any awe they experienced no doubt would have turned to amazement at what followed. The arbiter turned singer told them he never heard one hymn but that he wanted to hear another, whereupon, with their approval, he sang song number two. Then, telling his audience he understood there was luck in odd numbers, he sang a third hymn before they could protest or approve. And, finally, Elder Taylor ended his impromptu recital by singing a fourth hymn, assuring his dumbfounded visitors that if they would indulge him just once more, he would then consider their case. At the end, the erstwhile enemies, touched by the Spirit, were melted to tears and, standing to thank their host, shook hands and left without having said anything about the dispute that had brought them to his office. (See *Improvement Era*, May 1919, pp. 634-35.)

Such skillful handling of sensitive and potentially explosive situations became a chief characteristic of President John Taylor's administration. Numerous examples could be cited, but two will suffice to illustrate his adroit executive touch. The first involved a controversial stake president who seemed to have lost the support of his constituents and whose release had been strongly recommended by several apostles. To the dismay of the Twelve, instead of approving a reorganization, their leader directed two of the brethren to go to the next stake conference and to compose the differences between the stake president and his followers. Obedient to this instruction, the assigned pair called a meeting of the stake president's main detractors on arriving for the conference. There, after listening to their grievances, the senior apostle asked the critics whether the stake president had ever rendered a service for any of them or was responsible for any worthwhile activity in the stake. After a pause, one brother raised a hand, and, being recognized, recited how his leader had given him some hay during a time of great scarcity. Another remembered how he had conferred a much-appreciated blessing on a member of his family during a time of illness. Still another remembered a kindness his leader had shown that almost had been forgotten in the midst of the grievance he now had toward him. And so, around the circle, practically everyone present recalled some good deed or favor their president had performed or shown. And as these recitals continued, a realization settled upon the group of how their pettiness and lack of Christian charity had misled them into an untenable position. The conclusion of the matter was that the antagonisms of these brethren were dissolved into feelings of amity, the stake president was sustained with good feeling, and the two apostles returned triumphantly to report the happy outcome. On hearing their report, Elder Taylor commended the brethren and then surprised them by directing that they return in six months to reorganize the stake presidency, which, he explained, was a necessity that could now be accommodated without injury or embarrassment to anyone.

The other incident illustrating John Taylor's wisdom and tact as an executive occurred when he and Joseph F. Smith went to Tooele to install twenty-year-old Heber J. Grant as the stake president. At lunch following the morning session of conference where the sustaining occurred, Elder Joseph F. Smith questioned why Heber had failed to bear testimony in his acceptance speech. The answer of the young man that this omission was occasioned by his lack of a testimony prompted the questioner to say to President Taylor that he did not feel that anyone who lacked a testimony should serve as a stake president and to suggest that they ought to undo at the afternoon session of the conference what they had done that morning. After Brother Grant had endorsed this suggestion, in the course of which he recalled he had not sought the appointment, President Taylor intervened in a kindly way to say with a chuckle that Heber had a testimony; he just didn't know it yet!

So, with poise, aplomb, and persistence, John Taylor went about the mammoth task of administering the affairs of the Church. He was not only concerned about the broad philosophical and practical problems facing an international organization and its leaders, but he also interested himself in the concerns of those who played roles out of the glare of public attention and notoriety. Therefore, he quietly upgraded the allowances of his staff as he publicly arranged to upgrade the living allowances of the general authorities. Similarly, he took an interest in the economic status and working conditions of other employees of the Church and of Church-owned or Church-controlled companies. This aspect of John's leadership style is shown in his regular practice of going to Temple Square, where many artisans were at work on the sacred building, and to the tithing office, where many workers were busy receiving and distributing in-kind contributions. There he observed operations and commended and encouraged supervisors and workers alike. And occasionally he would call together the workers on the temple—stone masons, blacksmiths, carpenters, stonecutters, teamsters, and others—and tell them of the importance of their work, identifying it as a priesthood function and equating it with the more traditional priestly functions like proselyting and ordinance work. One can see in this unusual interest in and support of artisan skills the influence of John Taylor's early training and employment as a wood turner and cabinet maker and, inferentially, the influence of the Savior's occupation as a carpenter.

Meanwhile, President Taylor continued with the customary round of strictly ecclesiastical duties he had performed since his call to the Twelve. He regularly attended and spoke at Church gatherings, including sacrament meetings, stake conferences, and funerals. On January 26, 1878, for instance, he attended and spoke at funeral services for his brother James, who was about the last personal reminder of his early years in far-off England. These assignments were interspersed with frequent individual counseling sessions with brethren at headquarters and from the field.

On February 28, 1878, the President called together the Quorum of the Twelve, the stake presidents in the area, the Presiding Bishopric, and a few other leaders to discuss matters of organization and policy. He repeated and elaborated on the instructions given at the previous general conference, laying special emphasis on the responsibility of the stake presidents to lead out in their respective areas. It was an obvious move to delegate responsibility and to decentralize control and initiative.

Among the most important of his ecclesiastical duties during the interim when John Taylor led the Church as the president of the Twelve was the laying of the cornerstones of the Logan (August 3, 1878) and Manti (April 14, 1879) temples. In remarks delivered at Manti, he indulged his interest in history and the use of analogy: "Napolean," he began, "on a certain occasion told his army when in Egypt that there were forty generations looking down on them. But the heavenly hosts are looking down on us. The priesthood which has administered in the various generations and under the various dispensations from the commencement of the world have their eyes upon us." (*Deseret News*, April 15, 1879.)

Events of this kind were a welcome respite to President Taylor from the crowded routine of administrative chores and from the drumbeat of still another anti-Mormon crusade whose beginning almost coincided with the death of Brigham Young. As usual, the main objectives were the destruction of polygamy and the dissolution of the Church. The specifics of this new assault, once it had gained momentum, were elaborated in the *Boston Watchman*, a paper controlled by the Baptist Church. In an editorial published September 5, 1878, the *Watchman* proposed a four-pronged attack: To prevent Utah's statehood until polygamy was abandoned; to repeal the law granting suffrage to Utah women; to disfranchise all living in polygamous relationships; and to "rescue" the public schools from the control of the Mormons.

Within two months after the *Watchman* published this blueprint, there commenced a drama in Salt Lake City that was played on the stage of the national press and that focused microscopic attention on the Latter-day Saints and polygamy. On October 25, 1878, John H. Miles was arrested for alleged violation of the 1862 Anti-Bigamy Act, based upon charges made by his wife, Carrie Owens, who accused her husband of also being married to Emily Spencer. During the lengthy legal maneuverings involving this case, which spanned almost three years and finally ended up in the United States Supreme Court, the public was treated regularly to a rich diet of lurid stories and titillating gossip and speculation about the Church and polygamy. Indeed, as it progressed, the suit itself was swallowed up in the larger issue of Mormonism and afforded a national platform from which enemies of the Church renewed or increased attacks on the Saints.

In the course of these proceedings, President Taylor and other Church leaders were subpoenaed to testify about events connected with the alleged plural marriage performed in the Endowment House on Temple Square. President Taylor was called to testify on October 29. In deference, the court remained standing while he was interrogated about an alleged visit the defendant had made to his office. Considering John's minimal previous experience as a witness in court, he handled himself with apparent ease and self-confidence, parrying nebulous or devious questions with requests for clarification or with discursive, noncommittal answers. The prosecutor, in an attempt to establish that President Taylor had seen the defendant on Thursday of the preceding week, asked, "Did you see him about that time?" The witness, seemingly convinced that his questioner was playing a cat-and-mouse game with him, responded in kind, "If you will explain the extent of your meaning of the word *about* then I may be able to answer." When the lawyer failed to define his term, Elder Taylor continued, "I don't think I could tell precisely when I saw him, perhaps a week or ten days before last Thursday, I don't remember." Willing to divulge what the law required him to divulge under oath, the witness was unwilling to go any further, and, on the advice of counsel, he refused to testify about the content of a conversation he had had with the defendant on the grounds it was privileged communication between an ecclesiastical leader and one of his flock. (See *Deseret News,* October 21, 1878.)

Although John Taylor left no appraisal of the incident, it is logical to infer that his questioning on the witness stand gave him a greater empathy for his predecessors, Joseph Smith and Brigham Young, who, during their tenure as the head of the Church, had been repeatedly grilled and badgered by determined, resourceful, and antagonistic lawyers bent on their humiliation if not their destruction. And the incident may have given the witness an insight into the dark days that lay ahead as he and his people found themselves caught up in the entangling coils of the law. This much we know, that President Taylor was concerned enough about the John Miles case and its implications that he ordered the Endowment House temporarily closed in an attempt to minimize the exposure to public view of the sacred contents and purposes of the building through coercive legal process.

Since he was the one who was accused of performing the marriage, Daniel H. Wells, a former counselor in the First Presidency and, at the time, a counselor to the Twelve, was the chief witness among the Church leaders who were summoned to testify. Indicative of the scope of the attack and the objectives of the prosecution was the statement of one prosecutor who boasted he would reveal to the world through the witnesses the details of the ordinances performed in the Endowment House. In an alleged attempt to identify the polygamous wife, the prosecutor asked Elder Wells specific questions about the ceremonial garments worn there. These the witness declined to answer because, he explained, to do so would violate sacred religious obligations he had assumed. When Elder Wells persisted in his refusal to answer, he was held in contempt of court, fined a hundred dollars, and sentenced to the penitentiary for two days.

The consequences of this action could hardly have been foreseen by the prosecutors who fomented it and the judge who ordered it. With a nod from President Taylor and his associates in the Twelve, a gigantic demonstration was organized to celebrate "General" Wells's release from prison. The word was spread up and down the Wasatch Front to assemble in Salt Lake City on the scheduled day. Demonstrating typical Mormon efficiency and enthusiasm, trains rolled into the city, loaded with Church and civic leaders from Utah and Juab counties in the south and Davis, Weber, Box Elder, Cache, and Bear Lake counties in the north. Stake presidents, bishops, and high councilors joined with mayors and city council members and other leaders, men and women alike, to show their support of the prisoner and their outrage at the court that had sentenced him. Accompanying the demonstrators were several bands whose lively music added a holiday air to the scene.

President Taylor led a large delegation from the city that met Elder Wells and a small party that accompanied him about halfway between the prison and Temple Square. Riding in a handsome barouche, John, on meeting his friend, whom he had known intimately since the Nauvoo days when, before joining the Church, the released prisoner had been known affectionately as "Squire" Wells, stopped to extend greetings and a welcome back to the society of the Saints. As the members of both groups gathered around, and after the customary interchange of pleasantries, President Taylor stood in his barouche to make a formal statement to the released prisoner. There being a *Deseret News* reporter present, as there usually was when the head of the Church made a public appearance, President Taylor would have been aware that his words would reach not only those within the sound of his voice, but also the vast audience, both within and outside the territory, reached by the news media. So the remarks, seemingly off-the-cuff to those present, were undoubtedly made with careful deliberation of the effect they would have upon all friends and foes wherever they might be at that moment. He began with an innocuous word of welcome and greeting, expressing the confidence, the respect, and the honor in which General Wells was held by the people. With this expected banality out of the way, the speaker moved to the substance of his remarks. While disclaiming any intent or effort to interfere with the functions of the courts, he left no doubt about the low opinion he had of them: "We have come, General Wells," said the speaker, "to wipe away a stain sought to be placed upon you by the bigoted, unreflecting and thoughtless." Having tossed that bouquet of weeds to the prosecutors and the judge who had railroaded Squire Wells into prison, the speaker uttered a sentence that is regarded as the crux of this historic address and that held such portent for the future: "We have come," he said "to exhibit to you our esteem and to show you that whilst you are true to your friends, your principles, your country and your God, that your friends are equally true to you." (*Deseret News*, May 14, 1879.) The full impact of this statement, embodying relationships between Latter-day Saints, their country, and their religion as well as the idea of personal integrity would be revealed soon in another confrontation between the United States and the Mormons.

A perceptive observer would have detected the depth of Mormon feelings toward the issues involved in the Miles case, and Daniel Wells's imprisonment by noting what transpired during the day John Taylor welcomed the released prisoner. Through prearrangement, General Wells joined President Taylor in his barouche, where also were seated Feramorz Little, Salt Lake City's mayor; Angus M. Cannon, president of the Salt Lake Stake; and Edward

Hunter, the presiding bishop. It was not happenstance that in the carriage, which was seen and applauded by thousands as it was pulled toward the Tabernacle by a handsome team of four spirited white horses, was represented visually, in the persons of its occupants, the highest local officers of the Church and the territory, the highest ecclesiastical and temporal officers of the international church and the man who symbolized all Latter-day Saints caught in the vise of a deadly contest between church and state.

As the barouche carrying these dignitaries clattered onto Main Street, followed by a procession of horse-drawn carriages and mounted horsemen, there was exposed to view an extraordinary scene. Lining the street for several blocks were thousands of spectators who had come to see and to applaud the procession. That this gathering was not a spontaneous outpouring but rather was a deliberately planned pageant was shown by the presence of children from the city's Sunday Schools, seated or standing en masse, waving banners. Also present in groups were representatives of priesthood quorums, the Relief Society, and the improvement associations. Seen here and there were knots of converts, dressed in the attire of their native countries, among them stolid Germans and rosy-cheeked Scandinavians. The spectators who could not see the procession adequately from ground level sought vantage points higher up on balconies, in office or store windows, or even on rooftops. Ripples and then waves of applause greeted President Taylor's party, ebbing and flowing as his carriage approached, passed, then receded from points along the course of the procession until the dignitaries reached Temple Square, where they entered the Tabernacle. The building was packed to capacity and decorated with colorful banners and streamers that bore mottoes expressing the deepest feelings of the Latter-day Saints about the issues that Elder Wells's imprisonment had raised. "Prisons are made for thieves, vagabonds, and lawbreakers, not for honorable men," proclaimed one banner. "When used for such purposes, we honor the prisoner more than the persecutors." Another one announced, "Honor to the man who is true to his religion and his God, and who cannot be overawed by judicial tyrants." And still another spoke accusingly, "We honor the law and its just administration, but we despise petty tyrants." (CHC 5:549.)

Differentiating further between the government itself and those who administered its affairs, numerous American flags festooned the balcony and the walls of the Tabernacle or fluttered from the hands of members of the audience. And during the proceedings, emphasis was given to the idea when patriotic numbers were played by the seven bands crowded into the building or were sung by the choir, these numbers being interspersed with favorite Latter-day Saint hymns.

The talks delivered on this occasion merely elaborated on the themes sounded by President Taylor when he first greeted General Wells, or suggested by the mottoes on the banners and streamers that decorated the building. The overall message this well-orchestrated pageantry was intended to convey was obvious, as was the audience for whom the show had been staged. The message, aimed at territorial and national officialdom, denounced oppressive laws and their unfair administration while affirming the principles of earthly governance by laws, not men, and the subservience of man-made law to divine law.

It is assumed an event that occurred several months before Squire Wells's release from prison was the primary reason why President Taylor chose this time and place to make such a theatrical statement about polygamy and the conflict between ecclesiastical and civil law. It was on January 6, 1879, that the United States Supreme Court rendered its decision in *U.S. v. Reynolds*, which upheld the constitutionality of the 1862 Anti-Bigamy Act. One important result of that decision to the Latter-day Saints was to erode away their main legal justification for continuing to ignore the law over the intervening years. It was their contention that the law was unconstitutional and that it was therefore not binding upon them. So for seventeen years the Saints had squared their commitment to the twelfth article of faith, which enjoins obedience to law, with a deliberate noncompliance with this particular law on the ground that it was void because it abridged their constitutional right to freedom of religion. But with one flourish of the pen, the Supreme Court swept away that argument. The Saints now stood exposed to the stark reality of violating a law declared to be binding upon them by the final legal arbiter in the land.

As the setting sun marks the end of a day, so the *Reynolds* decision marked the end of the first phase of the federal government's mighty battle with the Mormons over polygamy. To some, it also marked the adoption by John Taylor and his followers of the anarchic concept of civil disobedience eloquently advocated by Henry David Thoreau and Leo Tolstoy, both of whom were contemporaries of the Mormon leader. As will be seen, however, the views of these famous men and those of President John Taylor have only a cosmetic similarity.

Chapter Twenty-One

Prophetic Ministry Begins

The year 1880 stands out in John Taylor's life as the one in which he was sustained as the third prophet and president of the Church. As with his predecessor, Brigham Young, this signal event followed three years of service in leading the Church as the president of the Twelve. The formal act of sustaining took place at the October general conference when the assembled Saints unanimously showed support of their new leader with uplifted hands. In a sense, this action was anticlimactic as President Taylor had been serving as the president in fact in the period since the death of Brigham Young. Yet the pageantry of the official ceremony of investiture was such as to arouse the interest and imagination of the Saints as well as the nonmember community.

It took place in the Salt Lake Tabernacle on October 10 in a special solemn assembly held in connection with the general conference. Officers and members of the various priesthood quorums, both Melchizidek and Aaronic, were seated on the main floor of the building in designated areas while representatives of the general membership occupied the balcony. There were preliminary votes by the various grades of priesthood, followed by a vote en masse when all in attendance stood to show visible approval and support. As happened when Elder Taylor was sustained as the president of the Twelve three years before, it was emphasized that those present were not "electing" the new president but were merely ratifying and approving previous actions of divine investiture.

The formal act of sustaining was preceded in the morning session by a scholarly address on the forms and order of the priesthood delivered by the bearded, white-haired apostle Orson Pratt. Carrying the weight of his years with dignity, this benign saint, who, but for the action of President Brigham Young taken five years before, would have played the role in this drama John Taylor then played, manifested in his bearing, his attitude, and his words the dominant spirit that pervaded these proceedings. That was the spirit of unity, illustrated by these concluding remarks that affirmed the structural integrity of the Church and lauded the work of the new president: "I rejoice that the time has again come," spoke the seasoned apostle, "when our Quorums in the Church of God will be completed as given in the Doctrine and Covenants. . . . There never has been a time, from the commencement of the history of the Church of Jesus Christ of Latter-day Saints when the organization has been so complete as during the last two or three years." (JD 22:38.)

In remarks delivered following his sustaining, President Taylor returned the compliment: "And now let me refer with pride to my brethren of the Twelve here," he began. After describing the smooth, strifeless way in which the Twelve had relinquished administrative control to the newly formed First Presidency, he added admiringly, "I very much question whether you could find the same personal exhibition of disinterested motives and self-abnegation, and the like readiness to renounce place and position in deference to principle, among the same number of men in any other place." (Ibid., p. 40.)

This show of unity among the highest councils of the Church was mirrored in the attitudes that existed in the lower echelons as well. It is true that over the years there had been pockets of dissension among the general membership, caused mainly by rejection of polygamy or dissatisfaction with the economic or political policies of the Mormon hierarchy. This had resulted in some attrition in membership as dissidents like the so-called Godbeites had become disaffected and were excommunicated. Far from weakening the Church, the exit of these dissidents in reality strengthened it by eliminating a negative, discordant element from its councils and by generating a greater internal unity as the remaining Saints banded together to defend against attacks from without. The process was not unlike the pruning by a husbandman who trims his vineyard to foster and promote future growth.

This sense of unity was greatly intensified during 1880 by the celebration of a Jubilee, marking the fiftieth anniversary of the organization of the Church. Imitating the example of the leaders of ancient Israel, President Taylor sought to relieve the debtors and the oppressed among the Saints of some of their burdens. The Church forgave half the indebtedness owing to the Perpetual Emigration Fund, amounting to $802,000. For some of the Saints who lacked the means to pay anything, this meant they were forgiven their entire indebtedness, while the debtors who had means were expected to repay the full amount owing. In like manner, one-half of the tithing indebtedness shown on the books of the Presiding Bishop was forgiven. Also, cattle and sheep were donated to the poor to replenish their herds, which had been decimated by the drought and later the harsh winter of 1897. Moreover, the Relief Society sisters, who had prudently stored grain during years of plenty, donated much of their stores to the needy. And as a means of extending this example throughout the Church, President Taylor urged members who were well-to-do to be lenient with their debtors and to excuse their indebtedness as far as it was feasible to do so.

Seen in retrospect, the sense of unity and commitment generated by the Miles case and the Church's Jubilee celebration represented a deliberate attempt by President Taylor to steel the Latter-day Saints against the storms of persecution that he foresaw ahead.

The storm clouds threatening the Saints centered around polygamy, of course, the problem with which John and his brethren had been grappling for decades but which, since the decision in the Reynolds case, had suddenly become fraught with complexities that seemed to defy resolution. At the foundation of the problem, as President Taylor appraised it, was the head-on collision between a civil mandate, the 1862 act, and a religious imperative, the revelation on plural marriage. In an address delivered a few months before the reorganization of the First Presidency, he had agonized in public over this perplexing issue. "Now, then," he told an audience in the Assembly Hall, "the United States pass a law that a man shall not marry wives according to the order that God has revealed. Now it is a fact that we should like to obey the laws of the United States, if we could do it." Then, giving emphasis to that assertion, he added, "If they could only tell us how to get out of the dilemma they have placed us in we should be very much obliged to them, we really should like to get out of it." (JD 21:70.)

As the speaker developed this theme, it was apparent where his primary loyalty would lie in any unavoidable confrontation between the law and his religious commitments. It was equally clear, however, that in any such confrontation, he would not advocate the cause of civil disobedience advocated by Thoreau and Tolstoy. "Let us be sincere worshippers of God and believers in him and in his law," he admonished the audience. "But," he then asked, "do we propose to govern, interfere with, or rebel against the Government of the United States?" His answer to this rhetorical question was positive and unequivocal: "No, we do not. That is not the programme." (Ibid., p. 71.)

In view of a commitment President Taylor later elicited from the audience, signified by the uplifted hand, "to abide by the laws of God," it is relevant to inquire into the "programme" President John Taylor would follow in attempting to compose this seemingly irreconcilable conflict between the power of the state and the compulsions of religious commitment.

In no single instance did President Taylor define precisely what this program entailed. However, viewing his presidential ministry as a whole provides an indication of its various elements. First, he argued that principles of equity should override the harsh and rigid application of the law that all too many of the enemies of the Church insisted upon. Steeped as he was in the history of his native England, John Taylor would have been aware that the growth of the principles of equity alongside the common law provided a necessary escape valve that prevented the iron-clad technicalities of the law from blowing the system apart. Therefore, he argued that in applying the law to the Saints the extenuating circumstances be taken into account—the "special" purpose of the 1862 legislation; its retroactive application to Saints who had entered into polygamy before its passage; its infringement of sacred religious teachings; and its destructive effect upon Mormon society.

Second, in seeking an equitable resolution of the problem, he sought not only to intellectually convince those administering the laws, but to bring spiritual influences to bear upon them. "We ought to pray for these people," he told the Saints,"for those that are in authority, that they may be led in the right way, that they may be preserved from evil, that they may administer the government in righteousness, and that they may pursue a course that will receive the approbation of heaven." (JD 21:69.)

Third, while President Taylor did not propose to rebel openly against the United States, neither did he intend to lend assistance in its callous enforcement of laws, considered by the Saints to be unjust, inequitable, and unconstitutional. So he counseled the Saints caught in the toils of the law to assert their rights to all the immunities and protections available to them and to refuse to cooperate with or to assist federal investigators and prosecutors where such refusal did not violate the law. In modern parlance, the Mormons, led by John Taylor, undertook a massive program of "footdragging" against the federal officials intent on applying the law with pharisaical exactness.

Fourth, in some rare cases where John felt the circumstances justified it, he asserted the preeminence of God's mandate over civil law by authorizing polygamous sealings in the Endowment House on Temple Square.

Toward the end of his ministry, President Taylor took the final initiative in his struggle with the might of the federal bureaucracy. He fled to the underground. From there he administered the affairs of the Church from a succession of "safe" houses, immune from the application of the 1862 legislation and the more repressive Edmunds Act passed by Congress in 1882. Related to this flight to the underground was the flight of the Saints from the United States to neighboring Mexico and Canada, where they sought refuge from the harsh strictures of the anti-Mormon legislation.

This five-act drama, compressed here into a few short sentences, was to be staged over the seven years of John Taylor's presidential ministry. It was to be played against the backdrop of continued growth of the Church at home and abroad; of increased internal cohesion of the Church hierarchy; of mounting pressures in family relationships; of deteriorating public relations with nonmembers; and of a frightening increase of enmity toward the Church by the hard core Mormon-haters.

Chapter Twenty-Two

The Storm Intensifies

While the Gardo House had been designated as President Taylor's official residence in April 1879, he delayed occupying it until December 1881, over a year after he had been sustained as president of the Church. John's reticence in moving his families from the modest dwellings along Taylor Row, where they had lived for years, to this palatial residence was rooted in a personal bias against ostentation and in consideration of policy and public perceptions. Although a man of patrician tastes and bearing, John Taylor had always lived in modest circumstances and had shunned any effort at showy display. Moreover, because most Mormons were still barely living on the sunshine side of poverty, it was felt that any mark of luxury would alienate those faithful Saints who were the backbone of the Church. It took his associates, particularly his first counselor, George Q. Cannon, many months to overcome these deep-seated prejudices against occupying the mansion, often called Amelia's Palace after one of Brigham Young's wives for whom it was reportedly built.

Considerations of security, convenience, and the status of the president of the Church urged upon him by his associates finally overcame John's reluctance, and the move of the prophet and his families into their lovely and spacious new home was accomplished in time to celebrate Christmas. A few days later, on January 2, 1882, the Taylors hosted a public reception when streams of well-wishers, both Mormon and Gentile, called to pay their respects, to view the impressive interior appointments of the new dwelling, and to sample the ample refreshments.

During the four-hour reception, the president and his family were serenaded intermittently and in turn by Croxall's Band, by Professor C. J. Thomas's orchestra, and by the Tabernacle Choir, which rendered, among others, the anthem "And it shall come to pass in the last days." One can hardly resist the speculation that as the full-throated Mormon vocalists sang this classic number to their president, he recalled the prophecy of his old friend Heber C. Kimball, who, in the days of John Taylor's poverty, predicted that one day he would occupy the most elegant home in the Salt Lake Valley.

While President Taylor's occupancy of the Gardo House was a joyous occasion, it was celebrated against the backdrop of another barrage of criticism leveled against the Latter-day Saints. The storm clouds these attacks generated were especially ominous, as they portended another effort to put more teeth into the 1862 Anti-Bigamy Act.

In nearby Ogden, the Methodists held a conference in the early part of the year where the Mormons and polygamy were the chief topics of conversation. Inflammatory speeches were delivered in which polygamy was characterized as a foul system of licentiousness practiced in the name of religion and where it was demanded that it be stamped out. Similar meetings were held elsewhere in the United States, including one at Farwell Hall in Chicago, where former vice-president Schyler Colfax added his influence to a demand for more restrictive legislation aimed specifically at the Latter-day Saints.

These efforts fueled increased agitation and activity in Congress, which responded on March 14, 1882, by passing the Edmunds Act, which was signed eight days later by United States President Chester A. Arthur. This punitive legislation, admittedly aimed at the Mormons, broadened the 1862 act by defining polygamous living as "unlawful cohabitation." In addition to providing criminal sanctions for violation of the law—fines and imprisonment—it excluded from jury service those engaged in polygamy and those who merely believed it was proper for a man to have more than one wife. It also vacated all registration and election offices and transferred their duties to a board of five commissioners to be appointed by the president with the advice and consent of the Senate.

The effect of this bill was to place the elective process in the hands of the avowed enemies of the Church, thereby ensuring the election of anti-Mormon judges, and to remove all faithful Latter-day Saints from juries, who would decide the guilt or innocence of those charged with violations of the Morrill or Edmunds acts.

The fifty-second annual conference of the Church convened in the Salt Lake Tabernacle less than two weeks after the Edmunds Act was signed by President Arthur. The leaders of the Church had been aware that this legislation would probably pass, but until it actually became law they had withheld public comment. That silence was broken by President Taylor on the second day of the conference, a day that was ushered in by a blustering spring snowstorm of the kind Mormons have come to expect at their general conferences. Again revealing his aptitude for analogy, President Taylor, in referring to the recent passage of the hated Edmunds Act, said in a jocular way, "Let us treat it the same as we did this morning in coming through the snow-storm—put up our coat collars (suiting the action to the word) and wait till the storm subsides. After the storm comes sunshine. While the storm lasts it is useless to reason with the world; when it subsides we can talk to them." (BHR, p. 360.)

At the afternoon session, the prophet took up this theme again, adding that in fact the storm was already "raging," that it had been for some time, and "that it would be well for us to keep up our coat collars and protect ourselves as best we could until the storm passed over." (Ibid.) The prophet then repeated counsel given at the previous general conference that the Saints pay all their debts "so that they might not be in bondage to anyone."

A week later, President Taylor delivered a two-hour sermon, which for its scope, its accuracy, and its purity of language is hardly equaled by any other of his public utterances. In it he traced the path of the restoration of the gospel, defined its basic principles, and explained the administration of the Church through priesthood authority. He then alluded to the numerous misrepresentations and untruths that had been circulated about the alleged ignorance and depravity of the Latter-day Saints and, as a means of showing their falsity, the president called on his secretary, L. John Nuttall, to read excerpts from the 1870 census report, the figures from the 1880 report not then being available. By way of explanation, it was noted that comparisons would be made in certain categories of statistics between Utah and "cultural" Massachusetts and between Utah and the District of Columbia, "which has the enlightening presence of the American Congress to add to its advantages, and is under its direct government." These statistics revealed that in terms of school attendance, literacy, and the availability of printed materials and church facilities, Utah was far in advance of the other two jurisdictions. And we can imagine the mock chagrin with which it was reported that there were three categories in which Utah was outshone: paupers (Massachusetts, 9 to 1; District of Columbia, 4 to 1); convicts (Massachusetts, 4 to 1; District of Columbia 3 to 1); and insane and idiotic (Massachusetts, 4½ to 1; District of Columbia, 7 to 1). With obvious relish and satisfaction, President John Taylor said, after Elder Nuttall had finished reading and had taken his seat, "We are ready, as I said before, to compare notes with them or the people of this or any nation at any time." (JD 23:60.)

Following this half-comical, half-serious interlude, President Taylor proceeded to analyze and criticize the Edmunds bill. In the process, he revealed the implacable quality of his own resolve and his abiding faith in the eventual triumph of the Saints through the blessings of God: "As American citizens," he assured his listeners, "we shall contend for all our liberties, rights and immunities, guaranteed to us by the Constitution; . . . we shall contend inch by inch for our freedom and rights." (Ibid., p. 61.) And again, "As a people or community, we can abide our time; . . . there is nothing of which you have been spoiled by oppressive acts or mobocratic rule, but that you will again possess, or your children after you." Then, moving from the general to the specific, the speaker added, "Your rights in Ohio, your rights in Jackson, Clay, Caldwell and Davis counties in Missouri, will yet be restored to you. Your possessions, of which you have been fraudulently despoiled in Missouri and Illinois, you will again possess, and that without force, or fraud or violence." The prophet then put this in a context that had become habitual with him and that reveals his deep spirituality and his faith in the power and purposes of God. "The Lord," said he, "has a way of His own in regulating such matters." (Ibid., pp. 61, 62.) At the conclusion of this sermon, after he had castigated the enemies of the Church and had canvassed several other subjects, President Taylor reverted to this spiritual theme, uttering words that at once calmed and fired his followers: "Be calm and quiet," he admonished them; "all is well in Zion. You need not be under any fears about anything that may transpire, as though some strange thing had happened. We have met such things before; we can meet them again. God has delivered us before. He will deliver us again, if we put our trust in Him and remain true to the covenants we have made with Him. Our trust is in God. You have heard me say before, Hosanna, the Lord God Omnipotent reigneth; and if this congregation feels as I do we will join together in the same acclaim. Follow me." President Taylor then repeated and was followed by the congregation, "Hosanna! Hosanna! Hosanna! to God and the Lamb, for ever and ever worlds without end, Amen, Amen and Amen." (Ibid., p. 68.)

President Taylor's young and able second counselor, Joseph F. Smith, spoke to the general conference on the same day, lending emphasis to many of the themes discussed by the prophet—the conflicts between ecclesiastical and civil law, and the persecutions, the faith, and the destiny of the Latter-day Saints. (Ibid., pp. 69-76.) But the voice of his first counselor, George Q. Cannon, was silent. At the time, John's influential and accomplished nephew, on whom he relied so heavily, was fighting for his political life in the nation's capital. Elected to Congress in the early 1870s as Utah's representative, Elder Cannon had been a powerful and effective spokesman for the Latter-day Saints over the intervening years and, through his skill and diplomacy, had ameliorated many of the harsh feelings and attitudes toward his people. But after the constitutionality of the 1862 anti-bigamy act was upheld in the *Reynolds Case,* the mind of official Washington began to turn against President Cannon, an acknowledged polygamist. This change in attitude culminated in a formal challenge to his right to be seated in Congress, a challenge whose success was assured by section eight of the Edmunds Act, which made it unlawful for a polygamist to hold office in any territory or under the United States. The final debate on the challenge began in Washington, D.C., nine days after President Taylor delivered his memorable "inch by inch" sermon in the Salt Lake Tabernacle. Apparently buoyed up by the bold and optimistic words of his leader and by his own stubborn will and self-confidence, the beleaguered congressman sought and obtained permission to speak during the debate, whose unfavorable outcome was never in doubt.

All of his colleagues were in their seats, and the galleries were crowded, when the lonely Mormon apostle stood in the well of the house chamber to deliver his valedictory speech. Elder Cannon had prepared himself well for the occasion, emotionally, intellectually, and spiritually. He was calm and deliberate, and he spoke clearly and easily without any trace of pique or outrage. It was a performance his mentor, John Taylor, would have lauded. Indeed, it was a performance that could doubtless be ascribed in large part to the president of the Church, whose example of courage and poise under fire had been a source of inspiration to George Q. Cannon who, through the years, had sought to emulate his distinguished uncle.

The placid image Elder Cannon projected on this occasion belied the biting, almost incendiary import of the sentiments he expressed, sentiments that had often been flung to a hostile world from John Taylor's pulpit in the Salt Lake Tabernacle. He began by casting his accusers in the role of those who condemned and crucified the Savior. "I am comforted, Mr. Speaker, by one reflection," he began quietly. "That Christianity which has been so much vaunted upon this floor, and which has been held up in contradistinction to that system which many of my constituents believe in, was itself a persecuted sect, and its founder was crucified between two thieves." Before his listeners had fully digested the implications of this verbal bombshell, wrapped in such a smooth, seemingly innocuous casement, the speaker calmly condemned his colleagues. "There has been no end of false statements made on this floor," he said disarmingly, "concerning the people with [whom] I am connected. But while this flood of false statements has been pouring over the country, concerning the people of Utah, scarcely a voice has been heard in their defense." For an hour, the speaker attempted to fill that void, defending his people eloquently and denouncing the illogical, narrow-minded, and, to him, illegal and unconstitutional foundation of the Morrill and Edmunds acts.

While the apostle's presentation was articulate and convincing, moving some of his listeners to tears, it had no effect on the outcome of the ouster motion, and by a resounding voice vote he was deprived of his congressional seat.

Elder Cannon's departure from Washington to take his place at President Taylor's right hand marked a critical turn in the uneven relationships between the Latter-day Saints and the federal government. In a sense, it symbolized a final severance of the tenuous cords that had bound the two together, cutting the Mormons loose from the last vestiges of national concern and protection and leaving them adrift on an uncharted sea, exposed to a mounting storm of government-endorsed prosecution and persecution.

It seems anomalous in a way that while these events were moving to fruition, foreshadowing the long night of the underground with all its turmoil and tragedy, John Taylor was quietly at work, during the occasional hours he could steal away from his arduous presidential tasks, writing his most enduring literary piece. Significantly, it was devoid of any reference to the stressful circumstances that confronted the author during its composition. Instead of dwelling on the transitory events that passed in view daily, he lifted himself above the confusion and chaos to focus on the object of his worship and loyalty, Jesus Christ. Moreover, he did not dwell on the Savior's many fine qualities nor on the details of his birth and ministry. Rather, he emphasized the central purpose of the Son's earthly mission, the redemption of all mankind. And this suggested the title for his masterwork, *The Mediation and Atonement*.

It was doubtless a marvelous therapy for the prophet to retreat from the strife and turmoil that marked most of his days as the president of the Church, and from the constant pressure of administrative tasks, to the quiet and seclusion of his study, whose walls were lined with the books and manuscripts he loved. There, John seemed to be in the element most congenial to his nature, where, using words and ideas as his basic tools, and tempered by the fire of spiritual illumination, he created a literary work as fitly framed as were the cabinets he had crafted as a master turner in his early manhood.

Taut, concise, and well documented, this book obviously was put together with the intent that it would stand the test of time as well as to serve an important current need. After almost forty years of pioneering following the martyrdom of the Prophet Joseph Smith, during which the main thrust of Latter-day leadership was to tame the wilderness, there was an obvious need to reemphasize the doctrinal foundations of the Church. And, what better place to start on such an internal rennaissance than a literary work about the central figure of Mormon worship involving the key element of his ministry and written by the earthly head of his church? Moreover, the book was no doubt intended for the Gentile audience as well, whose perceptions of Mormonism and its foundation and objectives had been clouded and distorted by an overemphasis on polygamy, on the temporal involvements of the Church and its members, and on other peripheral matters.

The Mediation and Atonement bears the clear imprint of a powerful intellect trained in the classical tradition and oriented toward advocacy. It begins with an explanation of the relationship between the Father and the Son. This is followed by a survey of the scriptures foretelling Christ's birth and ministry. Then comes a detailed description of the history of animal sacrifice as practiced by the ancients and an analysis of the relationship between that practice and the Savior's atoning sacrifice. This leads to discussion of the need for an infinite atonement and the relevance and interplay of the eternal concepts of agency, justice, and mercy. Afterward, the author surveys the idea of man's perfectibility through resurrection and exaltation, the latter gained by obedience to all the laws and commandments of God. In his concluding chapter, President Taylor capsulizes the effect of the atonement and of the promulgation and observance of the principles of the gospel: "Through its principles," he wrote, "and by its power the Kingdom of God will be established, righteousness spread, evil overcome, and Satan be vanquished; by it Zion and the New Jerusalem will be built up, Enoch and his city be received, the work of the Millennium be done, the renovation of the earth accomplished, and all God's glorious [purposes] will be fulfilled, until the vision becomes a reality which Daniel saw and wrote." (*The Mediation and Atonement* [Salt Lake City: Deseret News Co., 1882], p. 188.)

Added to the main work was an appendix advancing the idea that the widespread use of animal or human sacrifice among pagan societies represents a perversion of the true concept of Christ's atonement, which was announced by inspired prophets through the centuries prior to his birth: "The fact is clearly proved," Elder Taylor declared, "instead of Christianity deriving its existence and facts from the ideas and practices of heathen mythologists, and from various false systems that had been introduced by apostacy, unrecognized pretensions and fraud, that these very systems themselves were obtained from the true Priesthood, and founded on the teachings from the earliest ages to the advent of our Lord and Savior Jesus Christ." (Ibid., pp. 204, 205.)

Following George Q. Cannon's return to Salt Lake City after losing his seat in Congress, President Taylor, having both counselors permanently at his side, seemingly became conscious of the need to fill the two vacancies in the Twelve as the general authorities faced the uncertainties created by the Edmunds Act. The most recent vacancy in the Twelve had been created on October 3, 1881, when Orson Pratt had passed away. The death of this seasoned leader had been deeply felt by President Taylor, not only because of the steadying and strengthening role he played in the Twelve, but because of personal reasons that could not be adequately explained to anyone who had not shared the apostolic yoke as long as this pair had done. For over forty years, in good times and in bad, these two friends had met intermittently with members of their quorum to report their activities, to plan for the future, and to be refreshed and motivated by each other and by the spiritual influences that attended their councils. And they shared a special bond through common interests in history, philosophy, and writing. Moreover, Elder Pratt's death marked the end of an era, he being the last of the men called in 1835 to comprise the first Quorum of the Twelve in modern times. With Orson's passing, therefore, John Taylor stood not only as the president of the Church, but as the man who had held the apostolic authority longer than any man then alive.

It was expected by many that the vacancies in the Twelve would be filled at the October general conference. However, the conference came and went without even so much as a comment that the vacancies existed. Several days later, however, on October 13, 1882, President Taylor received a revelation that declared, "Let my servants George Teasdale and Heber J. Grant be appointed to fill the vacancies in the Twelve, that you may be fully organized and prepared for the labors devolving upon you." This revelation also admonished the leaders to perfect the other quorums and organizations of the Church; enjoined all members to humility, repentance, and diligence; and promised peace, prosperity, and safety to the Saints for their obedience.

President Taylor discovered that these two men added to the apostolic ranks had little in common, except that both were tall and spare, both were serving as stake presidents at the time of their calls—Elder Teasdale in Nephi and Elder Grant in Tooele—and both were dedicated to the cause of Mormonism. Aside from these similarities, they were a study in contrasts—Elder Teasdale was fifty, while Elder Grant was twenty-five; The older man spoke with a delightful accent denoting his English roots, while the younger man's speech betrayed his western American origins; and the first was almost professorial in the pulpit, while the speech of the latter was aggressive and fiery.

Perhaps recalling the concerns expressed by his counselor Joseph F. Smith when Elder Grant was sustained as stake president only two years before, and wishing to add prophetic support to the youngest apostle, President Taylor went to Heber's stake at Grantsville only sixteen days after the revelation and delivered a major address. He gave emphasis to the need for God's blessings and commented on the role of adversity in the lives of the Saints: "We have learned many things through suffering," he told his audience. "We call it suffering; I call it a school of experience. I never did bother my head much about these things; I do not to-day. What are these things for? Why is it that good men should be tried?" The speaker went on to answer these rhetorical questions by explaining that adverse influences ultimately serve a good purpose by leading men to place their "dependence upon God, and trust in Him and to observe his laws and keep his commandments." (JD 23:336.)

It was this forward-looking, buoyant aspect of President Taylor's personality, coupled with his dignified, patrician bearing and outlook and the Saints' own faith and convictions that caused them to follow him without hesitation into the trying and stressful circumstances of the underground years. B. H. Roberts, one of President Taylor's most ardent disciples, once wrote that the prophet's example would "breathe into other lives the inspiration of a kindred courage, and lead them to emulate its valor."

Another excerpt from President Taylor's Grantsville speech pointed to the ultimate security he and his followers sought to shield them from the storms of adversity that beat upon them: "Our desires must be for God and his righteousness," he told his listeners, "until we shall exclaim with one of old: O God, search me, and try me, and if there be any way of wickedness in me, bid it depart." Elaborating on this theme, he added, "It is for us, as fathers and mothers, to go before the Lord in all humility and call upon him that his peace may be in our hearts; and wherein we may have done wrong, confess that wrong and repair it as far as we possibly can; and in this way let every man and woman in Israel begin to set their houses in order, and forever cultivate the spirit of peace, the spirit of union and love." (JD 23:337.) As we shall see, John Taylor not only admonished his followers to cultivate inner peace and strength in the midst of adversity, but he showed them how to do it.

Chapter Twenty-Three

Politics and Priesthood

On October 8, only five days before he received the revelation that filled the vacancies in the Twelve, President Taylor convened a meeting of the First Presidency and the Twelve and all stake presidents to discuss what, on its face, appears to have been a purely political matter. That was to discuss combining their efforts to nominate someone to fill the unexpired congressional term of George Q. Cannon. To John Taylor and his brethren, the issue far transcended political considerations, however, and resolved itself more into the question of whether there would remain in Congress at least one voice to speak in behalf of the Latter-day Saints. There was an urgency to act promptly, as a territorial convention of the People's Party—the political group to which most Latter-day Saints belonged—was scheduled to convene only three days later. At their meeting, the Church leaders unanimously supported John T. Caine, the man who was ultimately nominated and elected. The achievements and experience of this man—a former personal secretary to President Brigham Young, a former assistant to Congressman William H. Hooper, a former managing editor of the *Salt Lake Daily Herald*, and a cofounder and lessee of the Salt Lake Theatre—made him a logical and popular choice. And his long acquaintance and association with all three members of the First Presidency obviously engendered in them a feeling of confidence that John T. Caine would adequately and accurately express the views of his constituents.

This native of the Isle of Man first heard the gospel in 1841 at Peel from the lips of John Taylor. Only twelve years old at the time, he was never to forget the impression conveyed by the dignified and convincing apostle. In 1854, after migrating to America, Elder Caine accompanied a group of missionaries to the Sandwich Islands (Hawaii). The group included sixteen-year-old Joseph F. Smith. And John Caine's Hawaiian experiences and involvement in politics and the newspaper business had brought him into frequent contact with George Q. Cannon.

John T. Caine remained close to President Taylor, often seeking his counsel and keeping him apprised of the stirrings and doings in the nation's capital. But despite that closeness, he was, after President Taylor's death, in the vanguard of those Latter-day Saints who advocated a discontinuance of the practice of polygamy. This is not to imply any sense of duplicity or disloyalty on the part of the congressman, but rather suggests a logical response to the radically altered circumstances that followed in the wake of the Edmunds-Tucker Act, which was passed shortly prior to President Taylor's death. Had John Taylor lived to see the ravages of this legislation upon the Saints and the Church, it is probable that his views would have altered as did those of his brethren and Congressman Caine, and such altered views, inferentially, would have led him to seek divine relief from the dilemma in which the Saints were placed, as did his successor, Wilford Woodruff.

Despite President Taylor's active participation in the political process as revealed in this episode and in his direction of Joseph Smith's presidential campaign, he strongly believed in the separation of church and state. This was confirmed by the mandates of the Articles of Faith and by negative experiences of his youth in a country with a state-sponsored church. To him, therefore, politics and civil government were not ends in themselves but rather were the means to an end that he sought with vigor and consistency. That end was to create the kind of environment in which the Church could flourish, enabling its leaders to expound the doctrines and principles of salvation unimpeded, and its members to live and apply them without hindrance.

It was to this task of preparing and perfecting the Saints that John Taylor had committed himself, especially after the apostolic mantle fell upon him. In the early years of his ministry, his efforts were devoted largely to proselyting, to harvesting converts, and thereby to enlarging the flock. In later years, especially from the time he became the president of the Twelve, his efforts were devoted almost exclusively to the internal affairs of the Church, altering that focus only now and then, as he did in the case of John Caine's nomination, and then only for the purpose of advancing his primary objective. The bias appears from the spate of activities that dominated his schedule in the months following the October 1882 general conference. On the fourteenth, the day after the special revelation was received, President Taylor convened the First Presidency, the Twelve, and the stake presidents again. The revelation was read and instructions were given to perfect stake, ward, and quorum organizations throughout the Church. Three days later, John was involved in sending off a large group of missionaries destined for fields of labor around the world. In the second week of November, he welcomed the last emigrant company of the season, most of which was comprised of converts eager to be assimilated into the main body of the Saints. Six days later, the prophet left with a group of his brethren for Utah, Sanpete, and Juab counties to the south, where numerous meetings were held, including instructional and motivational gatherings at Manti, Pettysville, Mayfield, Fayette, Levan, Nephi, Mona, Santaquin, and Payson. All along this route, the president of the Church elaborated the ideas that had preoccupied his mind of late—the response of the Saints to the new government crusade; the need to perfect stake, ward, and quorum organizations; and the challenge of cultivating inner peace and serenity in the midst of turmoil.

Although these were rural communities, there was little justification for calling them provincial. There was an international flavor about them, assignable to the fact that many of their residents were foreign born and that numerous others had filled missions abroad, bringing back to these remote valleys the language, customs, and cultures of distant lands. Also, the Mormon drive for excellence had inspired community and individual efforts in self improvement and in cultivating latent talents and skills. So most communities boasted a town band that was invariably employed to welcome visitors of high rank. Debating and drama societies were not uncommon, and literary and reading clubs were a spur to many in broadening their appreciation for good literature. Yet few of these Saints were professionals or merchants. Most were farmers, ranchers, or artisans. None of them claimed inherited wealth or royal titles. They came largely from the working and deprived classes of Europe and the eastern United States. But, through the upward reach of Mormon doctrine and practice, they aspired to something better, not only economically, but, more importantly, culturally and spiritually.

These intelligent, hard-working and aspiring people were the fruits of Mormon proselyting and preaching and, in a sense, were the laurel of Latter-day Saint leadership. On this account, John Taylor, who was one of the most conspicuous actors in the development of this distinctive society, was always refreshed and rejuvenated by direct contact with the Latter-day Saints in their home environment as he was during this trip. *Tourism* being an unknown word in the Mormon vocabulary of that day, there were no hotels as such in these small communities, which required that visitors from Salt Lake City be hosted in the homes of the Saints. Invariably, the visitor of highest rank would be assigned to stay in the home of the local bishop or stake president unless his accommodations were deemed inadequate, in which event the owner of the most elaborate dwelling in town would be honored to have the visiting dignitary as his guest. In this way President Taylor and the other brethren who were accustomed to traveling throughout the Mormon communities were regularly exposed to the grass-roots habits and living conditions of their people and thereby were better acquainted with their needs and resources and better able to provide relevant counsel and direction.

Returning home in late November, John took up the reins of his duties at headquarters, which entailed a steady flow of council meetings, board meetings, personal interviews, paperwork, and speaking engagements, these being interspersed with domestic duties, study, and reflection. Twice more before the end of the year, the prophet ventured out of Salt Lake City on special assignments, the first into Davis County for a series of meetings, and the second, a week later, into Cache Valley, where, in addition to the customary preaching services, he inspected the Logan Temple, which was then under construction.

After a brief respite at home to celebrate the holidays with his family—a celebration cut short by the unexpected death of John's good friend Captain W. H. Hooper, a former congressman from Utah and a local banker—the prophet resumed his travels in January, undertaking two out-of-town trips, one to Ogden, to the north, and the other south to Nephi. In both communities, President Taylor installed new stake presidents. Forty-eight-year-old Lewis W. Shurtliff, bishop of the Plain City Ward and local city-county official, was installed as the stake president in Ogden; and twenty-eight-year-old William Paxman, teacher and businessman, was chosen at Nephi. Also at Nephi, President Taylor installed as the bishop of the north ward David Udall, the father of a rising young man, David King Udall, whom President Taylor had previously called to help colonize a struggling Mormon community in Arizona, St. Johns, where he was installed as the town's first bishop and later as the first president of the St. Johns Stake, there becoming the father of a numerous and distinguished progeny.

As was true in the case of George Teasdale and Heber J. Grant, the calls of these two new stake presidents mirrored the diverse qualities and characteristics of the Mormon leaders called during the administration of John Taylor. There was no consistent pattern in terms of age, occupation, or background. While the experience, achievements, character, and personality of a candidate for a Church position were weighed by the prophet, the final decision rested upon the "impression" or "whispering" that came to him, a process that a modern-day personnel director might find somewhat baffling. The test of the effectiveness of this method of recruitment is suggested by the stability of the communities over which these men presided and the positive influences they exerted upon those whom they led.

A pleasant chore for John during January was to preside at the dedication of the then-new Eighteenth Ward chapel in Salt Lake City, located just "up the hill" from the Gardo House near the intersection of Second Avenue and A Street. Presiding in that ward was a promising young bishop and historian, twenty-eight-year-old Orson F. Whitney, a grandson of Heber C. Kimball and first cousin of the twelfth president of the Church, Spencer W. Kimball. Twenty-three years later Bishop Whitney would be called to the apostleship by Joseph F. Smith, then the president of the Church, who helped President Taylor dedicate the chapel.

While the prophet went deliberately about the task of perfecting the stake and ward organizations and instructing and motivating the Saints, the machinery created by the Edmunds Act ground away inexorably toward its goal of crushing the Church and destroying polygamy. The commission created by the act had moved promptly to formulate a test oath, which it required every person to affirm as a condition to either registering or voting. As to a man, it required an affirmation that he had "never" lived simultaneously with more than one woman "in the marriage relation." As to a woman, it required an affirmation that she was not the wife of a polygamist, nor had she ever entered into a relation with a man in violation of the laws of the United States pertaining to polygamy and bigamy.

The obvious effect of this oath was to withhold the vote from all who were then living or who ever had lived in polygamy, while allowing it to everyone else, regardless of the extent to which they may have committed adultery or fornication. Incensed at the duplicity of this action, John had denounced it as a bald, illegal attempt to open the ballot box to the "roué, the libertine, the strumpet and the brothel keeper" while closing it to sober, God-fearing people who were endeavoring to create wholesome homes in which to rear good citizens. To underscore this injustice, President Taylor told of one registrar, the son of a former Salt Lake City Mayor, Feramorz Little, who had to deny his father the right to register even though the father was single because he had once lived in polygamy with two women who were then deceased. The irony of the situation was made complete when, shortly thereafter, he was forced to allow the registration of a notorious madam. (See *North American Review*, January 1884.)

While the administrative provisions of the Edmunds Act governing registration and voting were speedily implemented, its judicial provisions were invoked more slowly due to the elaborate process of gathering evidence and obtaining indictments. By 1884 however, the prosecutors were ready with their first case. The defendant was twenty-seven-year-old Rudger Clawson, a son of Hiram B. Clawson, who had been one of Brigham Young's business agents, and one of whose wives was one of Brigham's daughters.

Five years before, while serving as a missionary in the south, Rudger had gained wide notoriety as the companion of Joseph Standing, who was shot and killed by a mob near Rome, Georgia. Young Clawson had then bared his chest to the mob, which had earlier threatened to kill him too. Whether sickened by the one murder, impressed by the young man's bravery, or fearful of being caught, the mobbers did not shoot again, and Elder Clawson lived to accompany the body of his dead companion home, where he immediately became much in demand as a speaker. It was likely his youth, his prominence, and his connections with leading families in the community that caused the federal prosecutors to settle on Rudger Clawson as the first defendant to be prosecuted under the Edmunds Act.

President Taylor was subpoenaed as a witness, not because he was in possession of any relevant facts, but because of the apparent desire of the government attorneys to heighten the publicity in the case by the appearance of the ranking official of the Church.

The packed jury (from which all Latter-day Saints had been systematically excluded) and the broadened language of the Edmunds Act guaranteed the conviction of the defendant, an exemplary young man who, fourteen years later, would be called to the apostleship. A few days after the conviction, President Taylor addressed a congregation in Ogden, where, still agitated by the injustice meted out to his young friend, he derided the court and the conditions that had made Rudger Clawson's conviction possible. This talk is one of the best examples of John Taylor's extraordinary skill in forceful yet dignified denunciation and satire. He began by sharing with his audience reflections he had had while seated in the courtroom at Elder Clawson's trial. "I could not help thinking as I looked upon the scene," John said, tongue-in-cheek, "that there was no necessity for all this." In mock seriousness he said Rudger need not have lived a moral and exemplary life as he had done, emulating "the ancient worthies whom Jehovah honored by making them His confidants, and revealing unto them the secrets of his divine purposes."; all that would have been necessary for him and his plural wife to have avoided the humiliation of a public trial, he told the audience, would have been to "walk in the way of the world today, unite with our modern Christian civilization, and if passion guide their actions, why call each other husband and wife, why hallow their association by any sacred ceremony—was there any need of such?" Then pulling out all the oratorical stops, President Taylor blistered the enemies of the Church with one of the harshest denunciations he ever uttered: "[Abortion and child neglect are] committed principally by those who go to high-toned churches and fashionable meeting houses in velvets and feathers, in silks and satins, and who with upturned eyes and hypocritical voices, insult the majesty of heaven by drawling out 'Lord have mercy on us, miserable sinners!' Yet they are murderers—murderers of the worst kind . . . whom the vengeance of God awaits." (BHR, p. 375.)

As a half-drawn circle foreshadows the appearance of the completed figure, so did the successful prosecution of the Rudger Clawson case reveal to John Taylor and his brethren what the future held in store for them. Absent some intervening circumstance, it was apparent their future would be marked by indictments, packed juries, biased judges, and, at the end of the road, imprisonment. If the young polygamist Rudger Clawson could not successfully defend against a suit for unlawful cohabitation, how could men almost three times his age, as to whom there was much more incriminating evidence, hope to escape? It was alarming to see the elaborate dragnet the federal officers had devised to ferret out information for use in the impending prosecutions. So-called "spotters" and spies were recruited and paid to monitor and report on the comings and goings of suspected polygamists. Children were accosted in the streets by federal investigators and questioned about the activities of their parents. And later, wives were subpoenaed and subjected to grueling and sometimes indecent and provocative questioning.

It was at this juncture that President Taylor decided on a lengthy trip to the southern settlements. Its purpose was three-fold: to counsel with the brethren in Arizona who were also being harassed by federal prosecutions; to explore the possibility of establishing communities of refuge in

Mexico; and to get away from the mounting pressures in Salt Lake City.

John left the Gardo House early on the morning of January 3, 1885, and was driven west several blocks, past the bishop's storehouse, past the still uncompleted temple, and past the palatial Devereaux Mansion to the imposing red-brick building at the end of Brigham Street that housed the Union Pacific depot. There, by prearrangement, he met his counselor, Joseph F. Smith, and Elders Moses Thatcher and Francis M. Lyman of the Twelve. Muffled in their warm coats to ward off the biting cold of a typical Salt Lake City winter, they waited quietly in the warmth of the depot until the northbound train was ready for boarding when, they walked briskly toward their private car. Inside, the apostles found every appliance of comfort and even luxury that modern railroad travel of the day could provide, including their own private kitchen, a cook, and a porter. President Taylor, who habitually viewed things from a historical perspective, could hardly have failed to contrast the pleasant, comfortable conditions of this trip out of the Salt Lake Valley with the comparatively crude and primitive conditions under which he had first entered it thirty-eight years before. And had he been able to look ahead with clarity thirty days hence, he would have realized that never again would he be able to move about openly in his beloved city without apprehension as he had done that morning. He would have seen, too, that his return home would have a covert, surreptitious aspect about it that would characterize the remainder of his life.

At Ogden, the prophet's private car was transferred to an eastbound Union Pacific train that carried its passengers through the rugged canyons of the Wasatch to the plains of Wyoming (then covered with a heavy blanket of snow) and thence by a spur line to Denver. From there they traveled to Albuquerque, New Mexico, where they transferred to the Santa Fe line, which took them as far as Winslow, Arizona. Debarking at this lonesome outpost, the party entered horse-drawn vehicles, arranged through telegraphic wire, and commenced a tour of the Mormon settlements in the area that had been established several years before on or near the Little Colorado River. Nearby Sunset had been used as a staging area for expeditions into the vast Navajo Indian Reservation to the north. Upstream from Sunset were other struggling Mormon communities: Joseph City, named after the Prophet Joseph Smith; Woodruff, named after Elder Wilford Woodruff; and Hunt, St. Johns, Springerville, Eager, Alpine, and Nutrioso, all of which were part of the Little Colorado or the Eastern Arizona stakes presided over, respectively, by Lot Smith and Jesse N. Smith. Two years later, most of these communities were to be included in the new St. Johns stake, presided over by young David King Udall. At the time of President Taylor's visit, the nucleus of the Eastern Arizona stake lay to the west, centered at Snowflake and other towns on or near a line connecting Holbrook and McNary—Taylor, named after President John Taylor; Heber; Lakeside; Pinetop; and Show Low. During his stay in this area, the prophet held regional meetings, giving the same counsel he had given to the Saints in Utah—to organize fully all priesthood quorums; to keep a low profile; to cultivate their spirituality; and to be vigilant in asserting their constitutional rights.

Leaving this area, President Taylor and his party went south, conferring with the Saints in the Salt River Valley, where Alex F. McDonald presided over the Maricopa stake, and in the Gila Valley, where Christopher Layton presided over the St. Joseph Stake. In these localities, the polygamists had endured the same harassment as their Utah brethren. Many of them had been convicted and sentenced to prison, either in the territorial penitentiary at Yuma or in the Detroit correctional facility. The domestic turmoil this had caused, the bleak prospect of any softening of the government's attitude toward the Mormons, and the close proximity of the border reinforced the prophet's inclination toward obtaining and building up communities of refuge in Mexico. Toward this end, John sent some of the brethren across the border to undertake negotiations with Mexican officials. Young Moses Thatcher, who played a leading role in this undertaking, was one of the most brilliant Mormon leaders of that day. He was adept at negotiation and spoke Spanish fluently, a skill acquired during his long service as the Mexican mission president. And in recognition of his services to the Arizona Saints in helping to negotiate for places of settlement across the border, they named one of their communities in his honor—Thatcher, Arizona.

Having sent these brethren on their diplomatic mission, John decided to venture into Mexico himself in order to become acquainted with the land and to gauge the spirit and temperament of the people. Traveling through some of the most ruggedly beautiful and picturesque country he was ever to see, the prophet visited Guaymas in Sonora, located on the eastern coast of the Gulf of California. On the return trip, he paused in Hermosillo, Sonora's capital, where he paid a courtesy call on Governor Torres, who received him graciously and who indicated unofficially that his people would be welcome in Sonora.

Arriving back in the Gila Valley, President Taylor conferred with his negotiators and on their recommendation authorized the purchase of a tract of land across the border in northern Chihuahua. Located near the Piedras Verdes river on the eastern slope of the Sierra Madre Mountains, this site was later named Juarez after the famous Mexican general. And not long after President Taylor's visit, Saints from Arizona and Utah began to migrate to Chihuahua, establishing a cluster of communities similar in appearance and organization to hundreds of those that had been previously founded by the Mormons in the United States—Colonia Juarez, Colonia Diaz (named after the president of the republic), Colonia Pacheco, and Dublan. And later, other Mormon settlements were established in Sonora—Oaxaco, Morelos, and San Jose.

As John Taylor left the Gila Valley for his circuitous return trip to Salt Lake City, it is doubtful that he foresaw the consequences that would flow from his decision to purchase lands in Mexico, a country in which the Latter-day Saints could live the law of plural marriage free from the legal restraints of the antipolygamy statutes that had been enacted or would be enacted by the United States Congress. During President Taylor's life, the reason justifying these Mexican colonies was that they were places of refuge from the harassments of the United States government. But after the Manifesto, that reason ceased to exist. Then these colonies took on a different meaning to a few members of the Church. To this minority, the Manifesto, announced by Wilford Woodruff, President Taylor's successor, was limited in its geographical application to the United States, whose restrictive laws had made it necessary. Therefore, they reasoned, the Manifesto did not apply in Mexico, whose laws tolerated polygamy, and that being so, it was permissible for Latter-day Saints residing in Mexico to continue to live the law of plural marriage. This interpretation would produce a deep schism in the Church, entangling some Saints, including President Taylor's son and namesake John W. Taylor, Sophia's youngest son, who eventually lost his standing in the Twelve and was excommunicated because of contrary views he held about the effect of the Manifesto.

President Taylor's travel schedule after leaving the Gila Valley settlements clearly reflects the ambivalence he felt about returning to Salt Lake City. He had been advised regularly by wireless dispatches about the conditions at home. Word that the tempo of prosecutions under the Edmunds Act had quickened and rumblings of efforts to indict more of the leading brethren had prompted President Cannon to suggest that the prophet delay his return. Heedful of that counsel, President Taylor took the long way home, traveling via Phoenix to Los Angeles and thence to San Francisco, enjoying, as best he could under the heavy burden of care he carried, the changing scenery from desert to mountain to seaside.

At San Francisco, he was feted by the local leaders, who

had never before had the honor of hosting a president of the Church and who outdid themselves in showing the prophet the sights of this Pacific metropolis in the hours between the meetings the visitor insisted on holding. So long had he been habituated to a nonstop schedule of meetings and counseling sessions that it was difficult for this seasoned warrior, now in his seventy-seventh year, to divert for long his attention from the duties of his apostolic calling. John Taylor did not excel as a tourist.

In apparent recognition of this shortcoming, the Mormon leader decided to return to Salt Lake City after only a few days in San Francisco, despite an urgent message from George Q. Cannon, delivered by a courier, Samuel Hill, that he not return. What concerned the counselor was the fact he had already been arrested and was free on bail, and a warrant had been issued for the arrest of both Presidents Taylor and Smith. Having made the decision to return, John boarded a train destined for Utah and traveled toward home and the last difficult epoch of his life.

Chapter Twenty-Four

The Night of Darkness

There was no fanfare when President Taylor returned to Salt Lake City on Tuesday, January 27, 1885, after having completed a trip of almost five thousand miles. The fear that the federal officials might spring the trap they had laid for him caused the brethren to forego the usual open welcome that customarily had greeted the president on his return from trips out of the city. He was met quietly by two brethren who doubled as security officers, Sam Bateman and Charles Wilcken, and taken to a secret rendezvous with President Cannon and L. John Nuttall. Joseph F. Smith was not present, as at President Taylor's urging he did not return to Salt Lake City but went on to Hawaii from San Francisco, where he was to remain in hiding for an extended period. Joseph F. probably would have been allowed to return with the prophet had it not been that he was in charge of the sensitive Endowment House records, and there was concern that were he arrested, incriminating evidence might be pried from him for use in suits brought under the Edmunds Act. This was of special concern because of the provision of the act that exposed the brethren to criminal action regardless of the time when their plural marriages had been contracted.

In counseling with George Q. Cannon and learning

firsthand of the hazards that faced him, President Taylor decided it was prudent that he go on the underground to avoid arrest and that he thereafter give direction to the Church through intermediaries. Before taking that step, however, he also decided to address the Saints one last time. This farewell sermon was delivered the following Sunday, February 1, when, without prior announcement, President Taylor appeared at a meeting convened in the Salt Lake Tabernacle, which was filled to capacity. With security personnel posted at the entrances to the building to intercept or to warn about the presence of federal officials, the prophet was left free to counsel his people, which he proceeded to do in a leisurely fashion and at great length. (See JD 26:148-57.)

He began by explaining his absence from the city visiting the Saints in the southern colonies. He painted a bleak picture of the harassments to which the members there had been subjected and condemned the insensitive, heavy-handed way in which suits against the Saints were being prosecuted. The speaker was especially critical of the practice of incarcerating some of the convicted polygamists in Detroit (rather than in the territorial prison), where visitations by family and friends were practically impossible. He likened this to the policy followed in despotic Russia of condemning prisoners to Siberia. "I was hardly prepared to-day to suppose that we needed an American Siberia under the form and in the name of liberty and the rights of man," the prophet told his audience. "But this is the fact. We have here in America today an American Siberia in Detroit, to which place, upwards of two thousand miles from their homes, men are banished for a term of years; and what for?" The speaker's answer to this rhetorical question was that the Saints insisted on worshiping God according to the dictates of their conscience and refused to "fall down and worship before the Moloch of an effete Christianity." (Ibid., p. 150.)

President Taylor went on to castigate those who had persecuted the Saints over the years, reaching deep into his rich store of civilized satire to denounce and berate them. He recalled how he had seen his brethren "shot to pieces in cold blood and under the protection of the State Government" in Illinois and alluded to similar acts of brutality and bloodshed against the Saints in Missouri, Georgia, and Tennessee. Then, to dramatize the double standard of justice American officialdom had always applied to the Latter-day Saints, he asked accusingly: "I want to know if any one of you can tell me of any individual that was ever punished according to law for killing a Mormon. Speak it out, if you know it." (Ibid., pp. 154, 155.)

Toward the end of his talk, President Taylor turned to the aspect of the government's new crusade that was most distressing to those caught up in it. This was the eroding effect it had had upon domestic relations. In a litany of woe, the speaker condemned the cankering irritations to which polygamist families were being subjected: "When little children are set in array against their fathers and mothers," the speaker began, "and women and children are badgered before courts, and made to submit, unprotected, to the gibes of libertines and corrupt men; when wives and husbands are pitted against each other and threatened with pains, penalties and imprisonment, if they do not disclose that which among all decent people is considered sacred, and which no man of delicacy, whose sensibilities have not been blunted by low associations, would ever ask; when such a condition of affairs exists, it is no longer a land of liberty, and it is certainly no longer a land of equal rights." With the fabric of human and constitutional rights in such tatters, the speaker saw only one solution: "We must take care of ourselves as best we may," he told his audience, "and avoid being caught in their snares." (Ibid., p. 156.)

The prophet acted promptly on the admonition given in this sermon, the last of his long and distinguished career, and almost immediately disappeared into the underground. He was never again to be seen or heard by a congregation of the Saints. Thereafter, he was merely an unseen presence whose instructions and admonitions were transmitted either in writing or by word of mouth. It was to be a lonely and confining existence for a man who was gregarious by nature and who valued freedom almost more than life itself. Yet even as he faced this last ordeal, which was to use him up physically, President Taylor revealed again the persistent optimism that had characterized his life from its earliest years. Like so many of those who shared his religious convictions, he looked upon adversity as a friend, not an enemy, because to him a world without adversity would have been a joyless world, devoid of a standard for differentiating between happiness and sorrow, good and evil. "Do you feel sorry for your people?" he had asked the audience in his last sermon. "Not at all, not at all," he had answered. "The Lord God has revealed unto us great and eternal principles . . . that we may be able to discern between the good, the virtuous, the upright and the holy; and the impure, the foolish, the vindictive, the corrupt, the lascivious, and those who are trampling under foot the laws and principles of eternal truth." (Ibid., p. 152.)

And, he approached the ordeal with a stoic fatalism reminiscent of the early Christians who faced the terrors of the colosseum with calm resignation. "Some of our young people think that the present proceedings are very remarkable," he told the Saints. "But many of us, grey-headed folks, have seen plenty of such proceedings, and have had many experiences of this kind; they are nothing new to us at all. And did we expect them to get better? We have not so understood it. We are told in the Scriptures, and we have kept teaching it all the while, that 'the wicked would grow worse and worse, deceiving and being deceived.' That is doctrine which I have believed in for the last 50 years and I have had a good deal of testimony and practical confirmation on that point." (Ibid., p. 151.)

So, it was not with a spirit of dejection or depression that President Taylor prepared to live a covert, nomadic life, never appearing in public, seldom with his family, and constantly exposed to the threat of capture, prosecution, and imprisonment. Quite the contrary, he was positive and even a little jubilant that he was privileged to share the mantle of persecution with other Christian soldiers of the past.

The idea of a Christian soldier in a more literal, militant sense found embodiment in the persons of Charles Wilcken (who accompanied President Taylor as he departed early from the meeting in the tabernacle on February 1, 1885) and Samuel Bateman. These were the two faithful bodyguards who were to spend more time with the prophet during the remainder of his life than anyone else. Brother Bateman, a native of Manchester, England, emigrated as a boy with his convert parents and, in 1841 at age nine, he witnessed the laying of the cornerstone of the Nauvoo Temple, where he also heard Joseph Smith preach a powerful, never-to-be-forgotten sermon. That exposure to the prophetic influence was the forerunner of a long career of service to the presidents of the Church. Sam, as he was fondly called by his intimates, served successively as a part-time security guard for presidents Brigham Young, John Taylor, and Wilford Woodruff, alternating that service with numerous other odd jobs at which he was adept—bricklayer, mason, miller, farmer, rancher, tax collector, machinist, and constable. An extroverted man who enjoyed prompting, or calling, for dances, Sam Bateman was a jovial, optimistic companion whom President Taylor admired and whom he relied on heavily.

Sam's associate in his guarding duties was tall, powerfully built, austere Charles Wilcken, a veteran of the Prussian army who had been decorated for bravery with the iron cross and whose bearing, address, and intimidating presence were of themselves a sufficient deterrent to anyone bent on harming the prophet. These men seldom left President Taylor's side during his remaining days spent on the underground, watching over him with almost parental care and serving him in a variety of ways, whether as protector, chauffeur, cook, butler, valet, or confidant.

Aside from his understandable desire to remain free

from legal restraints, there was a more compelling reason why John Taylor used every legal means, albeit devious, to avoid arrest. There were rumors, not without foundation, that the enemies of the Church hoped to incite the Saints to violence by humiliating and imprisoning their leader, thereby justifying a violent and bloody counterattack. This, went the reasoning, would disperse and neutralize the Mormons as a religious or political force. John Taylor had seen enough of government duplicity and doubledealing that this scenario was not beyond belief. Therefore, from the beginning of his underground days, the Mormon leader was determined to avoid detection and arrest. He changed his travel habits so that except in cases of dire emergency, he moved from place to place only under the cover of night. And, following the precedent of his deceased leader, Joseph Smith, set during the years of travail before the martyrdom, he began to use pseudonyms to mask his identity from his persistent pursuers.

Along with these radical changes in his life, which until then had been regular and conservative, came a complete revolution in his daily routine and regimen. No longer was he able to follow a consistent pattern in the timing of his meals and rest. Being a guest in the homes of others, he had to conform with their schedules and habits. Further complications in these matters were added when unplanned and sudden moves were required by the approach or proximity of the hunters. Diet, too, was a difficult problem, as the variety and quality of the meals differed from place to place. Moreover, consistent, healthful exercise was almost an impossibility under such cramped conditions, and recreation and entertainment were practically nonexistent except for good conversation and games of quoits, horseshoes, or checkers. And for one with a literary bent like President Taylor, a major deprivation was the unavailability of his library, his personal papers, and his staff assistants. Adding to all this the separation from his family that life on the underground entailed, one may catch a glimpse of the stresses and anxieties borne by a seventy-seven-year-old prophet as he contested with crafty, determined adversaries. It was these pressures and annoyances that would accelerate the aging process and hasten President Taylor's death.

After leaving the Tabernacle on February 1, 1885, the prophet was whisked off to a place of concealment in a barn behind the tithing office, where he remained until night had fallen. When a careful inspection revealed that the nearby streets were empty, he entered a nondescript carriage and was driven in a roundabout way to his first place of refuge, the home of Samuel Bennion, the bishop of the North Jordan Ward, whose home was near the Church leader's old Taylorsville farm. This kindly, sixty-seven-year-old Saint, whose slight accent still betrayed his North Wales origins, had first heard the gospel preached by John Taylor and Joseph Fielding in 1840 in a rented Liverpool chapel. Baptized two years later, the new convert soon migrated to the United States, leaving behind both his former protestant religion and his former occupation as a baker. In his new home he had, over the years, gravitated to positions of ecclesiastical leadership and to prominence as a farmer, a rancher, and a political leader. As these two native Britons embraced, there lay behind them long, tortuous trails that had often converged, then separated, extending back to their native lands and to their first happenstance meeting forty-five years before. Through the turmoil and shifting scenes of those turbulent years, the one thing that had remained constant was their shared conviction of the truthfulness of the restored gospel, a conviction they would carry to their graves.

Given their long acquaintance, the circumstances under which they had met, and their common loyalty to the Church and its priesthood, it hardly seems necessary to report that President Taylor was treated with regal hospitality in this home, as he was in most homes where he stayed during the underground.

He remained with Bishop Bennion for nine days and then went, successively, to the homes of Bishop Bennion's sister-in-law, which was nearby; of Charles Bagley in Big Cottonwood; and of Peter Hansen in Sugar House. During his first year in hiding, John was housed in eleven other places of refuge. The length of his stay depended on whether the host family had the facilities and the means to accommodate the visitor and his bodyguards, as well as his staff and counselor during their intermittent visits. A factor that originally militated against extended stays in any one place was the constant tension that enshrouded the hunted man and that reached out to infect and sometimes to frighten the other inmates of the house. These feelings were intensified by the cloak-and-dagger atmosphere created by the clandestine methods often used by the visitors in communicating with the outside world—the hoot of an owl or the bark of a dog at night; the call of a bird during the day; coded messages transmitted by the position of clothes hung on a wash line; or some other unorthodox means.

When the circumstances were just right, George Q. Cannon, L. John Nuttall, or other members of the president's staff would make personal visits to the places of refuge, usually at night. There the prophet would be briefed and would handle matters of official or personal concern. On these occasions, the Mormon leader disposed of the usual grist of correspondence and other paperwork and imparted instructions for transmittal to others on the outside. In a letter dated May 19, 1885, to Daniel H. Wells, who was then presiding in Liverpool, England, L. John Nuttall gave this insight into the methods used in administering the affairs of the Church under these difficult circumstances: "There has not been one day from that time [February 1, 1885] to the present but what we have been enabled to attend to the general duties, just as much so as though we had been in the office, with the exception of conversing orally with the brethren and holding public meetings. Our arrangements have been such that nothing has been neglected." In commenting on the condition of the prophet and the other leaders of the Church, Elder Nuttall noted, "The health of the Pr——t has been excellent and his spirits buoyant all the time. . . . I never saw such a spirit of calmness and serenity with the Presidency and Apostles as also among the people. There does not seem any degree of alarm or excitement in any quarter." To negate the idea that all was peace and light in Zion, however, the author added parenthetically, "Yet a great many are harassed and put to many inconveniences." (As quoted in *Messages of the First Presidency* [Salt Lake City: Bookcraft, 1966] 3:2, 4.)

Although he was never arrested and tried as were some of his brethren, it is doubtful that any Latter-day Saint of that period endured as much harassment as did President John Taylor, a conclusion suggested by the frequency with which he found it necessary to change his places of concealment. Yet with all this moving about and with the upset and confusion it necessarily entailed, the prophet continued to give strong leadership and direction to the Church. During his intermittent visits with George Q. Cannon and members of the presidential staff, and in the periods between, he spent much time preparing messages and instructions intended for the guidance of the Saints. These were usually read to Latter-day Saint congregations by members of the Twelve who were not being sought by the federal officials and who, therefore, could move about freely. In some respects, these vicarious sermons, like the classic letters written by the Prophet Joseph Smith from his confinement in the Liberty jail, had more impact than had they been delivered in person. The sense of drama and intrigue surrounding the underground and the feelings of empathy and concern of the Saints toward their leaders kindled an atmosphere of excitement and expectancy when the Saints gathered in general conference.

Such an atmosphere existed in Logan, Utah, as the Saints assembled there in early April 1885 for the fifty-fifth annual general conference of the Church. Logan was selected as the site for the conference because of the stressful conditions that existed in Salt Lake City due to the federal prosecutions in progress there. A secondary reason was the apparent desire of the leaders to afford Church members the opportunity to see and participate in services in the new Logan temple. During May of the previous year, President Taylor had dedicated this sacred building in special services attended by members of the Church from throughout the area. A third reason was to deprive the Gentile merchants in Salt Lake City of the increased business that always accompanied general conference, when thousands of Saints gathered from the surrounding communities. Of the four remaining general conferences held before President Taylor's death, one more was held in Logan, two in Provo, and one in Coalville.

When it was announced at the conference that Elder Heber J. Grant, a new member of the Twelve (and senior only to President Taylor's son John W. in that quorum) would read a message from the First Presidency (see MS 42:290-96) the audience gave rapt attention, as no official statements had been made by the Church's presiding quorum since President Taylor's last public sermon on February 1. After making expressions of gratitude to the Lord for His numerous blessings to the Church and of love for the Saints, the message explained the reasons for the absence of the First Presidency, alluding to the "deadly hostility" of the federal officials, which had produced a "reign of terror" and a consequent flight to the underground, where they expected to remain until there was "a prospect of receiving impartial treatment by the courts and juries." Referring to the prophet specifically, it explained that "he deemed it wise, under the circumstances, to withdraw for awhile to attend to his business in a more private manner. . . . This he has continued to do up to the present, writing, receiving and answering letters, giving counsel and instructions, and devoting himself assiduously to all the duties of his calling, except in delivering public addresses from the stand." It complained about illegal searches of the homes of the First Presidency, especially the home of President Joseph F. Smith, where, presumably, the searchers hoped to find the Endowment House records. In responding to a rhetorical question as to how long the First Presidency would remain in seclusion the message said, "We are as ready today, as ever, to submit our cases to a properly organized court and jury of our peers, to decide upon." There then was discussed an issue that had never before been raised and as to which a satisfactory answer was never provided. Noting that only about 2 percent of the male membership of the Church practiced polygamy, the message observed, "We consider it an act of great injustice to the ninety-eight per cent to be abused and outraged, and have all their business relations disturbed, values of every kind, unsettled, neighborhoods agitated and alarmed, and the property of the people generally jeopardized, because of this 'raid' upon these alleged breakers of the law." After denouncing the hypocrisy of adulterous enemies who persecuted the Mormons because of their chaste efforts to raise God-fearing and law-abiding families, the message ended with this admonition: "We exhort you, therefore, to preserve your bodies and spirits pure, to protect the virtue and honor of your wives and daughters, to live your religion, to deal honestly and honorably with all men, and to maintain inviolate these glorious principles which have been revealed unto you."

At the remaining general conferences held prior to President Taylor's death, similar messages from the First Presidency were read to the Saints. The last of these was presented on April 8, 1887, at the fifty-seventh annual general conference held in Provo, Utah. Being the most comprehensive of all the statements of the First Presidency delivered during President Taylor's underground days, this wide-ranging document covered such diverse subjects as the welfare of the young, amusements, sanitation, the selection of missionaries, secondary schools, and agriculture and tree planting. Most interesting and provocative of all, however, was a section entitled "A period of Transition," which must be read in conjunction with the action of Congress taken a month earlier in the passage of the Edmunds-Tucker Act, whose object was to plug the holes left by the Edmunds Act of 1882 and the Anti-Bigamy Act of 1862. This repressive legislation, which its sponsors intended would sound the death knell of the Mormon Church and polygamy, provided for the disincorporation of the Church as a legal entity, the forfeiture by the Church of all property in excess of $50,000, and the dissolution of the Perpetual Emigrating Fund Company. To strengthen the prosecutorial campaign against polygamists, it also provided for the compulsory attendance of witnesses at trials, decreed the legality of testimony by a wife against her husband, and empowered the president of the United States to appoint county probate judges. Other provisions that diluted Mormon influence or imposed political or legal impediments on Latter-day Saints included the abolition of women's suffrage, a new voting test oath, a provision for redefining voting districts, and abolition of the office of territorial superintendent of schools.

Fully conscious of the destructive effect this legislation would have upon the Church and of the harsh impediments it would lay upon the fulfillment of its ministerial responsibilities, the First Presidency announced to the Latter-day Saints that the Church was passing through a period "of transition, or evolution" such as appeared "to be necessary in the progress and perfecting of all created things." It explained that such periods generally had "their pains, perplexities and sufferings" and that the present was "no exception to the rule." With typical buoyancy, however, it assured the Saints that "out of apparent evil, Providence will bring abundant good, and the lesson which the signs of the times should teach us is one of patience, endurance and calm reliance on the Lord." It concluded with this optimistic forecast: "The result will be that we shall be stronger, wiser, purer, happier, for the experience gained, and the work of the Lord . . . will yet triumph gloriously over all its foes, and the infinite atonement of the Redeemer will accomplish its perfect work. The final victory of the Saints is certain; after the trial comes the reward." ("An Epistle of the First Presidency, *Deseret Evening News*, April 8, 1887, p. 2.)

This statement of the First Presidency, written after the effect of the Edmunds-Tucker Act had been fully appraised, foreshadowed the action taken three years later by President Wilford Woodruff in issuing the Manifesto. The "transition" alluded to logically refers to the terrible days of the underground, the result of which, it was predicted, would be to make the Saints "stronger, wiser, purer, happier."

For President Taylor, the crucible out of which these virtues were to emerge consisted of the restraining tedium of the places of refuge he occupied during the two and a half years of his exile. The instability of his living arrangements during 1885 continued throughout 1886 until late November. Through June he alternated between the homes of S. J. Sudbury, William White and sons, and Alfred Solomon in Salt Lake City, all of whom lived relatively close to the Gardo House. Then through July and August, he moved back and forth between the homes of James Livingston, James Godfrey, Bishop Stuart, and Henry Day in the South Cottonwood, Little Cottonwood, and Draper areas, located in the southern part of the Salt Lake Valley. At 3:00 A.M. on September 5, the prophet was aroused from sleep while at the Henry Day home and was moved hurriedly to the home of George Stringfellow in Draper because of a report, later proven to be false, that federal officers were approaching. He remained in the Stringfellow home only until that night when he was moved back to the home of William White in the Sixteenth Ward. After nine days in that hospitable place, the much-harried prophet was taken north to Davis County, where, except for a few days in early November when he returned to the William White home, he was to spend his remaining days.

The first place in Davis County where President Taylor took refuge was in the home of John W. Woolley in Centerville. A son of Edwin D. Woolley, bishop of the Salt Lake

Thirteenth Ward, fifty-five-year-old John W. was then a member of the Davis Stake high council and years later was ordained a patriarch in that stake. Experienced as a constable, a justice of the peace, a deputy sheriff, a deputy territorial marshal, and a major in the Nauvoo Legion, this hearty, outgoing man not only was a gracious and willing host to the president of the Church, but, because of his background in law enforcement, he also became an important link in the prophet's chain of security.

The Mormon leader was a guest in John W. Woolley's home on three occasions: the first from September 14 to October 10; the second from October 12 to November 3; and the last from November 9 to November 21. The short intervals between these visits were spent in the homes of Orren Randall in Centerville and, as mentioned, back in the home of William White in the Salt Lake Sixteenth Ward.

On November 22, 1886, President John Taylor made the last move in his long odyssey in search of peace and security on the underground. On that day he traveled a few miles north of Centerville to the farmhouse of Thomas F. Roueche located on the flatlands west of the peaceful community of Kaysville. The prophet's host, who had been Kaysville's first mayor, was at the time a selectman of Davis County and a counselor to Bishop Peter Barton in the Kaysville Ward bishopric. A native of North Carolina, this convert of over thirty years reflected a heritage of southern hospitality when he insisted that his famous guest and entourage occupy the main farmhouse while he and his family occupy the nearby cabin, which had been their only home during the years the land was being homesteaded.

As the farmhouse had four large rooms on the main floor and three upstairs, there was ample space for both President Taylor and President Cannon and for their clerical and security staffs. These accommodations made it possible for the prophet, for the first time since he had disappeared into the underground over twenty months before, to establish the office of the First Presidency on a basis that held out the prospect of permanency and efficiency. This arrangement obviated the need for the clerical staff to shuttle back and forth to and from the main headquarters in Salt Lake City and the constantly shifting places of refuge. Moreover, the location of the farmhouse on the flatlands, with comparatively few trees to the east, afforded a clear view of the Bluff Road, the main carriageway connecting Salt Lake City and Ogden, and the Utah Central Railroad to the east. Thus, a good set of binoculars during the day and a guard posted at the intersection of the carriageway and the farm's access road at night with instructions to fire warning shots if necessary provided adequate security against the approach of unwanted visitors. Setting up their books, papers, and files and with a daily courier service to and from Salt Lake City, the First Presidency and staff were able to operate the machinery of Church administration at the Roueche farmhouse with almost as much efficiency as in the pre-underground days.

Although President Taylor now had a secure and comfortable place of refuge with the necessary tools and staff to perform the duties of his prophetic office, there were missing two ingredients essential to a happy and contented life. The first was the freedom to come and go as he pleased. While the Roueche farm had the advantage of remoteness and a location that made it possible to detect strangers at a distance, yet the last factor also made it possible for an enemy with powerful binoculars to see and identify anyone walking about the property in the daylight. So, movement outside during the day was necessarily restricted to the use of the quoit court, which had been laid out on the west side of the house toward the nearby marshes of the lake and in such a position as to be shielded by trees from the view of anyone traveling on the Bluff Road to the north or the south. The occasional carriage rides the prophet enjoyed were always taken at dusk and in disguise, and then only after a careful scouring of the neighborhood by his security guards gave some assurance that Sam Gilson, the persistent federal marshal, and his aides were not skulking nearby. And, of course, one of President Taylor's greatest joys, worshipping with the Saints in their chapels, was out of the question, leaving him only the alternative of holding home services with his staff, which he did regularly.

President Taylor's greatest aggravation, however, while he lived in the Roueche farmhouse, indeed, during the entire period of his exile, was the separation from his family. Throughout the other trials of his life as a Latter-day Saint, except, of course, when he was abroad on Church assignments, John had been blessed with the companionship and counsel of the women to whom he had been sealed for eternity. These were women of wit, intelligence, and vivacity who not only were good mothers and homemakers, but who were good intellectual and spiritual companions as well, interested in and conversant with both Church and public affairs. While at this time Leonora and Harriet had passed on, his other five faithful wives, Elizabeth, Jane, Mary Ann, Sophia, and Margaret, were still alive and made periodic visits to see their husband and, in the intervals between, prepared and sent to him by his couriers items of clothing lovingly prepared with their own hands or culinary delicacies they knew would please him.

The loving concern shown toward him by his wives was amply reciprocated by the prophet. In addition to their periodic visits, he communicated with them regularly through letters that revealed with clarity the feelings of love and affection he had for them. On November 1, 1886, the occasion of his last earthly birthday, he addressed a letter to his family, who, he correctly assumed, would be gathered in the Gardo House for a vicarious celebration. He buoyed them up with the restatement of a philosophy of his with which all members of the family were well acquainted: "Some people suppose that persecution and trials are afflictions," he wrote reflectively. "But sometimes, and generally, if we are doing the will of the Lord and keeping His commandments, they may be truly said to be blessings in disguise." (As quoted in BHR, pp. 391, 392.) This led him to expound at some length on the law of compensation and to reaffirm his conviction that life's battles and complexities are intended by a loving heavenly Parent to assist in honing character and to help one to prepare for celestial glory. "I must fight, if I would reign," he quoted approvingly from John Wesley. "Increase my courage, Lord; I'll bear the toil, endure the pain, supported by thy word." He expressed pleasure to have learned "that the disposition and feeling of both wives and children is to fear God, to work righteousness, and to yield obedience to His laws." In commenting on his wives, he mentioned "the terrible affliction that has overtaken Aunt Sophia." By way of comfort to this faithful companion who had borne eight of his children, including John W. of the Twelve, he added, "I would here remark that in speaking of these strokes, I have been making careful inquiry about them since her sad affliction, and learned that it is no uncommon thing for people to be healed of this kind of disease. A lady of about her age that I conversed with quite recently, said she had had two strokes of that kind, and she is now quite well, hale and hearty." (As quoted in BHR pp. 391-99.)

As it turned out, Sophia did not fare as well as did the woman about whom her husband reported. She passed away quietly on February 27, 1887, while the prophet was at the Roueche farm. The mounting pressures being exerted by President Taylor's pursuers prevented him from attending the funeral. Only a few weeks before, Sam Gilson had posted placards all over Salt Lake and Davis counties, offering an eight-hundred-dollar reward for the arrest of John Taylor and George Q. Cannon. In a snide slap at the prophet, the placard explained, "$500 will be paid for Cannon alive, and $300 for Taylor."

A few days after these reward signs blossomed on telephone poles and fenceposts in the area, the Latter-day Saints were treated to an event that of late had occurred with great infrequency if at all—a legal victory. This was a favorable decision by the United States Supreme Court in the case of Elder Lorenzo Snow of the Twelve. This benign apostle, who had been convicted of unlawful cohabitation in three separate suits tried between December 30, 1885, and January 5, 1886, had appealed a year later to the Supreme Court on a writ of habeus corpus. The appellant contended that the territorial court had erred in basing his convictions on identical facts that existed throughout a single course of events. The high court accepted this argument and decreed there was but one offense and that, therefore, the trial court had no jurisdiction to impose sentence. In doing so, it pointed out the fallacy of attempting to divide a period of alleged unlawful cohabitation into several segments as Elder Snow's trial court had done: "On the same principle," the opinion noted, "there might have been indictments covering each of the thirty-five months, with imprisonment for seventy-four years, and fines amounting to $44,400; and so on, ad infinitum, for smaller periods of time."

The news of this decision brought a momentary sense of elation to Kaysville's distinguished exile, as it did to all Mormondom. Victories had been such a rarity of late that any kind of a triumph would have given the Prophet and his people an emotional and psychological lift. But this particular one was of special significance as it spotlighted for the entire nation the grossly unfair treatment the Latter-day Saints had received from the judicial system in Utah.

But this glimmer of success was obscured almost immediately by the dark shadow of the Edmunds-Tucker Act, which was then moving ponderously toward passage in Congress. Church attorney Franklin S. Richards and congressman Joseph T. Caine had monitored this legislation closely and had provided President Taylor with regular, detailed briefings that had kept him fully apprised of the expected content and the effect of the final version of the bill. Convinced from the reports that the bill would pass and that it would contain a provision severely limiting the amount of property the Church could hold, President Taylor, on advice of counsel, began to convey and assign to local ecclesiastical entities property he had held as the Church's trustee-in-trust. While the 1862 act contained a similar provision and relatively little had been done to insulate Church properties from forfeiture under it, there was a sense of urgency now because of other provisions of the new bill that would work a revolution in the local judicial structure by putting federal appointees on the bench of the territorial probate courts and by excluding most Mormons from jury panels through a required oath pledging obedience and support of the antipolygamy laws.

In tandem with these actions, President Taylor and his brethren began to appraise the nature and quality of Latter-day Saint life once the proposed legislation became law. The prospects were dreary under any scenario that could be imagined. Although the idea was personally repugnant to him, President Taylor considered, among others, a proposal advanced by John T. Caine that the Church leaders endorse another effort to obtain statehood and approve a provision in the proposed constitution outlawing polygamy. At first, John rejected this idea out of hand because of his tenacious commitment to the principle of plural marriage and to the noble women to whom he had been sealed under its provisions. But once the Edmunds-Tucker Act became the law of the land, his views on the subject began to moderate. One can only speculate as to the factors that brought about this change in outlook. A dominant consideration to one as thoroughly schooled in Mormon doctrine as was John Taylor would have been the recognition that to suspend the practice of polygamy would not require rejection of the underlying principle. He would have been cognizant of the teachings of Jacob in the Book of Mormon, during whose day the practice of polygamy was in suspension, but who affirmed that should God command his people, it would be obligatory on them to comply. (Jacob 2:30.) And he could not have failed to recall that for almost ten years after he had received the principle, Joseph Smith had refrained from living it or from admonishing his followers to do so. From this perspective, President Taylor would have been aware that the ultimate issue of whether the Saints would be required or allowed to live the principle or precluded from doing so lay in the province of God. Since he was obligated to live it under mandate from the Prophet Joseph Smith, and not having received a revelation from God to discontinue doing so, he adhered to the principle through the few remaining days of his life. Yet there were hints and suggestions that his mind was turning in the other direction. Mention has already been made of the "transition" statement contained in the First Presidency's message read at the fifty-seventh annual general conference in April 1887. More convincing, however, is the fact President Taylor approved the proposed constitution presented at the constitutional convention held a few weeks before his death, which document contained a provision forbidding the practice of polygamy. And shortly after his death, the Utah electorate almost unanimously approved this proposed constitution, an event that would have been impossible had not the Saints known that their late beloved leader had concurred.

But the revelatory direction for the Saints to discontinue the practice of polygamy was to await the maturing of events and the accession of the fourth president of the Church, Wilford Woodruff. In the meantime, John Taylor continued to battle against the constant and unremitting pressures of an exile that was now stretching into its third year and of the rapidly accelerating physical infirmities that beset him.

Chapter Twenty-Five

The Light Flickers Out

The months of forced seclusion had taken their toll. The step that had once been firm and quick was now unstable and slow. Although the prophet's mind remained clear and agile, his reflexes had slowed perceptibly, causing him to respond to questions and stimuli with an unaccustomed deliberateness and detachment. Moreover, the keen interest he had always shown in people and events faded into an attitude of calm indifference. Most of these responses are assignable to President Taylor's physical deterioration. The magnificent machine that was his body had almost worn out. He was now only a few months short of his seventy-ninth birthday, almost a decade beyond the traditional three score and ten. And, as already suggested, the two and a half years he had spent in exile had added physical burdens and disabilities far disproportionate to the amount of time that had actually elapsed.

But the obvious physical deterioration that was taking place does not seem to account fully for the speed with which the process of dissolution had been set in motion. That process appeared to accelerate noticeably as the time approached for the constitutional convention in late June. It may be inferred that President Taylor, having endorsed the convention as well as the anti-polygamy clause to be included in the proposed constitution, felt that in the process of transition alluded to in the First Presidency's statement at the recent general conference, it would be preferable to leave to another the task of announcing any new direction the Lord might dictate.

Whatever the reasons, President Taylor's condition took a dramatic turn for the worse in late June, so much so that George Q. Cannon sent an urgent message to his fellow counselor in Hawaii, advising of the prophet's condition and suggesting that he come home. President Joseph F. Smith responded by promptly undertaking the long and tedious journey to Utah. As we shall see, he arrived only a week before his leader passed on.

Meanwhile, the prophet continued to be as active as his deteriorating health would allow. He walked about the house for exercise but spent most of the time in his room, resting and conferring with the brethren. On June 20, he talked at length with L. John Nuttall about the questions of the day and especially about the constitutional convention. He expressed the hope that good would come from the labors of the brethren and that if the Lord so ordered it the proposed constitution would be adopted and Utah admitted to the union.

By July 1, President Taylor's activities had slacked off even more. George Q. Cannon was now handling most of the correspondence and other presidential matters, although his actions were discussed with his leader. When matters were brought forward, the prophet gave them careful attention and either approved or disapproved.

On the afternoon of July 1, Bishop Peter Barton brought word that deputy marshals had been seen at Farmington. So often had similar reports been received that the response was almost automatic. Some of the brethren were assigned to delve further into the matter and to report back, and the watchfulness of the guards around the farmhouse was intensified. The alert ended that evening when word came that there were only two marshals and that they had returned to Salt Lake City.

Two days later the prophet sent for his sons John W. and George J. to come to Kaysville to discuss matters pertaining to his estate. At that time he carefully reviewed and approved the arrangements for disposing of his property in a way that would be equitable to all members of his large family. Later in the day, it being Sunday, a fast and testimony meeting was held.

From this time forward until the end, President Taylor's condition deteriorated rapidly. Without exercise, his system became sluggish and his sleeping and eating habits even more irregular. The distinction between day and night lost all meaning for him. He might sleep fitfully during the daylight hours and then lie awake most of the night, tossing and turning, or resting in the easy chair near his bed. Also, the patient's appetite had now fled, and during this period of rapid decline he rejected nearly all food except liquids. The notable exception was ice cream, which he ate almost ravenously and with great relish. His eagerness for this delicacy could as easily be explained by the momentary relief from the summer's heat it provided as by his need or desire for nourishment.

On July 11, Mary and Maggie came to visit again, bringing George J. and Thomas E. with them. The prophet had mildly resisted their visit out of apparent concern that his condition would trouble the family, but he was pleased when they arrived.

By July 15, the aged leader began to experience considerable pain, which seemed to be alleviated by hot baths. On July 17, after one of these, he brightened up, spoke plainly, and answered questions distinctly. The following morning, however, his perceptions were quite dull, although in midafternoon they revived markedly with the excitement that attended the arrival of Joseph F. Smith from Hawaii. After exchanging hurried greetings with President Cannon and members of the prophet's clerical and security staffs, Joseph F., accompanied by George Q., entered the sickroom. Unable to evoke a response from the patient unaided, President Cannon took him by the hand

and, after referring to the return of his second counselor, said to the prophet that it was the first time all members of the First Presidency had been together since December 1884. Reviving at this, President John Taylor uttered the last recorded words of his mortal life: "I feel to thank the Lord," he said quietly, almost inaudibly.

Having spoken what could be described appropriately as a fitting benediction to an extraordinary life, the prophet did not speak again. The voice that had inspired many, chastised some, and intimidated or antagonized others had been stilled insofar as intelligible conversation was concerned. Over the next week, it was to be heard intermittently, but only as soft moans or occasional cries of pain.

On July 19, he seemed to be completely oblivious to everything going on about him. The next day the patient's legs began to swell, a condition that continued to worsen over the next several days. On July 23, the counselors sent word to the local leaders that in view of President Taylor's worsening condition, the Saints should forego the customary Pioneer Day celebration. And forty-eight hours later, John Taylor began the last day of his mortal life. By now he was breathing laboriously, which he continued to do until 7:55 in the evening when, without the movement of a limb, he breathed his last. At his bedside as life slipped away were his wives Mary and Maggie, presidents George Q. Cannon and Joseph F. Smith, L. John Nuttall, Samuel Bateman, James Malin, H. C. Barrell, Elizabeth Bailey, and members of the Roueche family.

The passing of President John Taylor was, in a sense, anticlimactic. Days before the event, it had been known by all close to the scene that the end was near. Therefore, his family and friends and his associates in the administration of the Church were fully prepared for the inevitable and were reconciled to carrying on with the work to which he had dedicated his life. So once the final curtain had fallen and those at the deathbed had vented their grief, they moved forward deliberately to perform the numerous tasks at hand.

The prophet's body was carefully bathed under the direction of Sam Bateman and was chilled with ice pending the arrival of the sexton, Joseph Taylor, who was summoned by telephone to take charge of the body and to bring his refrigerator. Meanwhile, there was busy activity among the First Presidency's staff, who packed their books and papers in anticipation of a hurried departure. The assumption appears to have been that once the news of President Taylor's death was published and word of his hideaway was made known, the Roueche farm would be swarming with marshals intent on ferreting out any polygamists who remained there or confiscating the records of the First Presidency still on the premises for possible use in pending or planned prosecutions.

By 3:00 A.M. the following morning, most of the arrangements for the move had been completed, including the reservation of a Utah Central Railway car to transport the prophet's body to Salt Lake City. Shortly thereafter, presidents Cannon and Smith left for the city, accompanied by Charles Wilcken, in order to supervise the numerous details connected with the funeral.

Telephone calls were made or wires sent to all of the general authorities and to stake and mission presidents advising them of the prophet's death and of the plans for the funeral on Friday, July 29. Also, a wire was sent to John W. Young in New York City, requesting that he attempt to obtain from the officials in Washington an exemption from arrest for President Wilford Woodruff to enable him to attend the funeral. This effort failed, as did any similar efforts in behalf of the counselors and other brethren who were under indictment. This circumstance limited those of the general authorities who could openly participate in the services to Elders Lorenzo Snow, Franklin D. Richards, and Heber J. Grant of the Twelve; Daniel H. Wells, counselor to the Twelve; and Seymour B. Young of the First Council of the Seventy. These brethren were not being sought by the federal officials.

The prophet's body was moved to the Gardo House on

the night of July 26, and during the two following days members of the family and their friends and President Taylor's associates in the ministry called to pay their respects. Among those who came was Wilford Woodruff, the president of the Twelve, who, by reason of the dissolution of the First Presidency at the death of John Taylor, then led the Church in fact, although his formal ascension to the prophetic office was to be delayed for two years. This stocky, energetic man with the piercing blue eyes and extraordinary spiritual perceptions and sensitivities arrived in disguise to avoid detection and arrest. There in the seclusion of the Gardo House, President Woodruff, who was a year older than his departed leader, shared with President Taylor's family his condolences and his reflections on the long association he had enjoyed with his friend, reflections he would have liked to express publicly but was prevented from doing so by an unfeeling federal officialdom.

The general membership of the Church was given the opportunity to bid farewell to their deceased prophet on Friday, July 29, 1887, the day of the funeral. Shortly before 7:00 A.M. on that day, the body was moved from the Gardo House to the Tabernacle and placed in front of the stand in such a way as to permit the Saints to file by in dual lines, one on either side of the casket. During four and a half hours they moved quietly past the earthly remains of their leader, some with moistened eyes, some with downcast expressions, and all with an attitude of reverence and respect.

While the native pine casket, polished brilliantly to resemble mahogany, and its occupant were the focal point of all eyes, there were other attractions in the building to claim the attention of the mourners as the lines moved slowly along. Most striking was the black crepe draped over the stand and the organ and around the graceful balcony. In front of the organ was a life-sized portrait of John Taylor, and on the sacrament table was a colorful floral offering that bore the title by which he had been known from the early days of his ministry, "Champion of Liberty."

Nearby was a sheaf of ripe wheat with the inscribed accolade, "Well done, Good and Faithful Servant." Setting the tone for the viewing and the memorial services to follow were the solemn strains of the huge Tabernacle organ played by J. J. Daynes.

At the beginning of the formal service, the conducting officer read a letter from President Taylor dated November 17, 1873, written on request to President Brigham Young, outlining his desires in the preparation for and the conducting of his funeral service. Most of the instructions pertained to the preliminaries of preparing and dressing the body, selecting a coffin ("sufficiently large to contain my body without pressure . . . of our own mountain pine . . . colored or stained . . . with a light cotton or woolen mattress or bed and a convenient pillow for the head"), and the procedure for burial ("coffin . . . placed in an outer strong box . . . a plain slab may be placed over the body, and a stone at the head and feet, on the stone to be given an account of my name, age and birth, as shall suit the feelings of my family"). As to the program at the funeral service, he asked merely for "such as prevails at the time among the Saints."

Given that direction, the family, counseled by the members of the Twelve who were present, decided that the prophet's stake president, Angus M. Cannon, should conduct; that his bishop, Millen Atwood, should offer the invocation; that the Tabernacle Choir should provide the music; that elders Lorenzo Snow, Franklin D. Richards, Heber J. Grant, and Daniel H. Wells and other associates and friends close to the deceased should speak; and that Patriarch John Smith should offer the benediction.

As one would have expected, the talks, viewed in total, lauded the character and ministry of the deceased, evaluated his contributions to the latter-day work, traced the power and influence of God as reflected in his ministry, and, as far as the Church was concerned, looked to the future, not to the past.

Elder Lorenzo Snow, the first speaker, set the tone for

the meeting by citing a quotation from Paul's second epistle to Timothy as his text: "For I am now ready to be offered, and the time of my departure is at hand. I have fought a good fight, I have finished my course, I have kept the faith." In comparing the lives of the ancient and the now deceased latter-day apostle, Lorenzo saw significant parallels. What was said of Paul could as easily be said of John: "He suffered imprisonment; he suffered the lash of his persecutors; he suffered every indignity, and finally died a martyr to those principles he so laboriously and so effectually carried forth among the human family."

This benign leader, who then stood second in apostolic seniority and who would later preside over the Twelve and then the Church, reminded his listeners that President Taylor, while a giant in his day and worthy of emulation, was but one brilliant piece in a grand mosaic. "Well, it is so ordered," said the speaker, "that one man's death, or the death of a dozen, though they stand in the highest positions in the Church, does not stop the work. The Latter-day Saints have advanced to that wisdom and that intelligence and that understanding, that this does not materially affect their interest. The kingdom of God moves forward. It is not dependent upon one man or a half dozen men." (As quoted in BHR, p. 444.)

Elder Snow's reference to President Taylor as a martyr reflected a common feeling among the Saints that his death had been hastened by the callous treatment he had received from his pursuers. This feeling had been formulated into the vague idea that what was commenced at Carthage, where he was wounded, was completed at Kaysville, where he was finally killed. Speaking of the close relationship that existed between John Taylor and the Prophet Joseph Smith, Elder Franklin D. Richards dwelt on the theme of martyrdom: "The story of that personal affection was consummated by the bullets he received in Carthage jail with the Prophet when he was slain," he told the audience. "President Taylor himself was disabled. In the scene that he then passed through he experienced all that pertains to martyrdom. He never suffered greater pain, or more severe pain than he experienced in the jail with the Prophet Joseph. But it was not appropriate for him to give up the ghost then. He had to wait another forty years." (Ibid., p. 449.)

Angus M. Cannon, in his closing remarks, gave an intimate glimpse into President Taylor's character and aspirations that revealed perhaps the most powerful drive that had propelled him along the course of his career. In reporting on his last visit with the prophet, the speaker said, "I saw him last in enfeebled health, and when I asked him if he would have me bear a message to his loved ones—to his family, his wives and his children—he said, "Yes, say unto them I remember them always. I love them individually, and never cease to plead with God for them." (Ibid., p. 459.)

It was to preserve the unity and sanctity of his family and of other polygamous families that John Taylor had waged such a tenacious fight with the federal bureaucracy. To him his glory and joy both on earth and in the hereafter were founded upon the happiness, well-being, and faithfulness of his wives and progeny. And he demonstrated these feelings in so many ways by both word and deed through the many years of his long life.

These feelings were uniformly reciprocated by President Taylor's family. They loved and revered him as he had loved and revered them. It was precisely this love and reverence that caused some of them to be misled after President Taylor's death and after the Manifesto that followed. Confused by seemingly conflicting demands of filial loyalty and priesthood commitment and discipline, and apparently unaware of the trends in his thinking and feelings during his last weeks, this minor segment of the prophet's family took a course that veered away from the one marked out by the presiding authority of the Church—something their honored parent never would have done had he been in their place. John Taylor was too well schooled in basic Mormon doctrine and procedure ever to have allowed himself to be found challenging and then rejecting the counsel and mandates of the one who held the keys of the ministry. He no doubt would have eloquently expressed any contrary views he may have held as he had always done; but once a decision had been made, he would have yielded to the one in authority. To say otherwise would require one to ignore his long, unblemished record of loyal obedience to prophetic direction and his conviction that exaltation is to be found only in submissive obedience to all of God's commandments received through or interpreted by the living oracle.

Once the final tributes and the benediction had been spoken over the remains of this great Christian warrior, they were gently borne to a waiting hearse, which led a long cortege of mourners, interspersed with six bands and a choir, to the Salt Lake City cemetery located high on the north bench overlooking the valley. There the prophet was laid to rest near members of his family who had preceded him in death and near many of his brethren with whom he had fought the good fight.

Appendix

The Philosophy of John Taylor

The Philosophical Credo of the Latter-Day Saint

He grasps at all truths, human and divine; he has no darling dogma to sustain or favorite creed to uphold; he has nothing to lose but error; nothing to gain but truth. He digs, labors, and searches for it as for hidden treasure; and while others are content with chaff and husks of straw, he seizes on the kernel, substance, the gist of all that's good, and clings to all that will ennoble and exalt the human family. (*The Mormon*, July 28, 1855, p. 2.)

True Philosophy Defined

What is true philosophy? It seems to me to be a true principle for men to try and find out who they are. I like to examine myself a little, and I sometimes ask who am I? where did I come from? what am I doing here? and what will be the condition of things when I leave here?

If there is anybody who can tell me anything about these things, I want to know. If I had an existence before I came here, I want to know something about it; and if I shall have an existence hereafter, I want to know what kind of existence it will be. I do not want to be frightened about hell-fire, pitch-forks, and serpents, nor to be scared to death with hobgoblins and ghosts, nor anything of the kind that is got up to scare the ignorant; but I want truth, intelligence, and something that will bear investigation. I want to probe things to the bottom and to find out the truth if there is any way to find it out. (JD 11:317, February 24, 1867.)

Are Mormons Philosophers?

Mormonism is philosophically true, but all Mormons are not philosophers—neither do we consider it necessary. A man may understand first principles, without knowing the mysteries; he may also enjoy certain influences and powers and priesthood, without being able to define the cause of those operations or their scientific bearings. . . . They may not be all philosophers, but they know it by inspiration through obedience. . . . God imparts his philosophy frequently to men of limited abilities; they follow his teachings—the result is, they confound the wise. It is not their philosophy, but God's; but being true to law, it is always obedient thereto. . . . Those principles would always overturn the puerile principles of a corrupt philosophy and the ridiculous fantasies of a false religion and vanquish them; they might not always understand why—it was the gift of God to them; but it was philosophical; such is Mormonism. (*The Mormon*, March 8, 1856, p. 2.)

Mormonism, the Philosophy of Heaven

Philosophy can not comprehend it; it is beyond the reach of natural philosophy. It is the philosophy of heaven, it is the revelation of God to man. It is philosophical, but it is heavenly philosophy, and beyond the ken of human judgment, beyond the reach of human intelligence. (JD 15:25, April 7, 1872.)

The Cosmopolitan Objective of Mormon Philosophy

We are cosmopolitans, citizens of the world, and have implanted in our bosoms the spirit of the living God, which prompts us to seek for the welfare and happiness of all the human family. (JD 11:55, January 18, 1865.)

The Philosophy of Eternal Progression

The present is only one stage of our existence. We existed before we came here; we exist here for a time, and when we depart from this mortal life we shall have a spiritual existence, an existence without the body, and then again with the body. And it is for those who manage and manipulate these matters to do as seemeth good in their sight, and it is for us to yield a willing and an obedient submission to the will of our heavenly Father, feeling always that whatever he does is perfect and right. (JD 22:354-55, January 29, 1882.)

The Philosophy of Perfection

But there are certain eternal laws by which the Gods in the eternal worlds are governed and which they cannot violate, and do not want to violate. These eternal principles must be kept, and one principle is, that no unclean thing can enter into the Kingdom of God. (JD 25:165-66, June 15, 1884.)

We are told that if we cannot abide the law of the celestial kingdom we cannot inherit a celestial glory. Is not that doctrine? Yes. "But," says one, "Are not we all going into the celestial kingdom?" I think not, unless we turn round and mend our ways very materially. It is only those who can abide a celestial glory and obey a celestial law that will be prepared to enter a celestial kingdom. (JD 26:133, October 6, 1883.)

Man is a dual being, possessed of body and spirit, made in the image of God, and connected with Him and with eternity. He is a God in embryo and will live and progress throughout the eternal ages, if obedient to the laws of the Godhead, as the Gods progress throughout the eternal ages. (JD 23:65, April 9, 1882.)

The Follies of Earthly Philosophers

One great reason why men have stumbled so frequently in many of their researches after philosophical truth is, that they have sought them with their own wisdom, and gloried in their own intelligence, and have not sought unto God for that wisdom that fills and governs the universe and regulates all things. That is one great difficulty with the philosophers of the world, as it now exists, that man claims to himself to be the inventor of everything he discovers; any new law and principle which he happens to discover he claims to himself instead of giving glory to God. (JD 11:74, February 5, 1865.)

Speaking of philosophy . . . I was almost buried up in it while in Paris. I was walking about one day in the *Jardin des Plantes*—a splendid garden. There they had a sort of exceedingly light cake; it was so thin and light that you could blow it away, and you could eat all day of it, and never be satisfied. Somebody asked me what the name of that was. I said, I don't know the proper name, but in the absence of one, I can give it a name—I will call it philosophy, or fried froth, [whichever] you like. It is so light you can blow it away, eat it all day, and at night be as far from being satisfied as when you began. (JD 1:27, August 22, 1852.)

Those men who profess so much intelligence that they cannot listen to the word of the Lord, and have so much egotism and philosophy that they cannot listen to sound reason and common sense, cannot be edified by these things, while we, who have not such lofty pretensions, enjoy them. (JD 5:241, September 13, 1857.)

An All-Encompassing Philosophy

We are open for the reception of all truth, of whatever nature it may be, and are desirous to obtain and possess it, to search after it as we would for hidden treasures. . . . If there are any good principles, any moral philosophy that we have not yet attained to we are desirous to learn them. If there is anything in the scientific world that we do not yet comprehend we desire to become acquainted with it. If there is any branch of philosophy calculated to promote the well-being of humanity, that we have not yet grasped, we wish to possess ourselves of it. If there is anything pertaining to the rule and government of nations, or politics, if you please, that we are not acquainted with, we desire to possess it. If there are any religious ideas, any theological truths, any principles pertaining to God, that we have not learned, we ask mankind, and we pray God, our heavenly Father, to enlighten our minds that we may comprehend, realize, embrace and live up to them as part of our religious faith. Thus our ideas and thoughts would extend as far as the wide world spreads, embracing everything pertaining to light, life, or existence pertaining to this world or the world that is to come. (JD 14:337, March 3, 1872.)

We talk sometimes about free will; is that a correct principle? Yes; and it is a principle that has always existed, and proceeded from God, our heavenly Father. . . . We may here ask, in acting under the dominion or control of the Priesthood are any of you forced to do anything you do not want to? If you think you are in any possible way, I absolve you from it to-day, every one of you. These are my ideas about the rights of men. It is "all free grace and all free will" as the poet has it. (JD 22:7-9, January 9, 1881.)

Would you allow everybody to worship as they please? Certainly. What? If you knew they were in error? Certainly. I would not wish to control the human mind; I would not control the actions of men, God does not do it, he leaves them to their own agency to combat with the trials, temptations, adversities and evils of every kind that are in the world, to which humanity is, or can be incident. He puts within their reach, however, certain principles and would like to lead them to himself if they would be led. If not, he then does the very best with them that he can. (JD 21:16, February 8, 1880.)

The Philosophy of Nature

The power that causes this earth to roll on its axis, and regulates the planets in their diurnal and annual motions, is beyond man's control. Their revolutions and spheres are fixed by nature's God, and they are so beautifully arranged, and nicely balanced, that an astronomer can calculate the return of a planet scores of years beforehand, with the greatest precision and accuracy. And who can contemplate, without admiration, those stupendous worlds, rolling through the immensity of space at such an amazing velocity, moving regularly in their given spheres without coming into collision, and reflect that they have done so for thousands of years. (*The Government of God* [Liverpool: S. W. Richards, 1852], pp. 3-4.)

Comparison between Earthly and Heavenly Philosophy

Man, by philosophy and the exercise of his natural intelligence, may gain an understanding, to some extent, of the laws of Nature; but to comprehend God heavenly wisdom and intelligence are necessary. Earthly and heavenly philosophy are two different things, and it is folly for men to base their arguments upon earthly philosophy in trying to unravel the mysteries of the kingdom of God. (JD 14:191, March 20, 1870.)

There is a philosophy of the earth and a philosophy of the heavens; the latter can unravel all mysteries pertaining to earth; but the philosophy of the earth cannot enter into the mysteries of the kingdom of God, or the purposes of the Most High. (JD 13:222, May 6, 1870.)

The Limitations of Earthly Philosophy

We have a great many ignorant, learned fools; but when you meet sensible, intelligent men, . . . they will acknowledge principle when it is presented to them. But many men have not the understanding to do it. Talking about saving themselves, who among the philosophers can save themselves? . . . What do they do when they have to grapple with the sting of death, and when it stares them in the face? Why, they take a leap in the dark. And this darkness is the end of all their philosophy and all their science. And the little they do know in divining the laws of God is only with regard to some very few of the fundamental principles of those laws that God has planted everywhere throughout the universe, and I do not therefore have that reverence for their theories, notions and vagaries, nor do I attach that importance to their intelligence that some people do. (JD 20:119, January 6, 1879.)

The Supremacy of Eternal Law

The world says, No, he [God] has no right; I am my own master, etc. Some of the Latter-day Saints almost say the same thing; not quite, but they would like to get near it. "I am a free man; I will be damned if I don't do as I please," etc. Well, I will tell you another part of that story. You will be damned if you do act as you please unless you please to do and to keep the laws of God. We cannot violate his laws with impunity nor trample under foot these eternal principles which exist in all nature. If all nature is compelled to be governed by law or suffer loss, why not man? (JD 21:114, November 28, 1879.)

The Leavening Effect of the Gospel

The gospel is like a little leaven put into a certain portion of meal, and it is working and operating, and the ultimate result will be that the whole lump will be leavened. (JD 24:124, April 8, 1883.)

We, under the inspiration of the Almighty, will introduce the laws of God that exist in the heavens and upon the earth, and form a nucleus of truth, of virtue and intelligence, of law and order, of principles pertaining to morals, to philosophy, to politics, to religion and to everything that is pure, exalting and ennobling, and the kingdom will be the Lord's. (JD 21:97, April 13, 1879.)

The Governing Power of Priesthood

What is Priesthood? Without circumlocution, I shall as briefly answer that it is the government of God, whether on the earth or in the heavens, for it is by that power, agency, or principle that all things are governed on the earth and in the heavens, and by that power that all things are upheld and sustained. It governs all things—it directs all things—it sustains all things—and has to do with all things that God and truth are associated with. It is the power of God delegated to intelligences in the heavens and to men on the earth; and when we arrive in the celestial kingdom of God, we shall find the most perfect order and harmony existing, because there is the perfect pattern, the most perfect order of government carried out, and when or wherever those principles have been developed in the earth, in proportion as they have spread and been acted upon, just in that proportion have they produced blessings and salvation to the human family; and when the government of God shall be more extensively adopted, and when Jesus's prayer, that he taught his disciples is answered, and God's kingdom comes on the earth, and his will is done here as in heaven, then, and not till then, will universal love, peace, harmony, and union prevail. (MS 9:321, November 1, 1847.)

The Kingdom of God

We talk a good deal about the church and kingdom of God. I sometimes think we understand very little about either. The kingdom of God means the government of God. That means, power, authority, rule, dominion, and a people to rule over; but that principle will not be fulfilled, cannot be entirely fulfilled, until, as we are told in the Scriptures, the kingdoms of this world are become the kingdoms of our Lord and his Christ, and he will rule over them. And when unto him every knee shall bow and every tongue confess that he is Christ, to the glory of God, the Father. That time has not yet come, but there are certain principles associated therewith that have come, namely, the introduction of that kingdom, and the introduction of that kingdom could only be made by that being who is the king and ruler, and the head of that government, first communicating his ideas, his principles, his laws, his government to the people; otherwise we should not know what his laws were. (JD 21:63, January 4, 1880.)

A Philosophy of Education

We want . . . to be alive in the cause of education. We are commanded of the Lord to obtain knowledge, both by study and by faith, seeking it out of the best books. And it becomes us to teach our children, and afford them instructions in every branch of education calculated to promote their welfare, leaving those false acquirements which tend to infidelity, and to lead away the mind and affection from the things of God. We want to compile the intelligence and literacy of this people in book-form, as well as in teaching and preaching; adopting all the good and useful books we can obtain. . . . And instead of doing as many of the world do, take the works of God, to try to prove that there is no God; we want to prove by God's works that he does exist, that he lives and rules and holds us, as it were, in the hollow of his hand." (JD 19:310, April 8, 1878.)

A Philosophy of Government

Will the concentrated intelligence of past ages, with the improvements of the present, advance man in the scale of being, and lead him to seek for improvement in the science of life? We think it will, for man is a progressive being. It is an era of transition, an age of active, busy preparation. Is it to the establishment of some vast permanent moral, political or religious government, or is it to eventuate in a combination of all in one magnificent structure, under which all the nations of the earth may gather? The idea of government, extending over the diversified tribes and nations of the earth, classifying, organizing and controlling the whole, has been considered chimerical, a sort of monomania raving of some besotted Alexander, hair-brained Peter of Russia, or unprincipled fatalism of a Napoleon—some bigoted believer in the Revelation of Patmos—Daniel, or some other old prophet of the dark ages. Changes of circumstances always require change in the administration; this would apply to individual States—why not to the world? (*The Mormon*, November 24, 1855, p. 2.)

The religion of Jesus Christ will develop the plan of putting down the high-handed power of tyranny and oppression which now pervades the earth, and how to establish the principles of peace, righteousness, and virtue upon the earth, and how to place the world of mankind in that position which God has destined they should occupy when his kingdom shall rule upon the earth, and when "every creature in heaven, on earth, and under the earth shall be heard to say, Blessing, honour, and glory, and power be unto him that sitteth upon the throne, and unto the Lamb, for ever and ever."

The germs of this peace are with us; the intelligence concerning these matters has begun to be developed. (JD 6:164, January 17, 1858.)

Let us now notice our political position in the world. What are we going to do? We are going to possess the earth. Why? Because it belongs to Jesus Christ, and he belongs to us, and we to him; we are all one, and will take the kingdom and possess it under the whole heavens, and reign over it for ever and ever. Now, ye kings and emperors, help yourselves, if you can. This is the truth, and it may as well be told at this time as at any other. (JD 1:230, April 8, 1853.)

The proper mode of government is this—God first speaks, and then the people have their action. It is for them to say whether they will have his dictation or not. They are free: they are independent under God. The government of God is not a species of priestcraft, . . . where one man dictates and everybody obeys without having a voice in it. We have our voice and agency, and act with the most perfect freedom; still we believe there is a correct order—some wisdom and knowledge somewhere that is superior to ours: that wisdom and knowledge proceeds from God through the medium of the holy Priesthood. We believe that no man or set of men, of their own wisdom and by their own talents, are capable of governing the human family aright. (JD 9:10, April 6, 1861.)

Mormon Stoicism

I do not desire affliction: I would pray to God to "leave me not in temptation, and deliver me from evil; for thine is the kingdom, the power, and the glory." But if the earthquake bellows, the lightnings flash, the thunders roll, and the powers of darkness are let loose, and the spirit of evil is permitted to rage, and an evil influence is brought to bear on the Saints, and my life, with theirs, is put to the test; let it come, for we are the Saints of the most High God, and all is well, all is peace, all is right, and will be, both in time and in eternity. (JD 5:114-15, August 9, 1857.)

The Eleventh Commandment

There are more people attending to the eleventh commandment in the city of Nauvoo, than in any other place of the same size on the globe;—that is *they mind their own business in Nauvoo,* without interfering with others. (*Nauvoo Neighbor,* April 7, 1845, p. 2.)

A Philosophy of Happiness

As we travel along through what is sometimes called this "vale of tears," there are many thoughts that occupy our minds, and many subjects for reflection present themselves, sometimes concerning the living and sometimes concerning the dead. However, it is with the living that we have to do at the present time, and it is "Life and the pursuit of happiness" that ought to occupy the attention of all intellectual beings. Mankind have various views and ideas in relation to the attainment of happiness upon the earth, and also after we leave the earth; and those views and ideas that are entertained by us in relation to these matters influence, to a greater or less extent, our actions and proceedings in life. We look at things through another medium, and judge of them from another standpoint, than which they are generally viewed by the inhabitants of the earth. We look upon it that the greatest happiness that we can attain to is in securing the approbation of our Heavenly Father, in fearing God, in being made acquainted with his laws—with the principles of eternal truth, and with those things that we consider will best promote not only our temporal, but our eternal happiness. (JD 11:87, March 5, 1865.)

Index

Index